MW00357087

Building School-Based Collaborative Mental Health Teams: A Systems Approach to Student Achievement

Building School-Based Collaborative Mental Health Teams: A Systems Approach to Student Achievement

Kathleen C. Laundy

Copyright © 2015 Kathleen C. Laundy
All rights reserved.

Published by TPI Press, The Practice Institute, LLC, Camp Hill, PA 17011
All rights reserved. Published 2015
Printed in the United States of America

ISBN: 0990344525
ISBN 13: 9780990344520

Library of Congress Control Number: 2015905950
Published by TPI Press, The Practice Institute, LLC, Camp Hill, PA

This book is lovingly dedicated to Christie, who started it all.

"Never doubt that a small group of thoughtful, committed people
can change the world. Indeed, it is the only thing that ever has."
—Margaret Mead

Contents

Foreword

Ralph Cohen

Building School-Based Collaborative Mental Health Teams: A Systems Approach to Student Achievement by Kathleen Laundy is a book that has been decades in the making. It is being published at a critical junction in U.S. education history, when licensed and certified mental health professionals are joining educators to promote well-being and academic achievement. The initiative to include marriage and family therapists (MFTs) as employed members of school-based mental health teams began in earnest in the mid-1990s, as a natural outgrowth of systems-based initiatives in education, starting with Response to Intervention. Rather than viewing problems as individually based, family therapists and other mental health clinicians focus on the *context* of presenting symptoms, looking at all of the layers that affect human behavior. Given the influence of schools in children's lives, it is important to include the school in the process of addressing children's problems.

As director of the Family Therapy Department at Central Connecticut State University, a psychologist and family therapist and a member of the Board of Directors of the Connecticut Association for Marriage and Family Therapy (CTAMFT), I chaired a committee to advocate for creating school-based positions for MFTs in Connecticut in 1995. During that time, counselors, MFTs, and social workers all achieved state licensure with the Connecticut Department of Health. After the initial start-up of that Advocacy Committee initiative, we encountered opposition by other mental health organizations to state certification. Many felt threatened that their jobs would be usurped by a new mental health discipline competing for limited positions in schools. At the same time, there were also pockets of strong support from school counselors, psychologists, and social workers who viewed the ability to work with families creatively as an asset to school collaboration. They recognized the added value of having systems-trained experts on their mental health teams.

Kathleen and I served on the board of directors together as she was elected president of CTAMFT. She later joined me as advocacy co-chair, bringing her passion and years of experience as a school social worker, clinical psychologist, and an MFT to the effort. In 2001, we put together a team of MFTs and others who were equally passionate about the importance of an MFT presence in schools. Over a period of 8 years, Connecticut became the first state in the country to legislate a school-based certification for MFTs. Since that time, several states have followed suit to build a full complement of mental health professionals on their school teams.

I then asked Kathleen to join me to create a specialty track in school-based MFT to meet state requirements for certified school-based practice in our Counseling and Family Therapy Department at Central Connecticut State University (CCSU). She did so with her usual energy and fervor, and we now have a curriculum in place. Many MFTs have become certified, and the work continues to educate school districts about the MFT certification, collaborative mental health teams in schools, and how MFTs can bring added value to their school-based teams.

A third area of our collaboration involves the creation of a course for Teacher Education students. Following the Sandy Hook tragedy in 2012, Connecticut teachers-in-training have been mandated by a new state law to obtain coursework in social emotional learning (SEL) before beginning their student teaching. I was asked by the dean of the School of Education and Professional Studies at CCSU to chair a task force to develop the course, and I put together a team of educators and multidisciplinary experts in the area of SEL to do so. Once again, Kathleen joined me in creating the curriculum for the course. She has been integral to that initiative by bringing her expertise and interest in working collaboratively with multidisciplinary teams to contribute to this curriculum for new teachers. With the widely publicized incidents of school-related violence across the country over the past two decades, a spotlight has been shone on the fact that violence can happen in schools in any neighborhood and that students' social, emotional, and mental health needs are often ignored or insufficiently addressed in the school milieu. The SEL coursework is designed to help general education teachers join special services staff to create safe and effective learning environments for all students.

Kathleen Laundy has taken her wisdom, years of experience, and collaboration with many colleagues to offer a look at the educational system from the kaleidoscopic lens of systems theory, examining layers of school milieu across special and general education. Her application of the LOGS model provides an elegant visual representation of how to approach educational complexities. She makes a strong case that creating a more systemic view of education will result in improving motivation, performance, and social skills of students, as well as stronger school achievement. This volume will provoke readers to examine their own views of what *education* means. It highlights the enormous responsibility that educators carry in creating healthy learning environments that address the needs of our students.

Kathleen often reminds me that the material in this book represents the endurance of not only our mutual commitment and collaboration over the years, but also the strength of the relationships we have built with like-minded colleagues and "converts" to a systems view that we have encountered along the way. Like the unlikely bunch that traveled the Yellow Brick Road to the Emerald City of Oz, our journey together has taken us through many twists and turns, trials and tribulations. We are now watching the fruits of our labor begin to bear seeds that are traveling far and wide. The material in this book is the result of a long process that has culminated in the promise of a new vision of education. That vision is inclusive, compassionate, adaptive, and respectful of the needs of students and those who support them in their process of becoming effective adults.

Acknowledgements

Although I am the primary writer of this text, material for this book was obtained from many sources. Multidisciplinary colleagues from education, medicine, and mental health all participated in its creation. I am indebted my Central Connecticut State University (CCSU) psychology and marriage and family therapy (MFT) colleague Dr. Ralph Cohen for sharing the leadership and stamina required to shepherd the first MFT school certification law in the country. Dr. William Nelson, Special Education colleague at CCSU, is also owed a debt of thanks for the collaborative writing of the special education chapter.

Our MFT students who train, graduate, and evolve the longitudinal overview of growth in systems (LOGS) model in schools are continued sources of inspiration for the collaboration initiative. Special thanks go to former students Michelle Ciak and Barbara Bennett, who have become colleagues in the development of the LOGS model, its application, and the workshops we teach about multidisciplinary school collaboration. Thanks go to all of the counselors, MFTs, physicians, school nurses, psychologists, and social workers who have worked and trained with us over the past decade and provide collaborative clinical services to school systems.

Several others were instrumental in the creation of this book. I am indebted to Thorana Nelson, who first suggested that I write about school-based clinical practice when I told her of our legislative success in Connecticut. To obtain qualitative data for the text, I conducted interviews with and researched the publications of medical family therapy colleagues. Thanks to Drs. Jeri Hepworth, Susan McDaniel, William Doherty, and John Rolland, who were all multidisciplinary pioneers in the creation of collaborative medical family therapy. Colleagues Beth Cooper and William Boylin were strong writing supports when I was running on empty.

I appreciate School Superintendent Joseph Onofrio's help in generating innovative ways for mental health professionals to create collaborative services in school systems. Joe's insight as a licensed professional counselor, a supervisor of MFTs, and a school superintendent has been an inspiration to me. Peg Donohue, former school counselor in Joe's district and now faculty colleague at CCSU, was also instrumental in developing collaborative services in that district and has been a valued colleague. Dr. Patricia Charles, Middletown Schools and former superintendent of Westbrook Schools, was instrumental in helping launch our first research project regarding family-based school practice and collaborative effectiveness. Ed Cassinari, school psychologist and family therapist, has successfully created a collaborative mental health system in his Newington school system and trains MFT, school psychology, and social work students there. I thank them for their vision.

Katharine Bishop was the first Connecticut principal to request MFT services to build her Westbrook Elementary School staff. She has been a wise and supportive special education colleague over many years. She and fellow principals Robert Travaglini, Peter DeLisa, and Michael Talbot, and Karen Riem and former State Department of Education Commissioner Betty Sternberg who are fellow faculty at CCSU, all gave me feedback about how the structure and process of identifying and servicing children with special needs has evolved over the past four decades.

Patricia Varholy was a consummate special education administrator who was instrumental in creating opportunities for mental health clinicians to offer comprehensive support to schools. She supported multidisciplinary service delivery to students with special needs in southeastern Connecticut for many years. I am grateful to have her as a colleague

I want to express my appreciation and lifelong attachment to Bob, Jennifer, and Jessica, my husband and children and fellow health care providers and educators. I have learned so much from you, and you continue to be my inspiration. You are the best multidisciplinary team that I know.

Finally, I want to thank State Representative Marilyn Giuliano for supporting our certification efforts in Connecticut. As a school psychologist, she saw the wisdom and utility of school certification for MFTs as a way to strengthen school mental health teams. Her legislative mentorship was instrumental to our success.

one

Introduction

The aim of this book is to provide information about the systemic, value-added services of family-centered, collaborative school mental health teams to educational achievement. The goal of the book is to help readers appreciate the shift from individualized approaches to student learning to a more cybernetic view of educational achievement in the past 50 years. Bateson (1972), the noted anthropologist-biologist who is considered a leader in the adaptation of systems theory to the behavioral and social sciences, profoundly influenced our thinking about how multiple genetic and environmental variables affect human behavior. This text is about how those variables all affect student health and academic functioning.

Seligman and Darling (2007) note that strengthening families helps boost resiliency in children, especially those with special health and learning needs. All professionals who work with children know that family support is necessary for children to thrive and achieve. This book is also about supporting family-friendly schools to promote academic achievement.

Although state certification for school marriage and family therapists (MFTs)[1] provided the original impetus for the book, *Building School-Based Collaborative Mental Health Teams* can serve as a useful handbook for all allied health care colleagues, teachers, administrators, and family members who wish to learn about the ingredients needed to engage in collaborative school practice.

---

1 Note that *MFT* is used in this book to refer to both *marriage and family therapy* and *marriage and family therapists*.

Colleagues from other mental health disciplines will see their own experience in case examples that are sprinkled throughout the book. Our skill set in mental health contains what I call *necessary redundancies,* which refer to common clinical skills that all six of our licensed mental health disciplines (counseling, MFT, nursing, psychiatry, psychology, and social work) are trained to provide. Readers of this text are invited to add any necessary redundancies they use to the growing multidisciplinary synergy of service in schools, as more systemic models are being developed to boost student achievement. I encourage you to read this text with a critical eye for where your skills may fit collaboratively with the school teams that interest you.

There are innovative collaborative models of health care provision in the field of family therapy that blend well with school-based practice. Adaptation of those models to the milieu of education can offer synergistic support to existing programs and services in schools for children with mental health and other special needs. Allied health care professionals must know how schools function to best integrate tools from their clinical training with the system of education. In turn, schools, allied educational colleagues, and families can all benefit from learning about the value-added services of mental health services in education. Professionals in the fields of health and education have similar goals of promoting full functioning for children and families. Their focus may be different, but their goals are complementary. Educators seek to help children learn and achieve, and healthy children are better prepared to achieve. Health care providers aim for children to lead healthy lives, which includes full access to education.

Because the focus of what we do differs, mental health clinicians wishing to provide multidisciplinary services in schools first need to become respectful "guests" in education systems to join effectively with a setting where education is the primary goal. The aim of *Building School-Based Collaborative Mental Health Teams* is to equip health colleagues, school professionals, and families with the information necessary to collaboratively promote academic achievement and resiliency in our youth. For some, the book will be a historic refresher. For others, it will be an introduction to the theoretical transition from individualized notions of student success to a broader systemic orientation to school culture and its layers of influence on child development. For still others, it will offer some practical examples that will be useful for your school-based practice. My hope is that there are elements of the text that will be useful for all readers.

Outline of the Book

After this introductory chapter, the first chapters introduce theory and history behind support for students with special needs. Chapter 2 traces the evolution in education from individualized services for students at risk for underachievement to more system-wide programs and services for all students. That chapter addresses the logic and power of adapting a systemic approach to school-based support for children to boost achievement and well-being, and it introduces the six licensed mental health groups that participate on multidisciplinary mental health teams in schools. It also introduces current systemic initiatives that are being developed across the United States.

The two longest chapters, Chapters 3 and 7, contain a great deal of theoretical information about special education and mental health. They are designed to orient new clinicians about the history and convergence of two systems of classification and diagnosis. To appreciate the context of those initiatives that evolved from individualized to systemic assessment more fully, Chapter 3 traces the history and development of special education laws in the United States. It orients the reader to the original, individualized culture of special education in school systems. It summarizes the history of federal laws and policies that address the special needs of children. Basic terminology and processes that schools use to assess and develop services for children with special needs are outlined to ground the reader in the nomenclature and culture of school systems. This chapter is cowritten with Dr. William Nelson, a fellow faculty member at Central Connecticut State University, who is an expert in special education history and practice.

Chapter 4 introduces an assessment and intervention tool called the *longitudinal overview of growth in systems* (LOGS) model, which provides a broader kaleidoscopic lens to conceptualize the special needs of children and families throughout their school career and beyond.

This chapter includes case examples designed to help the reader apply the concepts being addressed.

The LOGS model is based on a text called *Metaframeworks: Transcending the Models of Family Therapy* (Breunlin, Schwartz, & Mac Kune-Karrer 1997). This text is a distillation of central systemic concepts from the major models of family therapy. The LOGS model integrates layers of individual, family, school, community, and cultural systems from *Metaframeworks* and conceptualizes programs and services in schools across the course of children's school careers.

Chapter 5 integrates the LOGS model with key systemic concepts borrowed from the specialty practice of medical family therapy. Medical family therapy provides cogent support from the field of health care to the collaborative educational work that multidisciplinary teams provide in school systems. This chapter offers practical information and techniques from medical family therapy to adapt LOGS model components to school-based services to children and families. The goal of this chapter is to illustrate the goodness-of-fit among these diagnostic and treatment meta-models, which have the mutual goal of providing collaborative, integrated, and more comprehensive services to children through family-centered systems of care.

In Chapter 6, another educational initiative will be detailed that has parallel goals in health care and education. Following the No Child Left Behind Act of 2001, an initiative called the Response to Intervention (RtI) movement in education was created to promote evidence-based practice founded on good science. Evidence-based best practice in health care and the RtI movement in education both support and encourage the development of scientific, standardized outcome measures and findings to provide early, preventive, broad-based, and comprehensive services for children to improve their functioning. This chapter addresses the promotion of scientifically documented, evidence-based health care practice in schools. It will further demonstrate the goodness-of-fit among certain health and education models and the timeliness of hiring systems-trained clinicians in schools.

Chapter 7 is the second most detailed chapter. It highlights the major categories of special needs and disorders that children present in schools. This chapter builds a theoretical bridge between school-based and mental health assessment and equips school mental health clinicians to collaborate with professional partners in education. It is designed to be a reference for mental health trainees and clinicians as they encounter school policies and programs and begin their clinical training in education. Using the *Diagnostic and Statistical Manual of Mental Disorders*, Fifth Edition (*DSM–5*, American Psychiatric Association, 2013) from mental health practice and "Primary Disability" categorization system from education, special psychosocial needs in children are addressed from both a psychological and an educational perspective.

This dense chapter integrates psychiatric and educational nomenclature about special needs diagnoses to provide clearer understanding of disorders that children most commonly present in schools. Although some mental health professionals will not regularly use psychiatric terms in schools, the *DSM* represents the common language that all licensed mental health professions learn in their training. Knowledge about these dual "languages" will help enhance the collaborative skills of clinicians in schools.

Assessment measures that are used in schools to evaluate children and track their progress are addressed in Chapter 8. Clinical and school psychologists and neuropsychologists have historically provided the primary expertise in school systems when general assessment of children with special needs is required. However, as more special services such as speech and language, occupational and physical therapy, special education, and behavioral/mental health services have been incorporated into school systems, other disciplines have developed and provided assessment tools to schools to more fully assess and measure progress in students. Multidisciplinary school teams use a growing array of both direct observation and self-report assessment measures that are administered to students, teachers, and parents in traditional special education as well as current RtI school-based practice. All professionals who practice in schools need to have familiarity with measurement instruments to more scientifically establish an evidence base for the work we do, as well as to appreciate the unique contributions of these instruments. Chapter 8 addresses how multidisciplinary teams employ the measures and participate in the assessment process.

There are challenges and limits in every professional setting, and Chapter 9 addresses some of the dilemmas about engaging in multidisciplinary school practice. Connecticut's history of school certification for counselors, MFTs, and social workers is included in this chapter to illustrate examples of those challenges and opportunities.

Supervisors of mental health clinicians need familiarity with school systems and their procedures to support the growth of collaborative mental health practice in schools. Chapter 10 addresses the importance of supervision of mental health trainees, clinicians, and services in schools.

Finally, three appendices are included to serve as resources for interested readers. They are listed at the back of the book and include a list of assessments and assessment companies, a list of resources, and a glossary of terms.

Caveats

The names of all case examples in this book are changed to protect the privacy of the students and their families. The case examples were chosen to illustrate the range of situations that school-based professionals may encounter in their work, as well as the power of collaborative relationships and services.

Another important caveat needs to be inserted here. I mentioned that the original impetus of the book was to provide a guide for MFTs for school-based practice. Because Connecticut was the first state in the U.S. to enact school certification for MFTs, the majority of case examples comes from Connecticut and involves MFTs. Therefore, I admit that I have not focused sufficiently on the important contributions that each mental health profession makes to the success of children in schools. I express my regrets at the beginning for this omission.

Our experience has been that school needs, resources, and multidisciplinary teams vary significantly across urban, suburban, and rural regions and ages of students served in that school system. Teams vary across those diverse regions and across the developmental life span of students, and the composition of those teams varies as well.

Nonetheless, the clinical challenges for school-based mental health clinicians offer collaborative opportunities for all of us who work in schools, regardless of our training and our specific school settings. I have utilized skills I learned in all of my graduate training as we have worked to ensure certification for counselors, MFTs, school psychologists, and social workers in schools and promote multidisciplinary collaboration.

Therefore, I invite readers to use the case examples from this book as an impetus for sparking their own creative ideas for adaptation to the school systems where they practice or consult. As a licensed psychologist, family therapist, and social worker, I have come to appreciate the synergy of multidisciplinary mental health teams and their collaborative value, as well as how much they vary across school districts. The respect and support that such teams offer to families, especially those struggling with debilitating and chronic stressors, can make a critical difference in children's lives.

Now that school-based mental health practice is becoming better incorporated in the United States, texts are needed to train students, clinicians, and supervisors to provide comprehensive support to children and families in schools. Multidisciplinary collaboration and standardized, evidence-based practice can only serve to improve assessment and service delivery to children and families, both in health and education domains. This book should in some measure support attainment of those goals. I hope that *Building School-Based Collaborative Mental Health Teams* becomes one of many texts that address the evolution of mental health service delivery in education.

two

Why a Systems Approach?

Evolution in Focus From Individual to Systems

Education has historically focused on individual student achievement scores as the most important measures of student success and effective educational practice. Since the enactment of Public Law 94-142 in 1975, special education needs of individual students have been increasingly recognized and accommodated in U.S. schools, and a wider range of variables have also become recognized as important ingredients for student learning and achievement. P.L. 94-142 was instrumental in raising a collective U.S. consciousness about special learning needs of students, and a proliferation of special education programs and services has emerged in the U.S. since 1975.

The success of U.S. special education also generated challenges regarding the skyrocketing of special education budgets and the bifurcation of special education from the general education curriculum. School services are predicated on the local needs, events, resources, and leadership of each school district, and they vary significantly across the country. As specialized services evolved, the experience of school staff in general education became increasingly separated from assessment and service provision for students meeting criteria for special education services. For example, a school survey was administered soon after marriage and family therapy (MFT) school certification legislation was enacted in Connecticut (Laundy, Nelson, & Abucewicz, 2011). It was discovered that although marriage and family therapists were welcomed by the schools where they were placed, teachers and administrators in general education understood the roles that multidisciplinary mental health team members play in schools significantly less well than special educators did.

In the decades that followed, because of a wider understanding of what makes students achieve, the No Child Left Behind legislation of 2001 was enacted to integrate services more efficiently for all children within general education before referral for special education services. Broad-ranging initiatives such as Response to Intervention (RtI) and Positive Behavior Interventions and Supports (PBIS or school-wide [SW]PBIS) were developed to reduce the bifurcation of educational services in schools, equipping educators to support at-risk children through a variety of systemic interventions within general education. They were also developed to ameliorate some of the labor-intensive procedures from special education that were not proven to be sufficiently timely or effective. These initiatives are addressed throughout the book.

Educators have worked to address the widening range of factors that affect student resiliency and achievement since 1975. School systems have hired a growing array of health care providers to accommodate special needs in service of boosting student achievement. Evidence-based practice that examines such broader systemic variables as school climate, student health and education needs across a child's school career and family participation has recently generated a wider array of opportunities to address and measure student achievement than individual test scores alone.

In "A Framework for Safe and Successful Schools" (Cowan, Vaillancourt, Rossen, & Pollitt, 2013), a coalition of mental health professionals and school administrators offered policy recommendations that advocate for broader, more integrated assessment and service programs for children who are at risk for learning. Their summary addresses several important systemic recommendations, including blending funding opportunities for more mental health services within education, building incentives for collaboration among stakeholders within and outside of school systems, and supporting multitiered systems of support (MTSS) for students who need increased academic and behavioral services in schools (Cowan et al., 2013, p. 1).

MTSS have been developed to accommodate the categories of disabilities under P.L. 94-142. Depending on the requirements and resources in their districts, teams of educators and health/mental health clinicians have also generated MTSS for students with special medical and neuropsychological needs across the United States. These team approaches now offer increased assessment and service programs to a broader range of students. They mirror similar specialization trends in psychology and medicine over the past four decades, where services and programs have become increasingly specialized as new data emerge about treatment and management of those specific physical and mental health disorders.

Using an integrated systems approach such as universal screening and training general education teachers in social and emotional learning affords even broader and more collaborative ways of fostering student resiliency in today's education and health care climate. Evaluating the variables that impact student achievement can reveal the need for early intervention at multiple school levels and potentially save costly out-of-district placement costs later in a student's life. In contrast, simply adding on piecemeal services when emergencies occur in middle and high school without attending to how systemic layers of school culture work together can unnecessarily divert limited educational funds from other needed school programs and services.

In the past few years in the United States, school systems have experienced escalating crises of violence by troubled teens with undiagnosed and/or unaddressed psychiatric and behavioral needs. Some students without obvious disabilities "fly under the radar" of traditional school oversight, and their needs do not become well understood until after horrific violence occurs, such as happened at Sandy Hook Elementary School in Newtown, Connecticut.

In an article covering the demolition of the Sandy Hook Elementary School after the tragedy, the *New York Times* addressed the costs to the communities where violence occurred in Newtown; Littleton, Colorado (Columbine High School); and Virginia Tech. In all of these communities, buildings where the tragedies occurred were demolished or overhauled to create new schools or memorials (Barron, 2013). The emotional, social, legislative, and financial costs to students and their teachers, families, and communities were immeasurable. Many mental health professionals were called in to consult with children, families, school personnel, and others affected by the tragedies, and many students and their loved ones have continued to develop delayed psychological reactions long after the shootings.

In contrast, primary preventive tracking and collaborative service provision to at-risk students early in their school careers by state-licensed/certified school teams might prevent or at least mitigate some of that violence. All school crises cannot be prevented, of course. But comprehensive tracking across time of the multiple systemic layers of children's academic, social, and emotional functioning can help ensure that more vulnerable students get the early help they need and possibly save lives.

For instance, following the Sandy Hook tragedy, Connecticut passed a law that seeks to add collaborative training in social and emotional development of children to curriculum for all teachers-in-training, not just special educators or mental health clinicians. The law states that on and after July 1, 2012,

> any candidate entering a program of teacher preparation leading to professional certification shall be encouraged to complete training in competency areas contained in the professional teaching standards established by the State Board of Education, including, but not limited to, development and characteristics of learners, evidence-based and standards-based instruction, evidence-based classroom and behavior management, [and] assessment and professional behaviors and responsibilities, and social and emotional development and learning of children. The training in social and emotional development and learning of children shall include instruction concerning a comprehensive, coordinated social and emotional assessment and early intervention for children displaying behaviors associated with social or emotional problems, the availability of treatment services for such children and referring such children for assessment, intervention or treatment services. (State

of Connecticut Public Act No. 13-333 An Act Concerning Teacher Education Programs, para. i)

To that end, a multidisciplinary faculty team at the School of Professional Studies at Central Connecticut State University was appointed by the dean of education and the president of the university to develop coursework for all teachers-in-training, not just teachers preparing for special education certification, before their student teaching experience (G. Grey, personal communication, January 30, 2014). The syllabus for this course was created by a collaborative multidisciplinary team of faculty headed by Ralph Cohen from the departments of special education, counseling and family therapy, social work, and teacher education from the CCSU School of Professional Studies. (For more information about that course, contact Dr. Cohen at cohenr@ccsu.edu.)

The team task was to design training modules for teachers-in-training in general education to help them better understand the importance of social and emotional learning to academic achievement. The module is also designed to assess, manage, and refer children at risk for behavioral services that they might need beyond the classroom. Mastery of this curriculum is serving as precursor to their field experience and student teaching for teachers-in-training. Mental health professionals in schools have an unprecedented opportunity to create and participate in collaborative mental health practice in schools with this new law.

Cohen enlisted a faculty team from the Counselor Education and Family Therapy, Social Work, Education Leadership, Teacher Education and Special Education Departments to cowrite this curriculum. We used a systemic brief developed at the Center on Great Teachers and Leaders at American Institutes of Research called the *Teaching the Whole Child Research to Practice Brief* (Yoder, 2014) as a beginning guide to develop the curriculum. Our assignment was to help educators understand the importance of social and emotional health as a precursor to learning, echoing Yoder's statement that educators, policymakers, and researchers "know that effective teachers do more than promote academic learning—they teach the whole child" (Yoder,

2014, p. 1). We used that brief as a basis for developing a collaborative "best practice" curriculum for teachers-in-training before they begin their student teaching experience.

Specific goals involve helping teachers incorporate into their lesson plans such emotional and social learning variables as learning to work together in group assignments, learning to monitor one's mood and behavior, and making informed behavioral decisions as students grow and face increasing academic challenges in school. Educators know that these are necessary skills for students to acquire to achieve academically and to meet growing standards such as those contained in Common Core and in secondary and postsecondary educational curricula. Because special education has been historically separated from general education, many teachers have not had access to such emotional and social learning training beyond one required special education course. This collaborative initiative is designed to fill that gap in teacher training, as well as help reintegrate general with special education training.

Students need to develop emotional skills to regulate and manage the inevitable and necessary frustrations of academic, emotional, and social transitions through childhood and adolescence. These resiliency skills are necessary for success across the life span of all students. Rather than having this training presented as another "add-on" that teachers must incorporate into their already packed school day, the aim of this project is to give teachers the tools to *integrate* social and emotional learning principles with academics through preclassroom training and to raise their consciousness about how to obtain further help for students in need should a referral become necessary.

The significance of the Connecticut legislative decision to integrate what was formerly the domain of special education into general education curriculum is important. Social and emotional learning curriculum is critical to the knowledge base teachers need to teach confidently, as well as to access the resources necessary to educate students with special needs in their care. Mental health teams in schools can play active roles in helping integrate this curriculum in education.

Multidisciplinary teams have worked collaboratively in hospitals and residential and outpatient treatment centers for many years, and

school multidisciplinary teams have developed increasing appreciation of MTSS since 1975. With proactive systemic planning within
a broader range of school program and service tiers, the chances
that primary prevention will improve student outcomes are greatly
enhanced. Some may argue that their school districts cannot afford
to hire licensed multidisciplinary teams, but the cost of not addressing special needs of students rises significantly if those needs are not
met early. The value of addressing the aftermath of increasing school
violence tragically outweighs the preventive costs of hiring highly
qualified mental health school teams to help students improve their
readiness to learn.

**Why Add Marriage and Family Therapists to School Multidisciplinary
Teams?**

Some argue that schools already certify counselors, school psychologists, and social workers for school-based practice and that schools
do not need and/or cannot afford more mental health clinicians
than they currently employ. Mental health professionals practicing
in schools currently do provide valuable mental/behavioral health
services to students in public and private schools across the United
States. All of these mental health professionals are trained to provide
individual, group, and some degree of family counseling/therapy and
support to those in need of such services. In addition, licensed mental
health clinicians regularly contract privately with schools to provide
specialized mental health services to students. Why should we certify
MFTs for full-time employment in schools? Isn't mental/behavioral
health service in education about education for children rather than
treatment for couples and families?

There are several reasons why the time has come for the full range
of mental health professionals to become licensed and certified to
practice in educational settings. There are five advantages to developing a cadre of qualified school-based mental health teams in schools,
which are addressed in the following pages. The advantages include
the following:

1. Developing higher standards of mental health service through
   state licensure *and* school certification

2. Mitigating the loss of mental health services in residential, hospital, and other clinical settings by colocating those services in or close to schools

3. Affirming the value of a multidisciplinary mental health team approach to student achievement

4. Recognizing the importance of wraparound services including families

5. Using the systems-based training and multidisciplinary heritage of MFTs and other mental health disciplines trained in systems-based service

Raising standards.

First, all six mental/behavioral health professions (counseling, MFT, nursing, psychiatry, psychology, and social work) are licensed by U.S. State Departments of Health to provide diagnostic assessment and treatment services. However, not all of these professions are both licensed *and* certified by their State Departments of Education to practice in schools. For instance, in Connecticut only MFTs are currently required to be licensed by their state Departments of Health to become full time school-certified employees, and many counselors, school psychologists and social workers do not hold licensure.

But school systems are federally required by the Individuals With Disabilities Education Act (IDEA) to educate children with an increasingly complex array of social and emotional needs. School administrators need to have access to a *full* talent pool of qualified mental/behavioral health providers to determine the particular service *fit* that is best for their school system. Raising the standards of mental health professionals hired for school-based practice enhances the qualifications to match those provided in traditional health care settings. It also equips school systems to hire from a more highly trained talent pool. Although initially there may be financial outlay to hire more highly qualified mental health professionals, the preventive cost savings can potentially be substantial.

Mitigating losses through colocation in schools.

Second, providing cost-effective services to children and families within schools can mitigate the loss of mental health services to children and families that has occurred in the recent era of escalating school violence, managed health care, economic recession, and loss of jobs and employer-based insurance. The community mental health movement started by President John F. Kennedy in the 1960s was a first step toward decreasing the marginalization of those with mental handicaps through deinstitutionalization. But the development of and support for outpatient health care services for those with psychiatric diagnoses have not kept pace with the need for services for students at serious psychiatric risk.

Far too many children, adolescents, and adults have not received sufficient care or lost coverage during the last recession under the current U.S. system of health care. Kelson (2007) reported that

> children accounted for the largest share of the roughly 3.7 million people who lost employer-provided health insurance between 2000 and 2004. And while public programs have taken up some of the slack, medical inflation and state budget constraints are making it difficult for programs like Medicaid and the State Children's Health Insurance Program (SCHIP) to continue to absorb the growing number of uninsured Americans. (para. 41)

The ranks of underinsured and noninsured children and families in this country have grown in alarming ways, just as residential services and programs for more seriously ill children and adolescents has dwindled in the past decades. In her Economic Policy Institute Briefing Paper, Gould (2012) reported that employer-based insurance for children fell by 11.9 percentage points during the period from 2000 to 2010, and the gap in access to insurance coverage for children also widened substantially (p. 56). She added that the decline was felt across the United States and that it has been accompanied by an overall decline in health care insurance.

Health care service provision to children and families has also become fragmented under the U.S. system of fee-for-service health care practice, where specialized procedures are reimbursed and not enough collaborative wraparound services are compensated. Children and families too often lack sufficient insurance and therefore receive less primary preventive health care than they need to make full use of educational opportunities. According to a report in *Health Affairs* (Karaca-Mandic, Choi Yoo, & Sommers, 2013), the recent recession took a particular toll on families of children with special health needs. They found that the recession

> led to a decline in spending for children with special needs, who had much higher out-of-pocket spending at baseline. Adults had significantly lower out-of-pocket spending during the recession, which suggests that parents may reduce their own medical care in difficult economic times to meet their children's health care needs. (p. 1054)

Primary preventive health care has become less available for children and has become more emergency-based and expensive. Families who struggle with chronic health care needs are particularly challenged and are at great risk for marginalization and depletion of their resources. What better place to serve children with special needs than in schools, where they spend the bulk of their time? More about colocation of health care services within schools will be addressed throughout this text.

The historic value of multidisciplinary teams.
Mental health disciplines such as counseling, nursing, and school psychology became integrated into schools in the United States after World War II, when interest first emerged in assessment, health, and postsecondary school preparation and placement. Other disciplines such as social work were incorporated into schools in the late 1960s and early 1970s, when civil rights and inclusion became national priorities in education. As the newest of the mental health professions, MFT had its origins as a specialty service located in inpatient psychiatric hospitals, outpatient centers and private practices in the 1950s and

1960s, and school certification began in Connecticut in 2008. As with other mental health disciplines, MFT licensure and school certification has expanded across the United States, with all states now having licensure and several having school-based certification.

The mental health professions have unique as well as similar training and skill sets, which equips them well for collaborative work in schools. We have developed a Mental Health Matrix at our Counseling and Family Therapy Department at CCSU to illustrate to our graduate students the "necessary redundancies" that mental health professions share, as well as the specific skill sets that make them unique. The blend of these competencies affords potent opportunities for school-based mental health support. The Mental Health Matrix is illustrated in

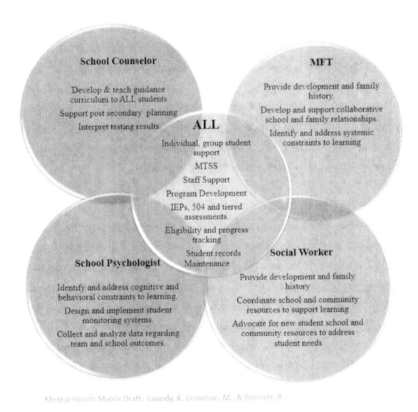

Figure 2.1. Mental Health Matrix. From Laundy, Donohue, and Bennett (2014). Reprinted with permission.

Each quadrant of the matrix lists the primary unique skills of the four primary mental health professions. School counselors are the closest discipline to school curriculum, and they typically teach guidance lessons to all students across primary, middle, and high school levels. Hence, they are the mental health discipline with the closest view of the school as a whole. They also provide valuable support for postsecondary school planning, and they help interpret testing results with school teams. MFTs typically provide developmental and family histories to the school team. They help interpret testing results to families and are primarily trained to encourage the development of collaborative home and school relationships. MFTs are also trained to address constraints to learning across all systemic levels of school culture, ranging from individual to school climate and culture levels.

School social workers are also trained to provide developmental histories, and they too serve as liaisons among social agencies, homes and schools. They have historically helped develop school and community resources to meet student needs, and they have a strong history of advocating for disadvantaged children and families. School psychologists are recognized as the experts in assessing cognitive and behavioral constraints to learning. They have been leaders in designing monitoring systems for student achievement, as well as analyzing collected data to promote student achievement.

All four disciplines have "necessary redundancy" in their training as well. As can be seen in the middle circle, all mental health clinicians who become school certified have at least masters' level training in individual and group counseling. They have skills based on their interests in multitiered systems of support, which includes individual and group services for student and staff as well as program development. All participate in formal assessment meetings to develop Individualized Education Plans (IEPs; also referred to as Individualized Education Programs) and 504 plans, as well as newer tiered interventions. They all participate in tracking and monitoring student progress and achievement, and the mental health professions are all trained in record keeping to document and maintain records.

Private practice professionals from all six licensed mental health groups have also provided clinical and consultative services and programs to children and families in schools through contractual arrangement for many years. For instance, school-based MFT, psychological, counseling, and social work services are routinely contracted through Youth Service Bureaus (YSBs) and child guidance clinics in many of Connecticut's 169 towns.

There is significant variability across school systems and districts in the United States regarding mental health services in schools, depending on resources, availability of staff, and leadership priorities of the school system. Each mental/behavioral health discipline has emerged from different settings, and they all serve schools in a variety of ways.

Physical and occupational therapy, speech and language pathology, nursing, and other disciplines have been invited into schools as the need for such special services for children with neuropsychological and physical handicaps became better recognized and made affordable by local districts in the last half of the 20th century. School nurses are important resources for linking medical with mental health services in schools.

The federal legislation mandating such services under Public Law 94-142 in 1975 and its subsequent 504 amendment strengthened the influx of allied health care services into public schools across America. The growth of multidisciplinary teams in schools is a tribute to how much they are valued by educators.

Wraparound, family-centered school services.

A fourth advantage to school certification for family-friendly multidisciplinary school teams is that family-strengthening services empower families who have children with special needs in ways that help those children learn, with wraparound support from home and school. Special health and learning needs are sometimes passed genetically from one generation to the next. When developmental problems (such as dyslexia, attention problems or autistic spectrum disorders) are also present in the parents, they too often struggle with negative experiences from their own educational backgrounds, when less was known about special educational needs.

Such parents often enter the school planning process with understandable trepidation. The resources of families who struggle with chronic health and education issues are continually challenged, and their energies can become depleted over time. Providing expert family wraparound support in schools by multidisciplinary teams can actually mitigate that downward spiral by empowering families to participate in the educational process in more informed ways. It can strengthen families to take more full advantage of IEPs. Paying attention to the "big picture" of health and well-being across time adds a critical ingredient to children's school readiness and ability to learn. Such systemic focus can save time, energy, and money in the long run by directing energy to primary prevention and family programs and services rather than remedial measures.

As alternative family structures and the health care needs have evolved over the past few decades and more has become known about children with complex medical and emotional issues, the services of health disciplines are being increasingly requested to provide a fuller range of services to children and families in schools. The availability and special skill sets of licensed mental health professionals in the United States varies significantly across urban, suburban, and rural locations. To have access to all disciplines that provide health services, school administrators need the freedom and flexibility to employ from among all six of the licensed and school-certified mental health professions as well as contract for services with clinicians in private practice or agencies to meet the specific needs of their district.

Training in systemic practice.

The fifth advantage to inclusive multidisciplinary school teams is the value-added systemic training that many current mental health professions receive. Systemic clinical training with a focus on families is the cornerstone of all MFT graduate education, making them well suited to the MTSS of contemporary education. The multidisciplinary heritage of the MFT profession is strong, and MFTs are oriented to address both the challenges and the advantages of collaborative multidisciplinary team service.

The MFT profession was originally created by a group of psychiatrists, psychologists, and social workers who became frustrated with the lack of success of individual psychotherapy with patients with severe mental illness and sought more systemic ways to support their needs (Becvar & Becvar, 2008; Hoffman, 2002). MFT began as a family-strengthening measure to help families join with the treatment team to help better manage their affected family member's health care needs. It grew quickly as a powerful treatment for chronic mental health problems and is now a standard treatment modality, along with individual and group therapy and psychopharmacology. In recent years, MFT has become its own mental health profession.

Connecticut, for instance, has five graduate training programs, which are accredited by the Commission on Accreditation of the American Association for Marriage and Family Therapy (COAMFTE). COMFTE reviews graduate programs in marriage and family therapy at masters, doctoral, and postdoctoral levels and grants accreditation to programs that meet and/or exceed accreditation standards. Currently there are more than 118 COAMFTE accredited programs in the United States and Canada (see their directory at http://www. aamft.org/mftaccreditedprograms). For more than two decades, MFTs have been trained as a unique mental health discipline to practice in a variety of clinical settings. Postdegree licensure is now granted in all states in the United States.

Building collaborative teams of all service providers and educators in schools who provide high standards of evidence-based assessment and care should prove to be a more effective way to educate and serve children and families in need. Evidence-based practice is part of the Response to Intervention (RtI) mandate enacted in the federal No Child Left Behind (NCLB) legislation of 2001. It will be more fully addressed in Chapter 5, but it is introduced here as an example of the shift from individualized to systemic thinking.

Public schools have been required by P.L. 94-142 to educate all children with special needs in the least restrictive environment (LRE) possible to maximize students' learning, according to the original special education legislation. The RtI initiative currently being incorporated into school districts across the country has as its aim to incorporate scientifically based research earlier into general educational practice. The goal of RtI is to help all children learn, without the inappropriate use of traumatizing labels, procedures, and placements that sometimes inadvertently occurs in special education (National Association of State Directors of Special Education [NASDE], 2005).

RtI is designed to address both educational and behavioral components of school through three increasingly intensive interventions, which are measured at regular intervals during the school year. An important shift is occurring in education under the RtI initiative in which schools are becoming more accountable for not only what they teach, but how well students learn (NASDE, 2005, p. 15). Schools are now federally required to not only provide specific and appropriate educational services, but they must also track and document service effectiveness. Blending evidence-based mental health and behavioral treatment with targeted and proven multidisciplinary educational services over time helps ensure that all children can become better prepared to learn in the LRE possible.

RtI seeks to incorporate evidence-based special services earlier within general education, before major educational problems develop and interfere with children's natural desire to achieve and before formal special education processes need to be enlisted. Making a full complement of multidisciplinary behavioral and educational services available early on to school systems therefore makes reasonable sense.

Multidisciplinary teams of licensed and certified mental health professionals are ideal resources to address the behavioral components of the RtI process in public schools. They help reduce the marginalization of children with special needs because three layers of RtI services are now offered to teachers and children in general education classrooms before formal special education assessment to determine the extent of support needed. For many children, that means less "special education" labelling, and for teachers it means more support within mainstream education. There needs to be more systemic utilization of evidence-based best practices across disciplines in health care and education to best promote and measure healthy functioning and achievement (Carr, 2000; Sprenkle & Piercy, 2005).

Such valuable collaborative assessment and service provision has been written into American education law since 1975 (Wright & Wright, 2007). Public Law 94-142 was enacted that year and mandated the creation of a multidisciplinary team approach to providing a free and appropriate public education (FAPE) to all children in public schools. Assessments and services are now available and provide for children from infancy to age 21. Special educators, learning disability specialists, speech and language pathologists, occupational and physical therapists, and counselors, school psychologists, and social workers have all become certified in schools, joining teams of general education professionals to provide more comprehensive services for students. Some urban schools across the United States have established school-based health clinics where integrated physical and mental health services are provided.

As described in several chapters of this book, chronic health problems have escalated and are being better diagnosed in the United States, but this has occurred at the same time as health care has become less accessible to children and families. School-based mental health services can help mitigate the dilemma of providing the health care services to all children so that they can fully access educational opportunities within their "educational home."

Health symptoms often show up in schools, and children need to be healthy to learn. The skills of mental health professionals are increasingly needed in schools to address chronic disorders that have both health and educational implications. Because some learning disabilities are inherited across generations, it is a strong advantage that professionals with family systems training can work with generational family patterns. Too often parents are wary of schools because their own learning needs were misdiagnosed as children and negative perceptions linger. Many mental health professionals are trained to address these processes and can strengthen families to participate more fully in school meetings.

Another timely contribution mental health professionals make is their ability to collaborate well with educators to comprehensively address children's needs. Education policy across America is shifting towards systemic and scientifically based ways of educating all children, based on 2001 NCLB legislation. Schools are integrating proven general and special education practices earlier and more effectively into regular education to better reach and teach all children. All mental health disciplines in schools are increasingly expected to collaboratively design and provide an array of behavioral health care services to children and adolescents in schools.

The intent of the RtI is to raise reading and other academic scores as documented proof that children are benefitting from intensive early interventions that are based on good science. RtI is designed to provide three tiers of intervention before making special education referrals in order to reintegrate special education into the whole school milieu. Mental health professionals are well versed in such evidence-based systemic practice and are trained to provide timely and value-added service to school teams. Together these professional teams can provide valuable diagnostic, treatment, tracking, and cost-saving services over a student's career.

The artificial and profit-driven boundaries between comprehensive health care and education need to be better recognized and eliminated in this country. A more collaborative and systemic approach to raising and educating healthy children is sorely needed, particularly in the wake of increasing school violence. Interest is growing in such collaborative concepts as the medical home (Keckley, 2010; McAllister, Sherrieb, & Cooley, 2009), and there needs to be coordination of such health care practices with education across the country to ensure more comprehensive service delivery. Integrating key concepts from medical family therapy with more systemically addressed education practices provides a bridge to better health care *and* education by building collaborative teams to comprehensively address children and families with special needs through wraparound services that are convenient to access. Such teams can create potent educational homes to boost student resiliency and achievement.

Before the value of systemic teams can be fully appreciated, however, the history of individualized specialized school-based support needs to be understood. The next chapter traces the history of special education in the United States as a "prequel" to subsequent chapters on current initiatives.

three

Special Education Law: Civil Rights, Inclusion, and Entitlement

Kathleen C. Laundy and William R. Nelson

History and Chronology

The education of students with special needs in America is rooted in three historical traditions. All are heavily embedded in federal civil rights and entitlement laws that have been enacted in the United States over the past several decades. Current interpretation of laws by individual school systems can seem confusing without an appreciation of the context of the federal laws that have been enacted for students with special needs. It is therefore important for all those who work in education systems to have familiarity with special education history. Such information helps determine how the skills of multidisciplinary professionals collectively fit together to form the multidisciplinary array of services that school systems provide to students with special needs.

This chapter chronicles salient events from that history, describes basic special education terminology, and outlines key initiatives over the past century that have been designed to educate all children. It describes the federal categories that schools use to classify special education and the services provided to students with disabilities. Finally, it addresses some constraints of the special education in the United States and introduces current initiatives that are being developed to strengthen special education legislation.

For our marriage and family therapy (MFT) graduate students at Central Connecticut State University, we developed a timeline to trace the recent history of education legislation, both federal and state, that enabled MFTs to practice in schools. Figure 3.1 illustrates how the federal special education legislation laws coincided with MFT state licensure and certification since 1975.

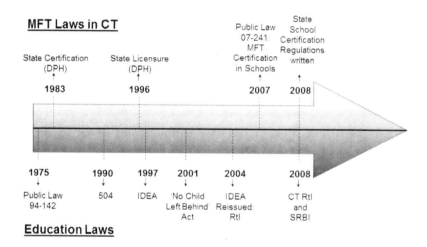

Figure 3.1. Timeline of education and marriage and family therapy (MFT) Laws. Reprinted with permission, courtesy of the author.

As can be seen at the bottom of the graph, Public Law 94-142, the groundbreaking federal special education law, was first enacted in 1975. As it has been amended, it has coincided with enactment of state legislation in Connecticut that has credentialed MFTs to become school-based mental health professionals to support the special needs of students. That legislation is chronicled across the top of the graph.

The full history of legislation to support the special needs of students extends significantly further back in time in the United States. Spurred by the leadership of Horace Mann, the United States has witnessed many efforts over the past century to educate all children (Wright & Wright, 2007). Collective education for the waves of children from immigrant families who arrived in this country helped promote tolerance and assimilation of families into American culture, according to Mann and other progressive educational thinkers. Education over the 20th century and into the 21st has come to include services for a wider variety of special needs that children present in school. But there has been significant historic variability in services within and among states for students with special needs. Special educational services were provided in primarily residential or private settings in the United States until the 1960s, and parents often shouldered the responsibility for developing and paying for those services.

In 1954, the U.S. Supreme Court issued the landmark *Brown v. Board of Education* decision. It determined that segregated schools were unequal for African American children and deprived them of equal protection under the law. The decision affirmed the civil right of African American children to attend integrated schools. Similar to ethnic and race discrimination, students with disabilities were often not considered "mainstream" students within the dominant school culture and were also excluded from educational opportunities. Over the next 20 years, class-action suits and other litigation followed to protect disabled students who were victims of discrimination. Turnbull (1993) stated that

> Although *Brown vs. Board of Education* established the right to equal educational opportunity on Fourth Amendment grounds, it was not until *Pennsylvania Association for Retarded Children (PARC) vs. Commonwealth of Pennsylvania, and Mills vs. D.C. Board of Education* that *Brown* became meaningful for children with disabilities. (p. 36)

Courts in both lawsuits relied on legal and educational authorities to support their findings that education is essential to enable children to function in society and that *all* children can benefit from education. The PARC group claimed denial of services to children with mental retardation as they sued the Pennsylvania Department of Education (Ysseldyke & Algozzine, 1995). The decision from *PARC vs.*

Commonwealth of Pennsylvania forced the school districts in the state to evaluate and plan appropriate educational programs for students with mental retardation who had been excluded from school. Rothstein and Johnson (2010) noted that "the general framework of the decisions was then the basis for the passage of a federal statute (the IDEA) and the detailed regulations developed pursuant to it" (p. 7).

The *Mills vs. D.C. Board of Education* decision was a judgment against the school board of Washington, DC, regarding children with disabilities other than mental retardation. Turnbull (1993) reports that

> Mills applied the equal protection and due process guarantees of the Fifth and Fourteenth Amendments to furnish this important right to students with disabilities. The court order from that suit stated that before any child with a disability eligible for publicly supported education may be excluded from a regular school assignment, the child must be furnished adequate alternative educational services suited to his or her needs, including (if appropriate) special education or tuition grants. (pp. 36–37)

The District of Columbia School Board was required to provide each disabled school-age child a free and suitable publicly supported education, regardless of the degree of mental, physical, or emotional disability. The school board was also enjoined from making disciplinary suspensions for any reason for longer than 2 days unless school authorities gave the child a hearing before suspension and continued the child's education while he or she was suspended. Because of civil rights legislation and other stakeholder movements during that period, parents became empowered to advocate that their children with special needs who were being similarly discriminated against and segregated because of their disabilities. The scope of understanding about determinants of school underachievement thus broadened beyond disadvantage to also include disability. The *Elementary and Secondary Education Act (ESEA)* was enacted by Congress in 1965 and amended in 1966. This law provided resources to help ensure quality education for disadvantaged students. The amended law in 1990 included incentive grants to stimulate the creation of programs to help students with disabilities across the nation (Wright & Wright, 2007).

The success of these suits and legislation paved the way for Public Law 94-142, which enabled a growing range of children with special needs to be included in public school education. With a foundation thus established by concerned families, government, and other leaders, P.L. 94-142 was enacted in 1975 and implemented in 1978. This landmark legislation is also known as the *Education for All Handicapped Children Act of 1975 (EAHCA)*. It revolutionized services to children with special needs across the United States. The legislation contained new and important provisions that form the pillars of special education law in schools. First, it ensured that all children were owed a *free and appropriate public education* (or FAPE; Hardman, Drew, & Egan, 2008) in the *least restrictive environment* (LRE) possible (Hallahan, Kauffman, & Pullen, 2009). That is, *all* children became *entitled* to be included in public education, regardless of their special needs.

Schools became responsible for assessing and designing through *Nondiscriminatory Evaluations and Assessment* appropriate ways to accommodate children's special needs, so that they could achieve according to their measured abilities (Hardman et al., 2008). From such assessment an *Individual Education Plan* (IEP; Hardman et al., 2008) was then developed for all children determined to be in need of special education. Parents became entitled to access to *due process* (Raymond, 2008), which ensured that they must give their permission for assessment and would have active, informed involvement in the special education process for their children. These fundamental elements form the pillars of the special education law and are defined more in detail later in this chapter.

P.L. 94-142 was critical federal legislation that began to direct and hold local educational systems accountable for providing such services to students. Because of that federal mandate, schools began to view children's functioning in school in ways beyond traditional reading, writing, and arithmetic. They began to incorporate consideration of a full range of adaptive functioning in children into measures of children's school success. School mental health staff added behavioral assessments to measure a child's adaptive functioning in addition to that child's cognitive ability and academic achievement levels. These behavioral assessments grew to include daily living skills, expressive and receptive language and communication skills, and social and emotional functioning. Schools have increasingly used such adaptive functioning data to plan comprehensively for children's needs.

Public Law 94-142 has been amended several times since 1975 to strengthen the law and its outcomes. In 1986 and 1990, Congress amended the law to include all preschoolers with disabilities, including infants, toddlers, and children aged 3 to 5 years. This is referred to as Part H, which mandates early intervention for infants and toddlers with disabilities and support for their families (Anderson, Chitwood, & Hayden, 1997).

P.L. 94-142 was further amended in 1990 as the Individuals With Disabilities Education Act (IDEA). Here, requirements for eligibility for special education services as well as protection for children and families entitled to those services were more clearly defined. Incorporating Section 504 of the Federal Rehabilitation Act of 1973, IDEA established due process hearing procedures, which were designed to better ensure the rights of handicapped children in public schools under the Americans With Disabilities Act (ADA). These laws and recommendations for curriculum accommodations further integrated civil rights with inclusion and entitlement components of federal legislation in education. Special education programs and services have grown exponentially over time, as have the special education budgets that fund such services.

Special Education Terms and Processes

We now turn to specific definitions of special education terms and processes that are essential to know to understand the language used in school systems. The following terms and processes are designed to familiarize the reader with the culture of special education and to introduce core concepts. To comprehensively serve the educational and emotional needs of students, productive collaboration with administrators, teachers, and parents requires an in-depth understanding of special education concepts and principles, as well as familiarity with the state and federal special education law mandates just described.

This fundamental understanding enables school personnel to participate appropriately in special service processes and to effectively fulfill the educational responsibilities of a public school system.

Free and appropriate public education (FAPE).

The federal special education law, IDEA, mandates a free and appropriate public education for all children (Hardman et al., 2008). This is to be provided at no expense to the parents, regardless of a student's disabilities. When planning programs for students who qualify for special education services, the fundamental question to be addressed is: Which educational program will help the student receive the maximum educational benefit to achieve according to his or her potential? As Hardman et al. (2008) suggest, this question presents many challenges because of the vast heterogeneity of students with special education needs. Effective programming demands skillful communication among all stakeholders in the education process, including the student, parents, educators, clinicians and school administrators.

Planning and placement team (PPT).

Special education services and programs are developed through a multidisciplinary team, generally consisting of the child's parents or guardians, the child's general education teacher, a special education teacher, a school administrator, a school psychologist, or other mental health professional such as an MFT, a school counselor, and/ or a school social worker. The composition of the multidisciplinary team is a reflection of the child's suspected area of disability (Kirk, Gallagher, Coleman, & Anastasiow, 2009). If, for example, the child demonstrates speech and language deficits, a speech and language clinician is needed on the multidisciplinary team. If a child has no speech and language delays but is demonstrating significant school adjustment problems, an MFT, counselor, school psychologist, or social worker would become preferred members of the team. For children with more pervasive disabilities, occupational therapists and physical therapists also play integral roles on the team.

Medical professionals are also included as team participants. School nurses typically attend team meetings, and pediatricians and psychiatrists, neurologists, or other medical specialists are invited to school meetings as needed to clarify and support the needs of the student and the plans made for that child and family.

According to the federal special education mandate of IDEA, it is only after appropriate academic and or behavioral interventions have been exhausted that a student is referred for a formal, individualized evaluation for a suspected disability. Therefore, prereferral activities must first be conducted and documented before a student is referred for an evaluation. Prereferral activities are designed to facilitate an increase in the child's productivity in the general education curriculum (Hardman et al., 2008). They do not represent significant changes in curriculum content or conceptual difficulty. For example, these accommodations may include changes in instructional delivery, expectations of student performance, or arrangements in the instructional environment (such as preferential seating). These accommodations are closely linked with Response to Intervention (RtI) and Positive Behavioral Interventions and Supports (PBIS) planning, which are addressed in Chapter 6.

Parents are invited to discuss the academic and/or behavioral challenges that their child is facing at school and are oriented to the nature of the prereferral interventions. Parents can also request further evaluation of their child. Such measures could include specific evaluation instruments, other sources of information including observations of the student, review of completed assignments, or discipline record information. Such processes must be approved by the child's parents or guardians.

When a full evaluation becomes necessary, the multidisciplinary team establishes procedures that address the area or areas of suspected disability. As part of the due process provision of IDEA, parents must agree to the evaluation and plans as established by the multidisciplinary team before the evaluation (Kirk et al., 2009). It is at this juncture that parents learn the scope and goals of the evaluation efforts. A challenge that the multidisciplinary team must address is how to construct the evaluation in a way that is jargon free, understandable, and agreeable to the parents. Ideally, questions about the student's strengths and needs from parents and school professionals will be incorporated into the evaluation together. At times, parents and educators may disagree about evaluation measures and results. This challenge must be met for parents to make an informed and committed decision regarding their child's evaluation. School planning for students with special needs is fundamentally based on school and family collaboration.

IEP development.

The multidisciplinary team assembled to assess the suspected disability or disabilities of a student is charged with developing an IEP that will address the specific educational needs of the student that have been revealed by the evaluation. An IEP is the result of front-loaded, multidisciplinary assessment and planning. It includes information regarding the student's current levels of functioning, identified long-term goals and short-term objectives focused on achieving the long-term goals, as well as information regarding the extent to which the student will not participate in the general education classroom and curriculum (Hardman et al., 2008). According to the major provisions of IDEA, the IEP must also provide an explanation of the services that are to be provided to the child as well as plans for initiating and evaluating the services. For students who are 14 years of age or older, transition services from school to work or further education must also be delineated.

In certain cases, the multidisciplinary team will identify the related services that a student with a disability might need to be productive in the program that is being established. Related services could possibly include support provided by audiologists, medical specialists, occupational therapists, physical therapists, vocational education teachers, interpreters, teacher's aides, paraprofessionals, and school mental health workers. Special transportation may also need to be provided. When a special education evaluation is completed, the PPT convenes and develops with the parents the comprehensive IEP to meet that student's unique special education needs.

Determining LRE.

Another responsibility of the multidisciplinary team in crafting an IEP is to fulfill the LRE mandate of IDEA. According to Hallahan et al. (2012), the major LRE provision of IDEA challenges the team to ensure that the student be educated in the least restrictive environment consistent with the student's educational needs and to the maximum extent possible with students without disabilities. The framers of the special education law recognized that the best role models are other students in general education classrooms. LRE is a legal term, which means that a disabled student should be separated from non-disabled classmates and from home, family, and community as little as possible. The multidisciplinary team must establish the LRE for a student's program. The team must answer the question of how much the student differs from average students, as well as what resources are available in the school and community. The LRE component of P.L. 94-142 is designed to provide as much of a mainstream education to children as possible and to protect students from unnecessary labeling or stigmatization while students' special education needs are being met.

In determining the LRE for a student with an identified disability, the multidisciplinary team reviews the spectrum of special service opportunities available that would be appropriate for the specific case. The team makes its decision by reviewing the continuum of most appropriate alternative placement options available.

According to Kirk et al. (2009), this continuum begins with the general education classroom and incorporates levels of intervention that are addressed in Chapter 6 on RtI. The choice of this option means that the general education teacher has knowledge of the specific disability and is skilled in meeting the instructional demands that the student brings to the classroom. The teacher is able to acquire any appropriate special materials and equipment essential to the child's productivity. Hence, students placed in general education classrooms where the teacher is solely responsible for the child's program are not receiving any special education services per se.

A slightly more restrictive option on the LRE continuum is when the multidisciplinary team has determined that the LRE for the student is the general education classroom with consultation services or coteaching available. With consultative options, the general education teacher receives consultative support from a special education, school psychologist, or other school professional. Special education teaching consultative activities might include modeling instruction and demonstrating the use of materials or equipment, and a marriage and family therapist might communicate to the teacher the family's capacity to provide homework completion support. These services are typically provided for students with learning disabilities and/or behavioral challenges to their learning.

The general education teacher and the special education teacher could arrange a coteaching experience in which both are providing instructional experience for the classroom. The special education teacher would emphasize instructional supports and modifications and accommodations for the students with disabilities included in the classroom, and the general education teacher would provide the major curriculum instruction. Or the general education teacher and a combination of special school professionals may arrange for group services within the classroom that meet the needs of students in that classroom. More is described about general education–special education collaboration in the next chapter on RtI. In both of these first two options, special education services are increasingly being incorporated within general education in comprehensive ways under the IDEA reauthorization that initiated RtI initiatives in 2004.

A somewhat more restrictive option on the continuum is the resource teacher or resource room program approach in which a student works with the resource teacher, a trained special educator, for a specified length of time and frequency as determined on the IEP. The resource teacher usually works with students individually or in small groups, using special materials and equipment in a separate classroom. The special education teacher maintains communication with the general education teacher regarding the specific skill development and needs of the students being served in the resource room. The students with disabilities participating in the resource room option spend the majority of their time in the general education classroom and move to the resource room for specialized instruction. Students who utilize these services typically have developmental disabilities, autism, or more severe behavioral challenges.

The self-contained special class is the next more restrictive option available for consideration by the multidisciplinary team. Students with disabilities placed in the self-contained special class option typically spend the majority of their school day in this special environment, while participating in music, art, and physical education with their nondisabled peers. All instruction in the self-contained special class is provided by trained special education teachers. At times they are assisted by paraprofessionals, who provide further instructional aid to students in the classroom.

The next restrictive option available for consideration by the multidisciplinary team involves placing the student outside the public school system in a special day school. In choosing this option, the PPT has agreed that the student's special educational needs cannot be met in the continuum options available within the child's public school system. Placing a student in a special day school is considered restrictive because it significantly separates the student with the disability from the nondisabled peers of his school and community. A special day school is often dedicated to a specific disability category, such as serving students with learning disabilities, emotional and behavior challenges, or those with pervasive developmental disabilities such as autism, blindness, and/or hearing impairments. The special day schools have a level of specialization that is necessary for meeting the educational needs of the students that they are dedicated to serving. Students attending special day schools return to their homes at the close of school.

The most restrictive placement option available for consideration by the multidisciplinary team is a residential school placement. Residential schools offer 24-hour care for students, where they provide appropriate instruction, special services as needed, and close supervision of the daily living environment of the students. This placement is generally reserved for students with profound impairments who cannot manage their thoughts, impulses, and behavior without the structured support that a residential school and staff can provide.

Nondiscriminatory evaluation and assessment.

Formal school evaluations and assessments are designed to document the learning strengths and needs of referred students and to prepare the multidisciplinary team for how to best service a child with special needs. Evaluation procedures typically include the following: ability testing (intelligence testing) conducted by a school psychologist; academic skill evaluation (achievement testing) conducted by special education teacher or school psychologist; academic work samples; social and adaptive functioning assessment conducted by school MFTs, social workers, and psychologists; neuropsychological screening/testing conducted by neuropsychologists and clinical psychologists; and curricular assessments conducted by the student's general education teacher in collaboration with a special education teacher (Hardman et al., 2008).

Should the multidisciplinary team determine that a child's needs warrant assessment input from a medical professional, an occupational therapist, a physical therapist, or a speech and language therapist, these specialists also become members of the multidisciplinary team assembled for the child. The team then administers tests and assessments relevant to their area of expertise as a part of the evaluation. All of these clinicians provide valuable expertise, particularly for students with complex and pervasive educational and health care needs.

Evaluations include observation of the student in school settings where the suspected disability is expected to be manifested. These observations are the often the province of the mental health professionals as well as teachers. Additionally, input from the parents or guardians regarding the manifestations of the disability in the home and community is essential. Typically, this is where a student's adaptive functioning is evaluated, as well. Obtaining this input necessitates meaningful collaboration and open communication among the parents and the multidisciplinary team. School-based clinicians with family counseling/therapy training can help ensure that parents fully understand the scope of the evaluation so that they experience the full partnership of the PPT process with school helpers.

Further evaluation procedures must fulfill the nondiscriminatory evaluation provision of the IDEA mandate. This requires that a student should be evaluated in all areas of suspected disability and the evaluation must be conducted in a manner that is free from bias related to the student's language or cultural characteristics or disabilities. In addition, no single evaluation procedure may be used as the sole criterion for placement of the student or planning of a student's program. That is because learning patterns emerge from the administration of multiple measures, and comprehensive assessment is better achieved by an assessment battery that reveals learning and personality patterns and profiles with more reliability and validity than single measures alone can provide. This matter is addressed more fully in Chapter 7 on assessment.

At times, an independent evaluation is needed and requested by either the school system or the family. Federal law mandates that parents are entitled to one independent evaluation funded by the public school system. An independent evaluation with a contracted provider outside of the school system is often requested to provide additional clarifying diagnostic information about a child. Sometimes it adds strength to a school psychoeducational evaluation, such as utilizing a full neuropsychological assessment to better pinpoint the nature and extent of a learning disability. Other times it may be used for obtaining new cultural information. For instance, students who speak English as a second language might be better evaluated by a contracted provider who speaks the students' native language if a child cannot be sufficiently evaluated in his or her language by an employed professional at the school.

Due process.

According to the special education mandate, parents are equal contributing partners in the processes of planning, program development, and evaluation of their child's special education programs and services (Raymond, 2008). Effective collaboration with parents is a continuing process that requires a thoughtful appreciation of parental understanding of their child's disability(s) and their continuing adjustment to having a child with a disability.

Raymond (2008) explains that parents need to understand the special education programming and related services that are being proposed and/or provided to their child. To develop and maintain a productive working relationship with parents of children with disabilities, a school system must be ever cognizant of the parent's view of their role in the processes of evaluation and program evaluation, as well as the dynamics of their parental and familial adjustment. Parents need to be fully oriented to the scope of school evaluations so that they can give informed consent for all evaluation procedures. Due process invites all stakeholders in a child's education to participate in his or her educational planning and programming.

MFTs, school-based family counselors, social workers, and school psychologists who are well trained in broader systemic processes such as building family-strengthening skills are essential team participants to promote positive and collaborative due process. Clinicians with this skill set have particular expertise in building strong school–parent relationships. They offer integral contributions to the success of due process in special education and can help avoid costly miscommunication and litigation.

The annual and triennial review.

IDEA further requires that the student's program and his or her productivity in that program be reviewed annually. It mandates that the multidisciplinary team reconvene every year to discuss and review the effectiveness of the program. At the annual review, the team, which includes the parents or guardians, determines whether modifications are necessary to ensure continued productivity that demonstrates educational benefit. These modifications include revisions in the student's goals and objectives and increased or decreased special education services, and/or modifications in related services to incorporate the LRE mandate. Parent or guardian consent continues to be necessary to make program changes resulting from an annual review of the student's program and progress.

Every three years, a reevaluation called a triennial review is mandated by IDEA. This means that an evaluation must be conducted that is designed to establish the student's current levels of proficiency in his or her designated area(s) of disability. Although a full reevaluation is no longer required, the team must consider what data are needed to provide a thorough assessment of that student's progress.

Disabilities Categories Identified by the IDEA

We now turn to the categories of special education included in IDEA. In this section, we introduce each category of special education and provide short descriptions of each. More discussion follows in Chapter 7, where the categories are integrated with disorders of childhood and adolescence that are listed in the *Diagnostic and Statistical Manual of Mental Disorders, Fifth Edition (DSM–5*; American Psychiatric Association, 2013).

IDEA (1997) defines a disability to mean a child with intellectual disabilities (formerly mental retardation), hearing impairments (including deafness), speech or language impairments, visual impairments (including blindness), emotional disturbance, orthopedic impairments, autism, traumatic brain injury, other health impairments, or specific learning disabilities. Although the federal guidelines list these categories, state requirements may vary in their own specific ways of classifying students. Nevertheless, these categories provide multidisciplinary teams with a focus for identifying areas of suspected disabilities. A study conducted by the Centers for Disease Control and Prevention (CDC) estimates that the incidence of all disabilities has increased 17.1% since 1997 and that disabilities occur in one for every six children in the school-age population (Boyle et al., 2011). These researchers found the following:

> Boys were reported to have a higher prevalence overall of select disabilities compared with girls. Hispanic children had the lowest prevalence of disabilities compared with non-Hispanic white and black children. Low income and public health insurance were associated with a higher prevalence of many disabilities. Prevalence of any developmental disability increased from 12.84% to 15.04% over 12 years. Autism, attention deficit hyperactivity disorder, and other developmental delays increased, whereas hearing loss showed a significant decline. These trends were found in all of the sociodemographic subgroups, except for autism in non-Hispanic black children. The number of children with select developmental disabilities (autism, attention deficit hyperactivity disorder, and other

developmental delays) has increased, requiring more health and education services. (Boyle et al., 2011, p. 24)

According to Kirk et al. (2009) and Learner and Johns (2009), these categories are further divided into *high-incidence disabilities* that occur frequently in the general school population, and *low-incidence disabilities* that occur more infrequently. The three categories of high-incidence disabilities include the Specific Learning Disabilities, Speech and Language Impairment, and Emotional Disturbance categories. Low-incidence categories include the categories of Visual Impairments and Blindness, Hearing Impairments and Deafness, Intellectual/Developmental Disabilities, Other Health Impairments (generally including such health conditions as asthma or diabetes), Traumatic Brain Injury, Orthopedic Impairments, Deafness, and Blindness. Two other disorders that have been traditionally considered low-incidence disabilities include autism and attention-deficit/hyperactivity disorder (ADHD). The incidence of these disorders has grown significantly over the past few decades, and those evolving changes are addressed in the following sections.

High-incidence learning disabilities.

The most frequently occurring disability found in the public school population is learning disabilities. IDEA (1997) defines a learning disability as a disorder in one or more of the basic psychological processes involved in understanding or in using spoken or written language, which may manifest itself as an impaired ability to listen, think, speak, read, write, spell, or do mathematical calculation. According to Hallahan et al. (2012), "just under 5% of children between the ages of 6 and 17 years have been identified as learning disabled by the public schools"(p. 141). Researchers from the CDC identified 7.66% of children diagnosed with learning disabilities between 1997 and 2008 (Boyle et al., 2011). Learning disabilities include such conditions as perceptual impairments (which include marked inefficiencies in any one of the five senses), brain injury, dyslexia, and developmental aphasia (a language impairment that affects the ability to understand, speak, or write language). According to Hammill, from the National

Joint Committee on Learning Disabilities (1990), learning disabilities refers to a heterogeneous group of disorders manifested by significant difficulties in the acquisition and use of listening, speaking, reading, writing, reasoning, or mathematical abilities. That committee postulated that these disorders are intrinsic to the individual and are presumed to involve dysfunctions of the central nervous system and may occur across the life span. Individuals with learning disabilities can also have problems with self-regulatory behaviors, social perception, and social interactions. However, the presence of these challenges does not in and of itself constitute a learning disability.

Speech and language impairments/communication disorders.
A second high-incidence disability found in the public schools is speech or language impairments. Students with speech or language impairments have communication difficulties. Hallahan et al. (2012) summarized speech impairment as disorders involving problems with voice and articulation such as lateral lisps and fluency problems such as stuttering. Language impairments are demonstrated by difficulties with the forms of language, the content of language, or the use of language. For instance, children with autism often have specific problems with the pragmatics of speech. Many children with autism have difficulty understanding language that is not literal and often do not comprehend the subtle nuances of certain kinds of humor such as sarcasm.

Many learning disabilities have a language component and can involve problems with understanding or expressing competence with language phonemes and syntax. For more information about these language impairments and disorders, the reader is directed to the American Speech and Language Hearing Association (ASHA.org).

A speech or language impairment must adversely affect a child's educational performance for the child to be eligible for special education services. Specific criteria and standards are used in the assessment process when students are identified as having a speech or language impairment. Hallahan et al. (2012) noted that speech disorders occur in 8% to 9% of preschool children and 5% of school children, whereas

2% to 3% of preschool children and 1% of school children have language impairments (p. 268).

Emotional disturbance.

The IDEA defines the high-incidence disability category of emotional disturbance as an inability to learn that cannot be explained by intellectual, sensory, or health factors (Raymond, 2008). According to the federal definition of this category, the child demonstrates one or more of the following: an inability to build or maintain satisfactory interpersonal relationships with peers and teachers, inappropriate types of behavior or feelings under normal circumstances, a general pervasive mood of unhappiness or depression, and/or a tendency to develop physical symptoms and fears associated with personal or school problems. One or more of these characteristics must be exhibited over a long period of time and must adversely affect a child's educational performance for the child to be labeled as emotionally or behaviorally disabled (Hallahan et al., 2012).

This category of disability includes several of the *DSM* psychological/psychiatric disorders addressed in Chapter 7 but is more general in nature than the *DSM*. This emotional disturbance educational category breaks down into externalizing, internalizing, and comorbid subtypes of several emotional disturbances. It is thought to affect 6% to 10% of the school-age population (Hallahan et al., 2012). These special education authors echo a 2001 finding from the Surgeon General's report from the U.S. Department of Health and Human Services that far too few children with serious emotional and behavioral disorders receive the help they need. Hallahan et al. (2012) conclude that

> only a small proportion of children with clear evidence of functionally impairing psychiatric disorder receive treatment. Once upon a time, when effective treatments for child and adolescent psychiatric disorders were rare, this was regrettable but not a major public health issue. Now it is. (p. 207)

In light of current tragedies across the country involving violence and death in schools perpetrated by young people, this educational disability category needs to be better understood and coordinated with mental health diagnosis and treatment. More preventive and comprehensive services need to be developed for young people with this disability to help them obtain the help they need. This category begs for early and comprehensive assessment and treatment by collaborative, multidisciplinary teams in schools. It is further addressed in Chapter 7 through discussion of the educational categories and the *DSM–5*.

Evolving Categories

Over the past decade, developments in neuropsychology, medicine, and education have had an impact on the some categories of developmental disabilities—namely, autism and other health impairments. These categories have evolved dramatically across the United States. Modern medicine has helped improve the survival rates of many premature and otherwise compromised children. Such children would not have survived without the medical technology available today. Due also to the success of special education assessment in response to new developments in medical and psychological diagnosis, many more children are currently being categorized with complex intellectual impairments in schools (Fletcher-Janszen & Reynolds, 2008). It is not clear what the relative contributions of occurrence rates and improved diagnosis and assessment are to the frequency of psychoeducational and psychiatric diagnosis of children. What is clear is that the educational categories of both high and low incidence have evolved exponentially from contemporary developments in health care and psychological, psychiatric, and educational assessment.

Intellectual/developmental disabilities.

This category is defined as significant subaverage general intellectual functioning, existing concurrently with deficits in adaptive behavior and manifested during the developmental period from birth to age eighteen (Hallahan et al., 201). Adaptive functioning variables include communication, socialization, and daily living skills, as well as maladaptive behaviors. The deficits in intellectual functioning and adaptive behaviors must adversely affect the child's educational performance for that child to be eligible for services. Generally, mild intellectual disabilities are considered high-incidence disabilities, and more severe intellectual disabilities occur less often and are considered low-incidence disabilities (Hallahan et al., p. 10). The CDC identified 13.87% of the school-age population as having some form of developmental disability from 1997 to 2008 (Boyle et al., 2011).

Autism.

The category of autism is defined as a developmental disability that significantly affects verbal and nonverbal communication and social interaction. Kirk et al. (2009) include Asperger syndrome in this category, and the cluster is referred to as the autism spectrum disorders (ASDs). Asperger syndrome has been similarly subsumed into the category of ASDs in the *DSM–5* (p. xiv). Symptoms of an ASD generally evident before age 3 years and must adversely affect educational performance to fulfill criteria for special education classification. That is, a child's ability to learn in school will be markedly compromised by that child's symptoms.

The IDEA definition includes several associated symptoms of autism, including engaging in repetitive activities and stereotypic movements, demonstrating resistance to changes in daily routines or the environment, and/or having unusual responses to sensory experiences. The IDEA categorical definition for autism does not apply if the child's educational performance is adversely affected primarily because of emotional disturbance.

The incidence of ASDs has rapidly changed in the past few years, and educational and clinical interest in this category is growing accordingly. Historically the prevalence of ASDs was considered rare, and the disorders were believed to affect children in profound ways. IDEA has historically classified ASDs in the low-incidence category of disability. The CDC noted in 2009 that the incidence increased 57% from 2002 to 2006, to 1 in 100, which includes Asperger syndrome. In their more recent Surveillance Summary, the CDC (Baio, 2014) reported that the estimated prevalence of ASDs has recently grown to 1 in 68 children in their Autism and Developmental Disabilities Monitoring Network (ADDM) sites.

The research on how the ASDs manifests is also becoming differentiated. Although the research has continued to reflect that ASDs are reported significantly more frequently in boys than girls (CDC, 2014; Hallahan et al., 2012), more children with average to above average abilities are now being reported, as are more girls and more children from minority backgrounds (CDC, 2014). The category of ASDs appears to be moving toward a high-incidence disability.

As with developmental disabilities, accounting for this phenomenon is complex. The CDC suggests that we are getting better at diagnosing ASDs earlier across age, gender, and intelligence domains across cultures in the United States. Wright and Wright (2010) suggest that greater general awareness is growing about the spectrum, and teachers, health care providers, and parents are advocating for assessment and treatment services for these and other disabilities (Yapko, 2003). All of these variables are involved in the increased diagnosis and categorization of ASDs; chances are that the relative contribution of each variable will be better known in time.

For instance, psychological and neuropsychological assessment has become more differentiated in several disability categories, including ASDs. In the 1960s, IQ scores were often measured by one number representing the *averaged* scores on *all* subtests of intelligence tests. Since that time, various domains of intelligence have become better understood as separate, although related, elements of intelligence. For instance, many children diagnosed with Asperger syndrome achieve Full Scale averaged cognitive functioning scores within the average range, and historically it has been hard to advocate for them as needing special education services. Yet many students with Asperger syndrome have left hemisphere scores that are markedly higher than their right hemisphere scores. Although many have Verbal Scale scores that are well developed, their ability to process and express information efficiently is compromised, and their ability to integrate information and express it efficiently within time limits is limited. Rourke's (Rourke & Tsatsanis, 2000) contributions to neuropsychological assessment have helped reveal the presence of a nonverbal disability in children with Asperger syndrome and other pervasive developmental disabilities that are not otherwise classified. He posits that brain inefficiencies in the corpus callosum make it difficult for children with Asperger syndrome to integrate information efficiently. He calls it an associative disorder in which children may be extremely proficient at processing information that is presented in sequential fashion, but they have difficulty integrated information that is presented simultaneously (Rourke & Tsatsanis, 2000; Tsatsanis & Rourke, 1995.

Other health impairment.

The IDEA disability category of *other health impairment* (OHI), according to the IDEA (1997), means having limited strength, vitality, or alertness. It includes a heightened alertness to environmental stimuli, which results in limited alertness to the educational environment. This category incorporates chronic or acute health problems such as asthma, ADHD, diabetes, epilepsy, a heart condition, hemophilia, lead poisoning, leukemia, nephritis, rheumatic fever, and sickle cell anemia. These conditions must adversely affect a child's educational performance for the child to be eligible for special education services. This is estimated to affect 1% of the school population (Hallahan et al., 2012).

Like autism, the diagnosis and categorization of ADHD by health care and education professionals have grown significantly in the past few decades, as have the medications and other treatments to manage children in schools with this diagnosis. ADHD involves problems with inattention, hyperactivity, or both. Because ADHD has not yet become its own category, its place in the OHI category of disabilities has swelled the incidence of children receiving the OHI designation in significant ways (Hallahan et al., 2009, p. 174). More girls are now also diagnosed with this disorder, which has increased the incidence rate. The ADHD prevalence rate is now estimated at 6.69% of the school-age population (Boyle et al., 2011). It is increasingly being viewed as a high-incidence disorder, as evidenced by the amount of children who are currently being medicated with psychostimulant medications in schools. More about the increased use of psychotropic medications for children and its effects on diagnosis and classification of disorders will be addressed in Chapter 7 on *DSM–5* and Primary Disability categories.

Low-Incidence Disabilities
Visual impairment.

The low incidence disability category of visual impairment including blindness is defined by IDEA as impairment in vision that, even with correction, adversely affects a child's educational performance (Kirk et al., 2009). This category includes both partially sighted individuals and those who are without sight altogether. The prevalence of children who are visually impaired is .05% of children aged 6 to 17 years (Hallahan et al., 2012).

Hearing impairment and deafness.

Hearing impairment and deafness, as described by Kirk et al. (2009), is also a low-incidence disability, which includes individuals with permanent or fluctuating hearing impairments. The impairment must, as with other disability categories of IDEA, adversely affect a child's educational productivity for an individual to be eligible for educational services. The U.S. Department of Education identifies about 0.14% of the school population from 6 to 17 years as deaf or hard of hearing (Hallahan et al., 2012).

Traumatic brain injury.

Traumatic brain injury (TBI) is categorized by IDEA as an acquired injury to the brain caused by an external physical force (accidents, falls, and/or abuse), resulting in total or partial functional disability or psychosocial impairment, or both. The impairment adversely affects the individual's educational performance. The term applies to open and closed head injuries resulting in impairments in one or more areas, such as cognition; language; memory; attention; reasoning; abstract thinking; judgment; problem-solving; sensory, perceptual, and motor abilities; psychosocial behavior; physical functions; information processing; and speech. Although the term does not include brain injuries that are congenital or degenerative or brain injuries induced by birth trauma, some states do include acquired injuries in this category. TBIs have also been increasingly diagnosed due to improvements in neuropsychological technology to recognize trauma and its effects over time (Hallahan et al., 2012, p. 372). Because of the increased diagnosis of

TBI, this category is sometimes discussed as a high-incidence disability (Stichter, Conroy, & Kauffman, 2008).

Orthopedic impairments.

Orthopedic Impairments are defined by IDEA as a severe orthopedic impairment that adversely affects a child's educational performance. The orthopedic impairments include those caused by congenital anomalies (e.g., clubfoot, absence of a limb such as an arm or a leg), impairments caused by disease (e.g., poliomyelitis, bone tuberculosis), and impairments from other causes (e.g., cerebral palsy, amputations, fractures or burns that cause contractures).

Multiple disabilities.

The multiple disabilities category as defined by IDEA means specific concomitant impairments (e.g., developmental disabilities/blindness, developmental disabilities/orthopedic impairment), the combination of which causes such severe educational needs that they cannot be accommodated in a special education program solely for one of the other impairments (Hallahan et al., 2009). The term excludes deaf-blindness because a separate category has been established for this concomitant impairment. About 1% of the school-age population is affected by the category of multiple disabilities (Hallahan et al., 2012).

Deaf-blindness.

The disability category of deaf-blindness as explained by Hallahan et al. (2009) includes individuals with visual impairments ranging from low vision (20/70 to 20/200 in the better eye with correction) to individuals who are totally blind. Hearing impairments can range from mild to profound deafness. Individuals who are deaf-blind have significant adaptive challenges because their ability to learn is compromised by the loss of two major perceptual senses in hearing and vision. Learning to communicate orally and in written ways requires intensive support. Often students who are deaf-blind have other disabilities and medical conditions such as orthopedic and speech and language impairments requiring assistive technology such as hearing aids, wheelchairs and other supports.

Special gifts and talents.

Hallahan et al. (2012) include learners with "special gifts and talents" (p. 427) as an important special education category. They quote from federal reports and legislation a 3% to 5% prevalence rate of giftedness in U.S. schools, depending on which criteria are used (p. 432). Although they note that there are several interpretations of what "special gifts and talents" means, they suggest that it generally involves high intelligence scores, early development of certain skills, unusual insight and/or aptitude, unusual creativity, and/or special talents or superior abilities in specific areas of performance (p. 431). Hallahan et al. state that although there is variability among school systems regarding how to define this group of students, they suggest that some of the issues that gifted students experience can be similar to some of the challenges that students with disabilities face.

Pfeiffer and colleagues (Olsewski-Kubilius, Limburg-Weber, & Pfeiffer, 2003) suggest that students have multiple intelligences; they add that giftedness often refers more to academic subjects, and talent is often viewed as aptitude in arts and music. They recommend that nurturing such special gifts in children requires a close partnership between children, their families, and their school system.

Pfeiffer's research with high-ability children at Duke University has focused on helping gifted children achieve while remaining well adjusted (Sams, 2012). His work has emphasized balance in such children's lives so that they are not overwhelmed by the academic pressures and can access their creativity. Because such children are often seen as bright and capable, their emotional needs may be at risk in ways that are not readily apparent and may be overlooked without careful observation.

Because there is often a discrepancy between the chronological age and the cognitive precocity of very bright children, such children can feel this developmental discrepancy, or the differences can be noticed by others. These children may be favored by some families and teachers but may not be as well accepted by other children. The potential for anxiety and/or depressive disorders exists for children in this IDEA category, especially in early adolescence, when differences may not be tolerated well by peers. Schools working with children who have such cognitive and behavioral profiles need to be alert to the need for supportive services to students who fall into this low incidence category.

Constraints of the Special Education Law

Despite the progress of special education services, there has been controversy about some of the policies and programs that schools have developed in response to P.L. 94-142. Over time, educators and parents have become alarmed at both the growing bifurcation of special education from regular education services and the surge of referrals of students into special education programs, up to 20% by some estimates (National Association of State Directors of Special Education, 2005). Although children with special needs have been supported well in schools, special education at times has become a "place to be" (National Association of State Directors of Special Education, p. 1), rather than a wraparound set of services to help children with special needs function within the context of regular public education. Some parents have even advocated for special consideration such as extended time limits for their children to improve college application testing scores. Some of those requests do not necessarily accompany a recognized, documented learning disability.

Special education programming began with the best of intentions but has evolved in unanticipated ways that at times became problematic even as more students were being serviced. For instance, the "discrepancy model" of determining the presence of a learning disability by assessing the difference between a student's measured abilities and achievement levels has come under scrutiny and critique (Fletcher-Janzen & Reynolds, 2008; Shaywitz, 2004). Although this psychological assessment model became the standard procedure for establishing eligibility for special education services nationwide after P.L. 94-142 legislation was enacted, student underachievement is not always accurately explained by this labor-intensive procedure alone. Trauma, family dysfunction, first-generation immigrant experience, poor instruction, motivation to achieve, mental health difficulties, and many other variables can all contribute to school underachievement.

When it is used, psychological testing to determine what special education needs exist has at times not been initiated in schools until after a child experiences a period of academic failure. Historically, children have not been assessed until approximately the third grade, a benchmark year for most children for developing beginning reading, writing, and mathematics proficiency. Some (Shaywitz, 2004) criticize the benefits of using the discrepancy model for high-incidence disabilities such as reading problems, those most commonly occurring in schools, because the model has not been scientifically proven to be effective for all children. It is often too late for some children who have struggled for several years before their learning needs are recognized and treated.

In other words, the discrepancy model, which utilizes the "wait to fail" approach, has not been well matched with evidence-based services. Evidence-based research on neurocognitive development of reading skills such as phonemic awareness suggests that precursors to reading are identifiable earlier in children's development than was originally believed.

Neuropsychological and educational research suggests that learning to read occurs much earlier than was formerly understood (Bradley, Danielson, & Hallahan, 2002; Fletcher-Janzen & Reynolds, 2008; National Reading Panel, 2000; Shaywitz, S., 2004). Functional magnetic resonance imaging (fMRI) has made possible direct observation of brain functioning. We now know that children can actually run the risk of developing additional emotional distress and/or behavioral problems such as low self-esteem and anxiety, if they don't receive early services for a primary disability such as dyslexia (Shaywitz, 2003). According to these data, the delay of early intervention misses important windows of opportunity for learning and that waiting until children fall behind wastes valuable remediation time, thus resulting in the "waiting to fail" phenomenon.

Conversely, earlier remediation is simpler and more cost-effective for students and teachers to achieve. Early intervention and instruction also appears critical to the prevention of emotional, social, and behavioral issues in children. Medical family therapy theorists also promote the notion of collaboration among the family members and teams who provide service to obtain comprehensive assessment. This is addressed further in Chapter 5 on medical family therapy influences. For school-based work, we have coined the term *frontloading* to refer to the specific collaborative team building that is necessary to create systems of care for children who are coping with health and education challenges. By frontloading, we refer to the practice of proactively building multidisciplinary educational *and* health care teams *at the point when students with needs are referred.*

Traditional early remedial special education services and programs have not been consistently grounded in scientific, evidence-based data with proven records of effectiveness. Nor have they been systemically incorporated with general education in sufficient ways to make them seamless, efficient, and accessible to all school professionals.

There is also significant variability in school systems regarding the depth and breadth of psychological and neuropsychological assessment that is actually provided to children. Some school systems have developed progressive ways of identifying children with special needs. Others have not kept pace with cutting edge assessment in children, despite the growing evidence base for the value of such assessment for learning disabilities (Fletcher-Janzen & Reynolds, 2008).

At the other end of special education service delivery, once a student has received a classification, exiting from a special educational program or class placement can also become complicated. Parents who have become comfortable with the protection of a small class placement may balk at the finding that their child now "tests out" of the class with higher achievement scores. Some students' disabilities do not ameliorate with intensive programming, while students from both groups can run the risk of remaining in special education classes and programs longer than necessary if proper evaluation and advocacy measures are not applied.

Once a student is declared a "special education" student, it can sometimes become difficult for that child to move efficiently back into regular class placement or to manage that label without adverse social consequences. For instance, a student may have experienced a measure of protection from bullies within the special education structure. A return to general education without adequate transitional preparation can potentially expose him or her to teasing and other maltreatment from students and teachers who do not know or understand that student.

Although education in the LRE is the goal for all students, gradual and prepared return to general education for a young person may be necessary. A student who has spent significant time receiving special education services or placed in a special school will need time and support to make a successful transition to general education. Without advocacy training and skills, that student may be vulnerable to difficult challenges, particularly during middle and high school.

Also, there continues to be an overrepresentation of minority students in special education programs. The numbers are disproportionate to the actual occurrence of "primary disabilities" warranting such special education services (National Research Council Panel on Minority Overrepresentation, Donovan & Cross, 2002). Special education has been sometimes criticized as an inappropriate compensation for poor education.

Discipline and Students With Disabilities
Students with disabilities in the public schools are afforded certain procedural due process rights in regards to discipline, according to IDEA. When a student who has an identified disability is involved in a disciplinary incident, a PPT team must be assembled to determine whether the student's disciplinary offense is the result of his or her disability. If the team determines that the student's offense is the result of the disability, the student is then not subject to the disciplinary procedures that are mandated by the school system. The team is required to use recent and thorough evaluation data to inform their decisions about the student (Yell, 2012). Alternative disciplinary approaches are then implemented in these situations (Raymond, 2008).

For instance, students who threaten violence are most frequently subject to automatic suspension or expulsion from school under current zero-tolerance policies in public schools. However, if it is determined that a child with Asperger syndrome who has limited social and communication skills is responding out of anxiety or stimulus overload, accommodations may be made to keep him or her in school through the efforts of the multidisciplinary team. Time-outs with trusted teachers and special service staff, counseling, small social skills groups, debriefing sessions, and behavior charts can all potentially serve to deter that student from emotional meltdowns that trigger extreme behavior.

Such proactive planning often serves a primary prevention function for students with special needs and actually serves to keep students from needing more restrictive learning and/or psychiatric placements. This is another key area of collaborative opportunity for mental health team members with systems training. For students with complex disabilities that contain maladaptive behavioral components, that student's needs are best served by a team of educational and psychological professionals who can intervene early and well together to serve that student, the school community, and the student's family. Yell (2012) notes that establishing a direct and substantial relationship between a student's misconduct and his or her disability is complex, and is a difficulty standard to meet (p. 348). Multidisciplinary teams making sufficient use of mental health and educational data are equipped to establish that standard.

Despite the constraints in special education law and practices, each of the special education legislative initiatives over the past half century has sought to provide a better FAPE to children in the LRE possible. Each law has been designed to effectively integrate the goals of meeting the civil rights, inclusion, and entitlement needs of all children so that they can take full advantage of educational opportunities in American public schools. Each law has come closer to comprehensively addressing the needs of children and schools so that all children can learn and achieve according to their potential.

Although there remain significant unmet student needs in schools, gains in identifying and servicing those needs have been realized through special education legislation in the past 40 years. The introduction and development of multidisciplinary health and education teams in schools affords more opportunities for students with special needs to achieve in school. When well-trained, multidisciplinary team members develop collaborative working relationships with each other and the children and families they evaluate, children can be more thoroughly assessed and serviced in school, the system where they spend a major portion of their childhood.

These elements are at the heart of the No Child Left Behind legislation of 2001, which prompted the RtI and other initiatives since that time. What the elements also reflect is a shift from creating individual plans and placements for individual students to an appreciation of how multiple, broader layers of systems of influence affect a child's ability to learn. That systemic shift is the subject of the next chapter on school-based systems theory, and the RtI and other initiatives are introduced in the next chapter.

four

School-Based Systems Theory,

Part I: The LOGS Model

Traditional psychological theory from the time of Freud has examined human behavior from an internal, individually oriented perspective. Over the past century, mental health problems in children, adolescents, and adults have been historically assessed and serviced through medication and individual therapy. Since the 1950s, an era of outpatient community mental health has emerged to replace residential treatment centers, with its accompanying new medications, treatments and services. Schools have followed suit with laws enacted to address the special educational needs of individual students. This chapter addresses how that history has evolved in recent decades.

Since the 1950s, it has also become clear that individualized treatments and services are not alone sufficient to address all aspects of mental illness and health. Group and family therapy emerged in inpatient institutions in the United States as a way to more systemically and comprehensively treat mental illness (Becvar & Becvar, 2008; Hoffman, 2002). Family therapy has relied heavily on systems theory as applied to human systems to address mental illness in a fuller way.

Two aspects of systems theory have been utilized in many creative ways by mental health clinicians in schools (Gerrard & Soriano, 2013). First, examining variables *among* as well as *within* individuals, groups, and families has elicited new ways of working to improve the mental health of children, adolescents, and adults, focusing on the family as a basic unit for study (Nichols & Schwartz, 2001). For instance, a child who comes to school from a newly immigrated family will be quite differently positioned to address reading assignments in class than a child from the dominant culture who has been read stories from that dominant language since infancy. Or a child from a home with an addicted parent and scarce resources may have come to school without breakfast. That child's attention in school will likely be quite different from a child from a home with consistent nurturance and resources. Many systemic variables besides internal ones have an impact on a child's performance in school and need to be addressed to promote optimal school resiliency and achievement.

Second, learning about the processes that exist among subsystem layers in individuals, groups, and social institutions as schools has revealed new areas for study and intervention to help improve achievement in schools (Boyd-Franklin, 2000). For instance, attending to the constraints among teachers coming from middle-class, suburban backgrounds and the children they teach in urban schools can help prevent teacher burnout and promote student achievement. Mental health professionals may choose to work in specific domains such as chronic illness, learning problems, and divorce. But they are all specifically trained to examine multiple layers of systems in their assessment and to provide targeted interventions at constrained areas of need in their treatment planning.

In the past generation of family therapy literature, theorists have evolved beyond creating *specific* therapy models to developing *integrated* paradigms for clinicians to employ *across* various settings. Systems thinkers in medicine and mental health frequently illustrate their family therapy concepts as concentric circles, which represent spheres of influence that have an impact on individuals and families.

Medical family therapists Campbell and McDaniel (1987), along with McDaniel, Doherty and Hepworth (2014) adapted Engel's biopsychosocial model of layers of influence on health into a circular pattern describing both the stages of family adjustment to illness and health, as well as players who need to be considered in health care. Those players include the patients, the health care system, and *family members*. McDaniel et al. referred to medical family therapy as a "systemic, holistic approach that asserts that mind, body, relationships and community all interact and affect one's health. In medicine, this approach is labeled *biopsychosocial*" (2014, p. 96).

Seaburn, Lorenz, Gunn, Gawinski, and Mauksch (1996) coined a medical treatment term, the *culture of collaboration* (p. 8). Their aim is to focus on the importance of creating a nonhierarchical web of teams that include medical and mental health care providers, patients, and families as participating treatment team collaborators. Seaburn and his team developed this concept as a contrasting alternative to the more triangular model in medicine in which the team is managed by a hierarchy of physicians.

Family therapists Boyd-Franklin and Hafer Bry (2000) developed a model for treatment that incorporates concentric patterns of circles representing the layers of systems that affect an individual's functioning. The layers of their multisystems model include immediate and extended family households, nonblood kin and friends, church and community resources, and social service agencies and other outside systems. The model illustrates those authors' notions about how to provide comprehensive family therapy in a variety of home-based, school, and community settings.

Our faculty and student team from the Family Therapy Program at Central Connecticut State University created a circular prototype for work in schools called the *longitudinal overview of growth in systems* (LOGS) model (Gerrard & Soriano, 2013). To fully consider the needs of children across their school careers, we needed a growth-oriented paradigm that incorporates temporal as well as dimensional elements. LOGS is a school-based meta-model that incorporates several systemic levels of influence across the life cycle of a child and his or her family. Elements for this framework are borrowed from the medical and family therapy literature just described, but LOGS is also based on another systemic meta-model of family therapy described in *Metaframeworks: Transcending the Models of Family Therapy* (Breunlin, et. al., 1997).

Metaframeworks includes individual, developmental, gender, and cultural dimensions of a person's life, all of which affect human systems.

Metaframeworks also incorporates sequential patterns of behavior that families show, such as rituals that families practice around holidays that occur every year. It also includes an explanation of the structural organization of an individual's family and social milieu. For instance, a family headed by a single parent in an urban setting may appear to function quite differently from several generations of family living together on a farm.

We have incorporated several ideas from the *Metaframeworks* and medical family therapy literature to demonstrate how the LOGS model guides mental health practice in school systems to remove constraints to school achievement. These clinical ideas are strikingly similar to what schools use in their multidisciplinary collaborative team efforts.

There are exciting parallels between collaborative family therapy practice and multidisciplinary team service in schools. Both can serve to benefit families and greatly reduce constraints to children's growth and learning. These practices have the potential to benefit students and families with chronic needs in both health care and education with greater effectiveness and efficiency. Developing evidence-based research to further validate and replicate these practices will hopefully affirm this hypothesis, as more collaborative, systemic solutions to education are sought and as health care reform evolves.

Our faculty team illustrates these elements in our LOGS model as an elongated log. It contains a trunk with concentric circles across one end that represent the rings within the tree's trunk that depict the age of the tree. The horizontal length of the trunk itself represents the life-cycle development of both the individual child and her or his family. The concentric rings represent the individual, family, school, community, and cultural dimensions of a child's functioning included in the *Metaframeworks* paradigm. Together these dimensions frame the concurrent developmental needs and processes that occur in children and families across time.

The LOGS model is useful for identifying, targeting and tracking clinical/interventions in schools. It helps to prioritize team interventions. The model is illustrated in Figure 4.1.

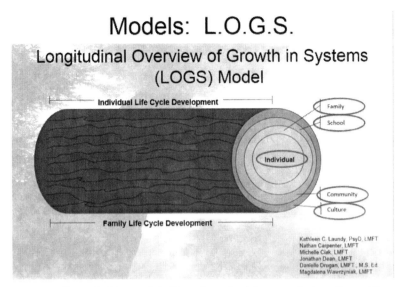

Figure 4.1. The LOGS model. Reprinted with permission from Gerrard and Soriano (2013).

The individual, family, school, community, and culture dimensions of LOGS represent both the internal forces as well as the varied contextual variables that have an impact on a person's life and help shape one's behavior. When a referral for services is made in schools by school personnel, parents, physicians, and/or other health care providers or agencies, traditional assessments begin with the individual child. After obtaining written permission to share confidential data about the case, data are then gathered about that child from those who know that child diagnostically. All the other concentric variables in that child's life can be explored to learn about that child, including her or his family, school, community and culture, as well as the stage of that child and her or his family's life cycle, to plan appropriate interventions.

LOGS represents an attempt to incorporate all the systemic variables necessary to consider when determining how best to address the constraints that interfere with a child or a family's functioning. For instance, a school team may choose to focus on providing a specific school-based service such as parenting classes, conducting a social skills training group, or providing individual therapy to a child. A school social worker may work with outside agencies to coordinate care for a student. A school psychologist's focus may be on testing the child, while a school counselor may work to modify the school curriculum to meet a student's needs. An occupational therapist or speech and language pathologist may design interventions to help that child learn to express herself or himself in more articulate ways.

The LOGS model serves as an ever-present reminder of all the relational influences in a child's life. It provides a fuller context for services and service providers to consider when determining best practices. As teams evaluate how they can best serve a student, the particular skills of the professionals on the teams can then be used in complementary ways. Together they form the synergistic, multitiered systems of support for each student they service.

A child is profoundly influenced by his or her family, community, and culture, represented by the three other concentric circles. As mental health clinicians and educators know, a child's ability to function in school is continuously affected by all of these influences. A child's needs also vary across the course of his or her school career and life cycle, and how those needs are addressed is mediated in part by where he and his or her family are in their life cycle. For children and families with chronic health and education needs, concerns about those needs escalate during predictable transitions in their lives, such as entering school, moving from elementary to middle school, or shifting from adolescence into young adulthood. The *Metaframeworks* authors view therapeutic change in as a collaborative effort between the therapist and the family to remove constraints that are preventing change from occurring (p. 281).

Children can also be dramatically influenced by unexpected trauma in their lives, such as death or divorce. These life-cycle issues in children and families are illustrated on the horizontal plane of the LOGS model. A child with pervasive intellectual disabilities, for instance, might be expected to develop in more uneven ways than a generally bright child without disabilities who experiences a family trauma such as a parental death. It has been my clinical experience that children with major disabilities develop with a wider range of strengths and needs than do children whose abilities are more evenly developed. Disabled students are often more vulnerable to the vicissitudes of life and take more time to recover when confronted with such trauma than children with more evenly developed aptitudes.

Interestingly, protective and necessary solutions that a family may enact during one period of a child's life can inadvertently serve to interfere with that child's development at another stage. A child who receives constant parental vigilance and care for his or her asthma as an infant, for example, may experience fewer hospitalizations during that child's early life because of their watchful care. But that child may come to feel "smothered" by parental "overprotection," as she or he wants to attend sleep-away camp as a young adolescent, even if the asthma is in remission. The parents and child need support to normalize their earlier coping skills, as well as update their skill set for the child's new developmental stage as they evolve as a family over time.

School-based mental health clinicians receive referrals based on any one or a combination of variables affecting a student's academic performance in schools, and the LOGS model helps prioritize and order the intervention and treatment choices the clinician makes about the case. The following case example illustrate in depth how we utilize LOGS in case planning and evaluation over time.

A second-grade boy was referred to the local youth service bureau by his school system. "Garth," as we will call him, was an attractive, verbal, and active youngster, but he experienced increasing difficulty settling in class and adjusting to the academic demands of the classroom. Although his behaviors had been challenging since kindergarten, his school was able to manage him until he entered second grade, when his developmental difficulties became more apparent. He had more difficulty with his fine motor skills than other children his age, and he could not hold a pencil correctly. He blurted out answers to questions in class rather than taking the time to discuss them with the teacher or his classmates in a more reciprocal way. He was indifferent and even condescending to students and teachers alike when school activities did not suit him. His behavior became increasingly out of control in the classroom, and his social skill development was not progressing like other children his age.

Garth had difficulty remaining in his seat for lessons, and he showed no social interest in other children or adults. He preferred to focus only on his preferred projects, which typically involved mechanical and science-based topics. Although he appeared bright and interested in learning, Garth could not manage his impulses sufficiently to adapt to classroom learning, even with paraprofessional, social work, and occupational therapy help. He indeed was "marching to his own drummer," and he was increasingly out of step with his classroom peers and teachers. His school system evaluated Garth, and his parents sought an outside psychological evaluation was sought after they consulted with his pediatrician. He was diagnosed with Asperger syndrome and attention-deficit/hyperactivity disorder (ADHD), and he began a medication trial of methylphenidate for ADHD.

A local youth service bureau (YSB) near Garth's school had developed several service programs for students on the autistic spectrum, and a referral was made to that agency for help. The marriage and family therapist (MFT) assigned to Garth was invited to the planning and placement team (PPT) meeting held at the school to help create a comprehensive educational plan for him. Unfortunately, Garth's behavior had already escalated to the point where he could not respond to verbal cueing and direction when his anxiety escalated. He would respond to attempts at limit setting by running from the classroom, which resulted in the need for physical restraint to restore order. The PPT team determined that Garth could not be managed in a regular school classroom. He was placed in a special day school where he could remain safe and receive individualized, targeted instruction.

When Garth began attending his new school, his mother began biweekly parent support meetings at the YSB, and Garth began a social skills training and summer camp experience there with other youngsters with autism spectrum diagnoses. Garth's parents wanted him to stay connected with his home school and community, but they grew increasingly frustrated that school and town services were not being provided for him. He was not able to participate successfully in town-sponsored group activities such as Boy Scouts and little-league baseball. Garth's parents felt abandoned by their town and school system, which became a frequent topic that they brought to the parent support meetings at the agency.

Garth's grandmother also died during the next year, and Garth and his family began family counseling to address their grief at the agency with their MFT clinician. When their therapist developed a trusting relationship with the family, she learned critical information that had significant impact on Garth's behavior and learning. First, Garth's parents revealed that they had both experienced chronic family distress and neglect in their nuclear families as children, which affected both their collective ability to function well in school as children and their confidence in authorities as adults. This experience provided a fertile context for their mistrust about school intentions regarding what was best for Garth.

The frustration Garth's parents felt translated to anger at school authorities for not providing sufficient services, which contributed to an increasingly adversarial atmosphere at school meetings. A tempting linear tendency for Garth's parents and school system was to blame each other for planning and placement difficulties. But it became clearer over time that Garth's situation was more complex than any of us first imagined.

Garth's mother then acknowledged to her therapist that she had also been diagnosed with Asperger syndrome as a late adolescent, which had not been revealed to the school team. Her difficulty with mental flexibility undoubtedly contributed to the school's misperception about her unwillingness to negotiate and compromise about Garth's school-based services.

Early the next year, the director of special services in Garth's home school arranged for his triennial evaluation. She realized that a better relationship needed to be established among members of Garth's family, home school, and treatment team. She asked me to complete an updated psychological evaluation of Garth, which was to include cognitive and achievement testing, as well as an evaluation of his adaptive and family functioning. She knew that I consulted with Garth's YSB and his other health care providers and wanted me to collaborate with them. By that time, the progress that the clinicians at the agency made with Garth's family enabled me to obtain signed release of information forms from Garth's parents to collaborate with all members of his health care and educational team. With this intervention, we began to build a family-centered multidisciplinary school/treatment team, which fostered more effective communication among all team members.

Significant measures of progress were realized during this evaluation. First, Garth's behavior settled enough over several months to reveal a clearer indication of his true abilities. Rather than refuse to complete many evaluation measures as he had in the past, Garth's distractive and oppositional behavior dissipated somewhat. His attention and concentration abilities improved with the help of medication to the level where he could complete test items previously left incomplete. His Verbal Comprehension Scores moved from the average to the top of high average range. He actually obtained superior range scores on a few of his Verbal Comprehension Subtests, a significant improvement in the 2 years since his previous evaluation. But a growing "scatter" in his scores also became apparent in this triennial evaluation: Garth's highest and lowest scores ranged from the superior to the borderline range of cognitive functioning.

He showed particular problems with word decoding and naming novel words, which affected his reading fluency. He also showed signs of dysgraphia, which undoubtedly contributed to his labored writing and reluctance to focus on expressive language skills on paper. As we formed more of a collaborative team, it became clearer why Garth was having trouble "showing what he knows." His brain was functioning at a rate far faster than his ability to demonstrate accuracy in reading and writing.

It became clearer in this evaluation that Garth's "diversionary tactic" of focusing solely on his own interests was more than simply being oppositional or misreading social cues, as children with Asperger syndrome typically do. It also had to do with Garth being a bright youngster who was constrained in his reading and writing work in school from achieving according to his true abilities. Garth experienced academic frustration at school because he was well aware of his uneven abilities. He was eager to distract himself and others from focusing on his vulnerabilities.

When the results were reported to his family before the PPT, his parents further revealed that although he is a competent mechanic as an adult, Garth's father had similar reading and writing problems in school as a child. Both parents acknowledged that they struggled with anxiety throughout their lives and had had difficulty trusting outside resources and agencies to help them manage. As they revealed important family history elements for the first time, the systemic pieces of the puzzle fit together more logically. Because of the clinical work and the leadership of his team at school, Garth's parents came to trust the school team more. As we gathered to discuss the results of Garth's updated evaluation, they allowed the team to have access to important family history information. As their anxiety dissipated and they began to feel more valued as part of the PPT, Garth's parents offered many creative suggestions about further evaluation and programming for their son.

Over the next year, Garth and his family made significant strides, with the support of the parent group and social skills programs offered at the agency. What made the difference is that Garth's mother began to trust her therapist and the school team. The team invested collaborative energy and worked diligently to support Garth and his family. A related variable is that Garth matured developmentally and socially as his family's anxiety dissipated.

Clinicians learned other important information from Garth's parents around this time. First, his parents achieved dramatic success in stopping addictive and destructive family patterns they had inherited from their families of origin. Despite their own lack of healthy parental modeling they succeeded at establishing healthy family relationships, routines, and structure with Garth and his younger sister Grace. They achieved this success anonymously at first, because they were understandably uncomfortable about sharing critical family information with their school team and others outside of the family. As school and treatment services became more collaborative, however, these critical elements began to emerge and be successfully addressed.

Garth's family. With the support of their school/health team, Garth's parents began to feel more accepted and supported in their efforts. They began to trust the process of collaboration.

We then completed further neuropsychological screening at his mother's urging, and Garth was diagnosed with dyslexia. A reading program that is specifically designed to help boost Garth's phonemic awareness and skill had already been introduced at his special school. The program was then applied with greater confidence by the whole team, and Garth began to respond to it with success and less anxiety.

By this time, the multidisciplinary team had grown to include Garth's home and special school team, his pediatrician, clinicians at the YSB, a neuropsychologist colleague, and myself. The family began to interact with team members with more ease and confidence, and the team began making plans for Garth to return to his hometown for middle school.

Garth made significant strides in his academic and social functioning during the 2 years we spent building a strong multidisciplinary team. Garth's father received a promotion at work, and his mother began graduate training in special education. Garth's parents later requested that I also evaluate their younger daughter Grace, who had not yet begun to speak by the spring of her kindergarten year. The special services director ordered the evaluation, and I diagnosed Grace with selective mutism. By the end of the school year, she began speaking in class, with ample support from her teacher and school team.

A plan was established to help Grace make the successful transition to first grade, and her parents worked with the school system more comfortably than they did during Garth's more difficult times. In some ways, it was as though Grace's reluctance to talk at school was a metaphor for her parents' historical relationship with school and other authorities. As Garth's parents developed more comfort to use their voices, so did Grace.

This process is called an *isomorph*, a term borrowed from chemistry. In family therapy, this phenomenon represents a parallel process across dimensions. It means that when phenomena occur in one aspect of a family's functioning, it can show up in other areas as well. For instance, when we first encountered Garth's mistrust of school helpers, we soon learned that his family shared that mistrust based on years of conflicted relationships with others in their world. We used that isomorph to create important family changes by fostering trust and giving Garth and his family more voice, which in the long run benefitted Garth and Grace academically.

For this case, we used the LOGS model and elements of collaborative medical family therapy in several ways. First, we identified the most pressing area of clinical need to be at the individual level on the LOGS model because Garth's behavioral dyscontrol was preventing him from functioning in groups and us from accurately assessing his cognitive and educational needs and strengths. Because of his diagnosis of Asperger syndrome, the case was assigned to MFTs who showed particular aptitude and interest in working with this population of students with pervasive developmental disabilities and their families. Because I consulted for the agency and also provided the triennial psychological evaluation, we were able to complete needed case collaboration about Garth and his family during regularly scheduled staff meetings.

We also saw a strong area of tension on the LOGS model boundary between the family and the school system. We utilized an active working relationship with Garth's school system and pediatrician, as well as understanding of the complexity and constraints regarding the culture of the community where Garth lived, to build a collaborative relationship between Garth's family and his school and health care systems.

We employed the dimensions of the LOGS model to design various specific services for Garth and his family and coordinate services with his school system and other providers. Because of the complexity of the case, it was tempting to lose focus and become overwhelmed by the needs and constraints involved. Using the LOGS model, we helped prioritize the interventions and sequence of services we offered this family and school system in a more logical and coordinated way. We based our plans on which problems presented first and how constraining those problems were. Such priority ranking gave us direction and reassurance about our treatment plan. It helped us recognize that Garth himself had major needs that were imbedded deeply within his family history and his life-cycle stage. Rather than seeing his

underachievement as a one-dimensional phenomenon such as behavior dyscontrol, we looked into several systemic layers of Garth's world.

For instance, we employed both individual and family life-cycle
aspects of LOGS to normalize the family's concerns, support their
attempts to parent their children well, and help them advocate appropriately for their academic needs at school. Because of the trust that
developed among the education staff, the health care clinicians and
Garth's family, significant strengths and needs were discovered that
had impact on the outcomes of Garth's educational plan and treatment. Despite the adversarial relationship that had initially developed
between Garth's family and his home school system, the YSB clinicians
were able to learn over time about the important family commitments
Garth's parents had made to raise their children in a healthier family
system than either of them had experienced as children. Garth and
his sister were clearly loved by his parents, provided healthy structure
and routines at home, and had strong, positive family time together.
We used this information to advocate for them at school meetings to
alleviate some of the discomfort Garth's school helpers had understandably developed.

We also learned that one of the unfortunate vestiges of Garth's
extended family history was that his parents had difficulty trusting any
authorities for whom care of their children was entrusted. They had
banded together to arrest unhealthy patterns from their past, but had
developed an "us against the world" style in their relationships with
their school system and community. Their solution during their children's infancy actually became a problem as Garth and Grace entered
school. In other words, what worked well at one stage of the family's
development became a constraint at another, because they had developed an entrenched pattern of mistrust of outside authorities.

When we began working together, Garth's family was struggling to
engage with authorities in new, healthier ways. In *Metaframeworks,* this
is referred to as an S4 sequence, in which long-term experience with a
behavior pattern becomes ingrained and can create a similar parallel
process in the next generation of the family system. The interventions
we created in our work with Garth's family were specifically designed to
ameliorate this parallel pattern of mistrust. As Watzlawick, Weakland,

and Fisch (1974) so aptly described, "the intervention is directed at the solution, and change can then take place" (p. 88).

Active use of the LOGS model also provided a framework to develop collaborative relationships with Garth's family and school system. The director of special services at Garth's school was an innate systems thinker who fostered the development of a strong multidisciplinary team to support the process of Garth's diagnosis, education, and treatment. She saw the value of primary prevention and long-term planning for Garth.

Although we were not successful at preventing an out-of-district placement for Garth, we were confident that the growth and progress he showed in the months after the collaborative efforts were applied would bode well for Garth and his family's future. The confidence that the team developed about Garth's academic and social progress succeeded in interrupting the negative cycle (and S4 sequence) of mistrust of school authorities. Garth is now functioning better academically and presents as a happier child. He is managing his behavior better.

Productive collaboration among his family, teachers, and health providers has continued to develop and grow. It is a tribute to the educational team as well as Garth's mother's passion for her family that she has chosen to pursue graduate training in special education. It is hoped that future costly residential placement and potential litigation borne from mistrust and conflicting points of view may be prevented.

The LOGS model fits well in education. It illustrates the possibilities of integrating *all* services provided to children in schools and serves as a template for how each service fits together on a child's behalf over time. Concurrent school services for a child may include, for example, a paraprofessional in the classroom to help a child sustain attention; occupational therapy to improve fine motor skills; a social skills group led by an MFT, school psychologist, counselor, or school social worker; a parent support group led by a school-based mental health clinician; and psychological testing provided by a school psychologist, as occurred with Garth's case. The LOGS model accommodates all of those services and helps locate where and when they can be offered during a child's school career.

Services may change yearly through a child's Individual Educational Plan, 504, or Response to Intervention plan, or other tracking mechanism. Individual, family, school, and other variables will inevitably change over time. But the LOGS model is a useful mnemonic to help integrate the services extending throughout a student's academic career, particularly for those students with chronic educational and health needs. Any teacher or clinician may apply their particular skills to a specific service or need in a linear, sequential way, such as a social skills group or a behavioral management feedback system. With the LOGS framework, a professional or parent can easily fit his or her expertise holistically into the full context of the child's education over the course of the school career.

five

School-Based Systems Theory,

Part II: Medical Family Therapy Influences

Why is it important to include a chapter about health care and medical family therapy in a book about collaborative mental health services in school systems? As outlined in the Introduction and described throughout this book, many students with special educational needs have accompanying long-term health care issues, and many children with special health needs also develop special education needs. In addition, early childhood distress caused by adverse childhood experiences such as child abuse and neglect can have damaging effects on the developing brain and can affect learning, behavior, and health across the life span (Austin & Herrick, 2014). This chapter addresses systems-based collaborative theory and practice patterns that have emerged from medicine to address chronic disorders in children. Many of these are adaptable for school-based practice, and special emphasis is paid to the term *medical home*, which is explored shortly.

Children need to be healthy to learn with consistency. It seems logical to provide services in the primary system where children function and where learning services are already being delivered in their "educational home." As an example, some schools have begun to incorporate health clinics within their buildings to provide the basic medical and dental care necessary for children to attend school regularly.

A growing number of hospital and community practices are emerging that incorporate policies and programs across the fields of health care (McCarthy, Mueller, & Tillman, 2009). They use multidisciplinary collaboration to comprehensively educate, diagnose, and treat children and families who struggle with chronic illnesses and disabilities. Here I introduce some best practices from medical family therapy that are adaptable for school systems and will demonstrate how such practices fit with current national educational initiatives.

Modern medical research and practice in the United States has resulted in higher survival rates for children born prematurely with chronic and life-threatening health conditions. But children who experience prenatal and perinatal distress are often vulnerable to the development of chronic conditions such as asthma, attention-deficit/ hyperactivity disorder, and other disorders, according to Genel et al. (2008). These authors suggest that the financial and emotional costs of managing these disabilities is growing. Health care providers (Feldman, 2011) and others are calling for sustainable and cost-effective systems of service for children and families with intense health care needs. In Gerrard and Soriano's edited book (2013), I suggest that "the success of diagnosis and treatment of chronic disorders is predicated on the development of *specialized collaborative care across settings, based on good science, which is well coordinated* over time" (p. 742).

In the American medical milieu of the past two decades, such collaborative practice has been difficult to employ outside of inpatient settings where clinicians practice in close proximity to each other. Health care professionals in outpatient clinical settings and private practice are typically reimbursed by specific procedures related to their specialized training. This practice is called *fee-for-service*, and medical and psychological providers have been paid by insurance companies or the government to perform specific tests and procedures. In the health care market of the past decade, fee-for-service health care providers have seldom been reimbursed for multidisciplinary collaboration across settings. Collaborative practice has often become a disincentive for outpatient clinicians who struggle with rising practice costs and low reimbursement rates for a limited range of reimbursed services.

Fortunately, collaborative educational and health care practice patterns are beginning to emerge as health care reform unfolds in the United States in response to the Affordable Care Act of 2010 (ACA; see HHS.gov/HealthCare). One trend is a move away from providing reimbursement for specialized and often fragmented fee-for-service toward support for more systems-based delivery and evaluation of health care services and programs. Rather than simply documenting that specific health care programs and procedures exist for services to be reimbursed, the ACA has spurred a shift of attention toward examining the outcomes and results of such services. That is, attention is shifting from simply tracking increasingly specialized service provision to evaluating whether collaborative services actually improve health outcomes.

Another important trend is that many previously uninsured or underinsured families have obtained insurance by enrolling with health care exchanges under the ACA. But children and families from underinsured homes remain high. For many children in rural, urban, and suburban areas, schools are the milieu where health care needs are first recognized and addressed. Rones and Hoagwood (2000) reported that schools are commonly regarded as the de facto providers of mental health services to many children and youth, providing an estimated 70% to 80% of psychosocial services to those children who receive mental health services.

The growth of multidisciplinary educational teams in schools (e.g., Planning and Placement, Response to Intervention) mirrors the growth of multidisciplinary teams in health care. Medical teams strive to support patients and families who struggle with chronic illnesses in ways similar to multidisciplinary school-based practice. The medical specialties of pediatrics and family medicine led the creation of the *medical home* concept, which was first developed in 1967 by the American Academy of Pediatrics (AAP; Keckley, 2008). The goal of the medical home model is to reduce the cost of unmanaged chronic health disorders by streamlining and coordinating services over time. Noting that 45% of the population of our country has a chronic medical condition of some sort, physicians endorsing the medical home concept recommend that primary care professionals provide the bulk of diagnostic and treatment services, as well as coordinate the care of their patients over time (Keckley, 2008).

The American Academy of Family Physicians, the AAP, the American College of Physicians, and the American Osteopathic Association published the *Joint Principles of the Patient-Centered Medical Home* (2007).

Representing more than 300,000 physicians, the group posited four principles to describe the characteristics of a medical home. The principles include having each patient linked with a personal physician; the physician leading a team of clinicians who provide ongoing patient care; fostering a delivery service where all of a patient's health care needs are addressed or are arranged to be addressed; and coordinating and/or integrating care across the whole health care system, utilizing the latest information technology.

The concept of medical home has several goals. First, the model seeks to utilize such technologies as electronic health records to streamline communication to free up more productive face-to-face time between patients and health care providers. Another goal is to improve caregiver cooperation to empower patients with chronic illnesses and their families. By making services patient and family centered, the medical home seeks to generate rapid and favorable health outcomes.

Preliminary research findings about health and educational outcomes utilizing the pediatric medical home are encouraging. In a report of a 3-year pilot study of 300 families in 10 pediatric practices utilizing medical home practices in New Hampshire (McAllister, Scherrieb, & Cooley, 2009), parents of children with special health needs reported that their children experienced better school attendance and fewer hospitalizations. The parents also reported less worry about their children's health. A review article of 30 studies by Homer et al. (2008) provided support that medical home practices improve health outcomes for children with special needs and their families. Improvements were noted in improved health status, efficiency of service provision, and family functioning and satisfaction.

The American Psychological Association recently appointed a task force headed by Hiroto and Kazak to collect data on psychology's role in patient-centered medical homes (PCMH). Novotney (2014) summarized their initial report in *Monitor on Psychology* as follows:

> The PCMH approach results in fewer primary-care and hospital visits, improved patient functioning, and reduced costs, and it allows the team to reduce its workload by decreasing the

number of repeat visits by patients and to feel more satisfied with their work. (p. 39)

Concurrent with the emergence of interest in medical home practice groups of family physicians, psychiatrists, pediatricians, psychologists, family therapists, and social workers began to formally collaborate and advocate for inclusion of families in treatment models for complex medical and psychological disorders and the family (Campbell & McDaniel, 1987; McDaniel, Doherty, & Hepworth, 2014; Seaburn et al., 1996). Their generative work resulted in the emergence of medical family therapy as an innovation in health care.

Medical family therapy seeks to incorporate both the medical team and the family as resources for diagnosis and treatment of chronic illnesses and relies heavily on the strength of collaborative teams to track and adapt best practices for the management of those illnesses. The work of these hospital-, agency-, and clinic-based teams has paved the way for the development of collaboration across a growing range of health and education-based systems. Elements of their work are relevant for school-based mental health practice and are described in this chapter.

In their edited casebook, *Family-Centered Medical Care*, Doherty and Baird (1987) first conceptualized five levels of involvement that medical practitioners have with their patients to improve patient outcomes. These levels ascend from Level One, which refers to the traditional practice of biomedical focus on the patient alone, with minimal family contact. Level Two involves the provision of ongoing medical advice and information. Level Three involves providing emotional support, which requires that the clinician utilizes stress management skills. Level Four involves developing systematic assessment and interventions and requires sophisticated collaborative clinical training. Level Five, which involves conducting joint family therapy sessions with families, is the most complex level of involvement and requires even more medical and family systems training. Each level involves the provision of increasingly active collaboration among the members of a patients' treatment team. Each level also incorporates increasingly sophisticated family therapy techniques, designed to more fully support and empower families of patients with chronic health problems through collaboration.

For example, Level Four, which refers to the practice of providing systematic assessment and planned intervention (McDaniel, Hepworth, & Doherty, 1992), is strikingly similar to the processes of medical home. It is also similar to the practices of the Planning and Placement Teams (PPTs) in special education, as well as to the Response to Intervention (RtI) techniques and levels of intervention that are now being incorporated across the country. (PPT and RtI teams and practice patterns are addressed in the next two chapters). In both medical and educational domains, systems-based multidisciplinary collaboration among teams of professionals is a central feature. Collaborative practice is designed to comprehensively assess, monitor, and evaluate services to patients/ students and families with special health care and education needs.

McDaniel, Hepworth, and Doherty's (1992) seminal book, *Medical Family Therapy: A Biopsychosocial Approach to Families with Health Problems*, first described medical family therapy as an innovative contrast to traditional individually oriented medical practice. The authors noted that *family-centered* health care for those families struggling with chronic medical illnesses is a core component of medical family therapy. Many of the ideas addressed in the first edition of their book reinforce current notions about the medical home. Medical family therapy techniques also incorporate elements that schools use to help children with chronic special needs obtain the educational services they need to succeed.

McDaniel et al. (1992, 2014), Seaburn et al. (1996), and other medical family therapists support the notion of creating multidisciplinary teams to diagnose and treat people with chronic disorders and their families. Seaburn et al. report that the top 10% of medical utilizers account for one third of outpatient resources and one half of inpatient resources. One half of these patients had mental health as well as medical needs. They note that collaboration is particularly useful for families with children who have chronic pediatric conditions such as diabetes, asthma, and attention-deficit/hyperactivity disorder. Families struggling with these disorders are often high utilizers of care, and they need support to promote and maintain healthy functioning and treatment compliance. These authors suggest that collaboration over time can alter the meaning of the illness in that family in positive ways and can help promote positive treatment outcomes.

As was described in Chapter 3 on special education, schools typically create multidisciplinary child study teams to begin the assessment process, which involves obtaining informed consent forms from families. When schools contract with providers of specialized diagnostic or treatment services, they routinely obtain signed release of information forms from the families of the child they refer. At the first appointment, health care providers and other professionals who contract privately with schools for service also obtain signed release forms that enable us to collaborate with informed consent from the student's family.

We typically begin building the health care/educational team at that point. We stress that health care and education is too complicated for any one of our disciplines alone and that we want to provide as much support to the child and family as we can. We use the term *frontloading* to support the family from the point in time when the child is referred, whether we are working within schools or are in practice outside of school systems. We use the data we collect to comprehensively assess, track, and evaluate the interventions we provide. *Frontloading* is the first step in building evidence-based treatment strategies, which is being increasingly incorporated in evidence-based interventions in education and health care.

McDaniel et al. (1992) promoted two other key medical family therapy goals that we have adopted for use in school-based professional service. The first involves the promoting the concept of *agency*, first coined by Richard Totman, to describe active involvement in one's own health care. McDaniel et al. expanded this notion to include supporting and strengthening the *family's ability* to actively manage chronic health problems in a family member. Building a sense of *agency* strengthens a family's confidence and competence to manage its family member's chronic illness or disability.

A related concept is that of enhancing *communion* in families experiencing health care crises. This notion refers both to the psychological family bonds of communication that are nurtured over the course of a chronic illness, as well as the resilience that can foster better health outcomes through team collaboration. As McDaniel et al. (1992) note, "the quality of social relationships appears to be the most powerful psychosocial factor in health and illness" (p. 10). Serious medical crises can isolate families and challenge their ability to communicate within and outside of their family.

But according to the McDaniel et al. (1992), "serious illnesses and disabilities provide opportunities for resolving old conflicts and for forging new levels of healthy family bonding" (p. 10). Promoting *agency* and *communion* through medical family therapy can help mitigate stressors and actually strengthen families over the course of the illness by alleviating distress and building options for management of the illness. In their second edition of their book, McDaniel et al. (2014) explain that medical family therapists are a

> welcome resource to help clarify the misunderstandings, help families obtain information and resources, decrease role strain for both families and health care systems, and help families and clinicians create more compassionate and sustainable systems of care. (p. 31)

Rolland (1984) is another medical family therapy pioneer and psychiatrist who developed a valuable way to conceptualize the impact of chronic illness over time. He categorized long-term medical illnesses into a schema that is useful for clinicians who treat families coping with chronic health disorders, illustrated in Figure 5.1. This typology of disorders includes a consideration of one of the three ways a chronic illness can manifest itself. The first category is *progressive*, where the illness follows a downward path of deterioration. A disorder such as Alzheimer disease, which follows a path of deteriorating cognitive functioning, classifies as progressive. The second category is called *relapsing*, where episodes of acute distress may be followed by a return to baseline functioning. Asthma falls into the relapsing category. Another disorder, such as multiple sclerosis, may be ultimately progressive, but may initially follow a relapsing path. Here, episodes of the disorder may be followed by return to baseline functioning for quite some time before loss of functioning occurs. A third type of manifestation is a *constant* type of disorder such as familial hyperlipidemia. Here, the abnormally high lipid levels that occur congenitally in some families are constant, although adverse symptoms may be entirely silent until a coronary event occurs (Laundy, 1990).

Rolland next classifies chronic illnesses according to the symptom *severity*, and then according to whether they are *incapacitating*, such as a myocardial infarction, or *non-incapacitating*, such as atopic dermatitis, commonly known as eczema. He then breaks down illnesses further into more specific categories, including *fatal, shortened life, possibly fatal, and nonfatal.* The *fatal* category includes illnesses such as Stage IV metastatic cancer. An example of *shortened life, possibly fatal,* includes Type I childhood diabetes mellitus, and the nonfatal category includes disorders such as mild asthma. Rolland's model is illustrated in Figure 5.1.

Chronic Illness Typology

| | | Incapacitating | | Non-Incapacitating | |
		Acute	Gradual	Acute	Gradual
Progressive	Fatal				
Relapsing					
Progressive	Shortened Life Possibly Fatal				
Relapsing					
Constant					
Progressive	Non-fatal				
Relapsing					
Constant					

Source: Rolland, J.S. (1987, June). *Chronic illness and the life cycle: A conceptual framework.* Family Process, 26, 203-221. [CD-ROM]. Family Process, 1–46. Copyright 1998.

Figure 5.1. Chronic illness typology, by J. Rolland, 1998. Reprinted with permission from Blackwell Publishing Ltd.

Rolland's chronic illness typology helps readers conceptualize how to think about the different challenges facing patients and families over time. It helps clinicians to target interventions for which they can provide the most potent support for people with chronic illness and their families. The examples that follow provide case illustrations of Rolland's typology.

Case Examples

"Damien," a 7-year-old second-grader, was referred by his school system for a psychological evaluation after a difficult year in school. He experienced significant problems with attention, and he was not progressing well socially. Damien appeared dependent on his teacher for directions in class and had difficulty working and playing independently. His school wanted to know how much control Damien had over his behavior and whether his attention/concentration difficulties warranted medication and/or other interventions to help him focus more independently on school work.

Damien was small in stature, and he was diagnosed as a toddler with diabetes insipidus, a rare condition. This disorder, unlike the more common diabetes mellitus, is not insulin dependent. Rather, it is a condition that involves excessive thirst, as well as the need for frequent discharge of diluted urine. According to *Taber's Cyclopedic Medical Dictionary* (Thomas, 1993) diabetes insipidus "is caused by inadequate secretion of antidiuretic hormone from the hypothalamus or its release by the posterior pituitary gland" (p. 526). Damien typically carried a water bottle with him at all times, and he needed frequent snacks to help maintain energy.

The treatment for this condition involves frequent monitoring of fluid intake, as well as vasopressin replacement therapy. A child's growth can be affected, and a growth hormone is often added as part of the treatment. Frequent bathroom breaks are essential. Diabetes insipidus, in Rolland's typology, classifies as a constant chronic illness that is not life threatening, if properly treated. Although much of the etiology of diabetes insipidus is unknown, trauma to the head that damages the pituitary is one of the causes. Damien experienced such physical trauma and neglect with his biological parents.

Damien became the foster son of his aunt and uncle that school year. His biological mother was declared psychologically unable to care for him by the courts, and his biological father was incarcerated for illegal drug-related and assaultive behavior. Damien's biological parents were separated from each other. His aunt and uncle agreed to care for Damien, and he relocated to his current state with his new family at the beginning of the school year. The onset of Damien's medical disorder occurred when he was a young child, but his new family became active in helping make his illness less incapacitating.

What precipitated the referral was that Damien's aunt recently removed him from his public school and placed him in a private Montessori school, following a classroom incident with his teacher. Damien's teacher, not fully understanding the nature or treatment for diabetes insipidus, required him to complete an assignment before he was allowed to take a water break and use the restroom. When Damien's aunt learned of the incident, she angrily removed him from that school.

It was tempting to examine the family history for information related Damien's inattention and dependent behavior. Utilizing the chronic illness typology first, however, gave me critical clues to integrate with the evaluation findings. Without medical research and collaboration about his condition, my evaluation and recommendations would have been incomplete as well as inaccurate.

My first intervention, therefore, was to collaborate with his school system to learn what they actually knew about diabetes insipidus. As it turned out, they welcomed a full orientation to the disorder. Because his aunt and uncle had been commissioned during a family crisis to care for Damien and transfer him to our state, they did not have sufficient time to fully orient his school system about what they understood about this chronic disorder. We scheduled team meetings with active help from the school nurse and worked to build a collaborative relationship among his teachers, his family, and other team members. Damien was eventually returned to this home school, where he learned to function with more success.

There were complex cognitive, emotional, and environmental variables that contributed to Damien's difficulties in school. But fostering a better understanding of his medical needs among members of his family, medical, and school team was a critical first step in creating a comprehensive assessment and plan for Damien's needs. Building informed and collaborative relationships among Damien's team members contributed to better academic and health outcomes. It boosted his aunt and uncle's trust as caretakers and enabled them to work more actively with his treatment/education team on Damien's behalf. Utilizing the collaborative strength of the team, we became better able to track Damien's progress and adjust his services.

Rolland's typology integrates well with the LOGS model described in the last chapter because it includes temporal as well as cross-sectional dimensions that are useful for conceptualizing patient and family needs. The two frameworks together provide helpful guides to plan timely clinical interventions based on how chronic illnesses manifest themselves over time. In Damien's case, his disorder is of a constant nature that, with proactive treatment, does not need to be incapacitating. The team interventions needed not to be intense or frequent. But to make timely and accurate interventions on Damien and his family's behalf, his team needed to be informed.

A few collaborative planning meetings when Damien first entered school might have established team relationships on more solid grounding and could have possibly prevented the disruption in his education. But even with these constraints, once we *frontloaded* Damien's team with information and health care team members and fostered better *communion* with his family, his aunt and uncle developed a stronger sense of *agency* for their family. They began working actively with his team, and Damien's health and educational outcomes began to improve. His aunt and uncle began to view his school as more of a medical/educational home. Integrated care across medical, educational, and family settings will likely make a difference in Damien's life and will help support his family to better address his complex needs over time.

Where and when to provide integrated school and health care services for children with chronic illnesses and disabilities will vary widely across time and specific illnesses. Some children with chronic disorders will require intense team vigilance, collaboration, and integrated care over time, such as the next case example.

"Meredith" is an adopted daughter whose parents presented at my private practice after experiencing exhaustion, depression, and anxiety after several years of escalating behavioral dyscontrol in their daughter. Meredith was born a drug-dependent baby to biological parents who had chronic polysubstance abuse problems. Meredith was placed with her foster family at the age of 3 weeks and was later adopted by them.

Her adopted family has three grown biological children. Meredith's adopted parents had also cared for two profoundly disabled boys, one biological and one a foster son. Both of the boys died several years ago, just as Meredith entered their family. I have provided intermittent family support to them over the past several years as they managed their children's illnesses. We did intensive work together as they coped with the deaths of their sons. They recovered from their losses with strength and dignity, and their older children were in the process of establishing their own households.

Meredith's family had developed a solid relationship with their local school system and special education team over the years as they raised their disabled sons. They were eager to provide a good home and education for Meredith, who did not appear to have the profound daily living skill challenges that her stepbrothers had experienced from birth.

Meredith is a physically beautiful child. Early in her infancy, however, she began having health and behavioral symptoms, which included asthma, feeding and sleeping difficulties, and problems with self-soothing. As she became a toddler, Meredith's behavioral dyscontrol escalated to the point where she could not restrain herself with her family. Although she could function reasonably well at child care and school, Meredith regularly defied behavioral limits with her family after school. She engaged in frequent altercations with them, particularly her mother. She developed increasing insensitivity to the consequences of her actions, and she regularly defied bedtime and other household rules.

Meredith was diagnosed with reactive attachment disorder as well as childhood bipolar illness as a young child. She was put on several medications (including antipsychotics, mood stabilizers, and antidepressants), experienced two psychiatric hospitalizations, and was recently placed in an inpatient therapeutic treatment center. Meredith's parents were exhausted, and they needed time to recover from several years of stressful caretaking.

Meredith's inpatient treatment was designed to stabilize her medications, provide intensive restorative therapy, and help her develop adaptive coping skills. Inpatient treatment included educational tutoring, as well as individual, group, and family therapy to address Meredith's reactions to her adoption and help her build adaptive relationships with her family. My work with the family at that time focused on helping her parents address their grief, disappointment, and exhaustion about their parenting experience with Meredith, particularly on the heels of losing their two other sons. I met biweekly with her parents to help them work through their distress and monitor their recovery from burnout.

The areas of the LOGS model that we targeted that year were her family system, and the boundaries where communication with her school and residential treatment team converged. The goals were to reenergize Meredith's depleted family system and to build *communion* with Meredith's residential treatment team and her special education team in her home school. We held several phone consultations and in-person meetings to track Meredith's progress in treatment and plan for her return to her family home and school system. Special education teams from her home district, inpatient hospital, and a special education school nearby attended these consultations. The multidisciplinary staff included teachers, psychologists, family therapists, and speech and language pathologists, as well as paraprofessionals and administrators. To promote agency and communion, we developed a collaborative phone and e-mail relationship with her pediatrician and outpatient psychiatrist and held several conferences with Meredith's public school team to make informed decisions about her educational reentry to her home community and school system.

To ease Meredith's adjustment and success, several rehearsal visits to her home and school were arranged. Because she was now 1 year older than when she left her public school system, her special educational setting was in a new school. Although she was challenged with adjusting to a new, unfamiliar school environment, some of her friends whom she had known before also attended her new school and made the process less stressful.

Meredith matured developmentally during her year away. She made strides in her ability to monitor and take responsibility for her behavior, as well as to make amends when her behavior was unacceptable to her family and teachers. The restorative model of inpatient treatment worked well for Meredith, and she also achieved progress regarding her adjustment to the history of her adoption.

The emotional and behavioral focus of Meredith's residential treatment augmented her academic progress, which was addressed at the special team meetings at her public school. Remedial tutoring and mentoring were arranged to help her catch up, while her team also agreed to help Meredith move into mainstreamed classes as she became ready. Individual and family therapy was also provided for Meredith and her parents.

During her hospitalization, Meredith's parents reclaimed the resilience they showed over the years with other family challenges they had faced. *Frontloading* and *communion* played significant roles in helping Meredith's parents appreciate that they were not alone in their quest to provide the best treatment and education for Meredith. As their energy returned, they both played vital and active roles in tracking Meredith's progress and return to her home school setting. They interviewed three other placement opportunities along with other treatment team members, and they were central collaborators with her physical and behavioral health and educational teams throughout her treatment. Meredith's parents demonstrated a strong sense of agency on their daughter's behalf, which made our collaboration richer and more productive.

At Meredith's team meeting at school 6 months later, she demonstrated significant behavioral and academic gains. Meredith succeeded in adjusting to her special and regular education classes, and she showed significant academic improvement. She made significant behavioral gains in her ability to recognize and manage her impulses in class and other group activities that year.

But over the next few years, Meredith experienced regression in her development as she entered early adolescence. Her ability to manage her emotions and behavior deteriorated at school and at home as she entered puberty. She began to have physical altercations with her parents, and she attempted to run away several times. Her escalating symptoms taxed the resources of her family and required renewed collaborative treatment planning.

Unfortunately, we were not able to prevent another residential placement for Meredith because her mood dysregulation and behavior dyscontrol escalated as she entered puberty. But we did prevent burnout for her parents by continuing to provide collaborative service to them across school, residential treatment, and private practice settings. With team support, her parents learned to accept the limits of the structure they could provide to Meredith at home.

The relief they experienced from knowing she was safely housed and cared for in a residential setting was significant. It helped them address the developmental needs of Meredith's older step-siblings who were marrying and beginning their own families. It also helped Meredith's parents realize and articulate their own needs as a couple, and they were successful at recognizing that they needed vacation breaks to recharge their parental batteries. While the direct work with Meredith addressed the LOG model's "individual" domain and the family work addressed the "family" domain, the communion dimension of our team collaboration addressed her school needs, her functioning in the community, and Meredith and her family's life-cycle needs over time.

Much of this could not have happened without collaborative teamwork that promoted frontloading, communion, and agency for Meredith and her family. Meredith's developmental course has been rocky and is a testament to the damaging effects of prenatal substance abuse. But the active team planning and close communication Meredith's parents had with her treatment team helped them muster the agency to prevail as the heads of their family on Meredith's behalf.

The research on the long-term biological effects of parental substance abuse on children's learning and behavior compelling. Feinstein (2014) summarized Streisguth and others' research about the damaging neuropsychological effects of alcohol on various areas of the brain, including the cerebellum, hippocampus, corpus callosum and basal ganglia. She notes that other organs in the body such as the liver, heart, and kidneys have also been observed in children with fetal alcohol spectrum disorders. Feinstein notes that these damages may be less apparent and more subtle than those originally observed in children with fetal alcohol syndrome, who often have noticeable head circumference and shape abnormalities, gait difficulties, and extreme difficulty with social interaction. But the more subtle effects can also cause chronic problems with children's psychoeducational, motor, and social functioning.

Because Meredith is one of those children with documented prenatal brain toxicity yet no observable physical stigmata, it is not clear how her functioning will specifically evolve. During her young life thus far, Meredith's physical health (asthma, sleep and eating problems) has significantly improved as she has grown and her symptoms have been treated. Her motor coordination is within normal limits, and she is physically an attractive young adolescent. But her learning difficulties are marked. And her psychological and behavioral symptoms have been relapsing, according to Rolland's model of chronic illness.

What is clear is that the collaborative medical, psychiatric, and educational team established for Meredith has provided her with timely and comprehensive treatment. Planning, monitoring, and providing services as a team have strengthened her caretakers' confidence. It has boosted Meredith's compliance at times when she could muster her strengths. Her team became increasingly well equipped with practice over time to communicate with one another and calibrate small changes in plans as needed.

Accompanying changes in Meredith's medications at school and at her residential placement have been more efficiently monitored, as have her response to those changes. Her team incorporated many quality and efficiency aspects of medical home as it spanned systems of health and educational care for Meredith and her family. It is hoped that the results of such integrated care will ultimately foster some favorable outcomes for her, which is a dream we all share for Meredith and her family.

Genel et al. (2008) note the following long-range benefits of collaborative research and practice on children's behalf:

As stated by James J. Heckman, PhD, the recipient of the Nobel Prize in economic sciences in 2000 and his colleagues, we need to invest in the very young because early learning begets later learning and early successes breed later success. In contrast, the later in life we attempt to repair early deficits, the costlier the remediation becomes (p. 844).

Further integration of medical family therapy concepts with education are addressed in Chapter 6, which addresses a national initiative, Response to Intervention. This initiative and the concept of medical home have compatible elements, which lend themselves well to the incorporation of medical family therapy into school-based multidisciplinary practice. Collaborative health care and current educational policies both focus on building competence and improving outcomes through systems-based collaboration, based on sound scientific, evidence-based research and practice.

six

Response to Intervention

In the past two decades, a shift has occurred in education for all students. First, as is happening in health care, there is growing interest and attention being paid to evidence-based practice and education, based on data that prompted the No Child Left Behind (NCLB) legislation of 2001. Policies and procedures are being enacted that more closely match scientific, research-based methods of service that are proven successful and are considered "best practices." High-quality instruction/intervention that is targeted in differentiated ways to help *all* children learn is receiving increasing focus in current education law and policy. Attention is shifting from simply ensuring that the provision of specific services occurs to measuring whether such services are integrated and are actually working (National Association of State Directors of Special Education, 2008). These elements constitute the foundation of the Response to Intervention (RtI) initiative.

This chapter outlines the RtI initiative, its history, and its components. I also integrate the expertise of mental health clinicians and educators with the systems-based requirements of the RtI initiative, suggesting that mental health school certification and licensure are a good fit with current educational trends. Finally, this chapter provides case examples of how RtI is being incorporated in a sampling of Connecticut school systems, with special emphasis on a model called Positive Behavioral Interventions and Supports (PBIS). For more detailed information about RtI, the reader is referred to documents published by the National Association of State Directors of Special Education (2008, 2014). For more information about PBIS, a good resource is Sugai and Horner's (2006) article in *School Psychology Review* on school-wide positive behavior support.

RtI History

As was mentioned in the special education history in Chapter 4, the discrepancy model has been used for many years to examine the significant differences between a child's measured abilities and his or her actual achievement. Score discrepancies have been used to determine the presence of a learning disability and to help classify its nature. Over time, however, there has not been sufficient evidence to prove that the discrepancy model identifies *all* children with special needs, and educators and legislators have sought comprehensive ways in the past few years to address this dilemma. Using research methods across medicine, education, and psychology, many more evidence-based measures are being currently developed for use by school teams to evaluate and track school progress for a wider variety of students with learning inefficiencies.

New Individuals With Disabilities Education Act (IDEA) legislation came from the NCLB Act of 2001. The law was enacted to ensure that all children have the opportunity to obtain a high-quality education, as evidenced by reaching minimum proficiency scores on state academic achievement standards and state academic assessments. It is a reauthorization of the Elementary and Secondary Education Act of 1965. NCLB provides key definitions of reading, components of reading instruction, reading assessments, and scientifically based reading research (Wright & Wright, 2010). A President's Commission on Excellence in Special Education was appointed in 2001 to make recommendations to improve the law. Three recommendations that came from that Commission were to

1. focus on results, rather than the process,
2. focus on prevention, and
3. first consider children with special needs within *general education.*

A further reauthorization followed in 2004, with the Individuals With Disabilities Education Improvement Act (IDEIA). This act added provisions to IDEA that removed the requirement of aptitude/discrepancy assessment to determine a learning disability and the need for special education. Authors of these provisions affirmed the research findings that "waiting for children to fail" to achieve in reading can miss an important window of learning opportunity. It can create a cycle of failure that is difficult to correct later.

The goals of the 2004 provisions were to screen children earlier and help schools comprehensively identify all children who were not responding to reading instruction. The objective was to proactively shift student monitoring and assessment from special education teams to general education for children who were at risk for failing to learn to read. This systemic shift is called the RTI initiative.

In 2006, federal guidelines were established to operationalize early screening methods for identifying learning disabilities. These methods are designed to use standardized, proven assessment measures that are more evidenced-based than those used before that time. In 2008, the Connecticut State Department of Education (CSDE) published its response to those guidelines. Their document titled *Using Scientific Research–Based Interventions: Improving Education for All Students: Connecticut's Framework for RtI* is being incorporated into the policies and procedures of educational districts throughout the state (CSDE, Bureau of School and District Improvement, 2008). Other states throughout the United States are also adapting the law to meet the specific needs of their local districts.

RtI seeks to screen children with learning inefficiencies earlier, helping schools to more quickly identify children who are not responding as expected to reading and other instruction. RtI aims to shift focus from special education for specific children identified with categorized learning difficulties to broader, system-wide attention to achievement levels of all children. It also represents a shift to using *results* of a wider range of scientifically based assessment/teaching methods to design and monitor interventions, rather than relying on traditional forms of assessment and teaching, which have not always been based on rigorous or proven standards.

Under RtI, assessment and support services are being designed and delivered in more systemic ways. Broader individual, family, school, and environmental data are beginning to be collected, thus creating more thorough evidence-based data to help students learn. The RtI initiative seeks to screen children who are at early risk for failure to learn to achieve in academics such as reading and mathematics. It also targets social and emotional behaviors such as aggression toward other children or teachers (or both), school attendance, and language differences that can affect school achievement.

RtI seeks to identify children who are not responding to instruction before they need formal evaluation for special education services. The responsibility for evaluations shifts in RtI from special education departments to general education to provide a smoother continuum of services to support academic success. As an assessment tool, RtI is designed to address those children with neurocognitive delays or disabilities as well as children whose educational needs have not been historically, culturally, or psychologically met in general education classrooms. RtI targets "invisible" and subtle variables that affect learning including cultural, family, or social factors such as bullying. All can interfere with children's resiliency and achievement in various ways.

As was discussed in the Chapter 3, full psychoeducational evaluations are labor-intensive, and they are at times not used until too late in a child's academic career to be optimally useful. Under RtI, new evidence-based measures are being developed to evaluate how those variables contribute to student learning and behavior and how students respond to targeted interventions to address those variables. These measures involve frequent monitoring of performance to make effective decisions in response to "child data" (NASDSE, 2005, p. 3). Core principles of RtI are that all children can be effectively taught, early intervention is critical, and problem-solving techniques use scientific research-based interventions.

The RtI Triangle Model

The RtI model, illustrated in Figure 6.1, is represented as a triangle that with three major tiers for intervention. Each tier is progressive, and movement through the tiers of RtI involves increasing intensity of services that are adapted to specific student needs within regular education, before formal referral for special education assessment and services. The tiers contain interventions that correspond to ascending levels of primary, secondary, and tertiary prevention.

Primary preventive interventions at Tier 1 are delivered to all students in general education classes. Secondary prevention at Tier 2 involves targeted group interventions for students at risk, either in or outside of the classroom. Tertiary prevention provides individual assessment, support and monitoring at Tier 3 for students at risk, either in or outside of the classroom.

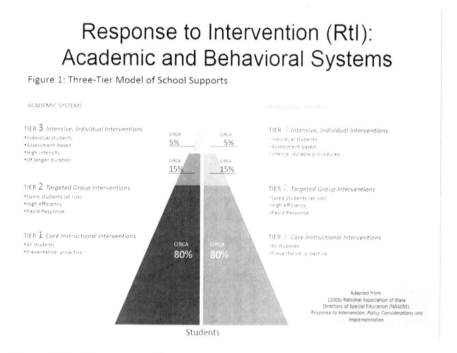

Figure 6.1. Response to Intervention (RtI). Reprinted with permission from the National Association of State Directors of Special Education, Inc., 2005. www.nasdse.org

Tier 1 involves universal screening and group interventions to assess and monitor progress in learning to all students. The goal is for 80% to 90% of students to achieve the benchmark levels of progress through interventions at Tier 1, as assessed by monitoring those levels at least three times per year. Monitoring can include report cards, screening measures, and teacher feedback, for example.

Students not achieving those benchmarks are to receive targeted, short-term interventions to help them achieve on the next level, Tier

2, of the RtI model. Multidisciplinary school teams are critical service providers at Tier 1. They design and help provide services that can involve supplemental instruction, social skill interventions, teacher consultation, and other evidence-based problem-solving measures on a small-group basis for students in need. These services are to be monitored closely, at least biweekly, and the interventions are to be time-limited, lasting generally between 6 to 10 weeks. Students who succeed are to be reintegrated into regular education. This group is speculated to contain about 15% of the general population of students.

If students are still having difficulty achieving according to expectations, longer term instruction and intervention can be offered at the next level, Tier 3, which is thought to include a significantly smaller percentage, from 1% to 5% of the general population of students. Here students receive more intense individual and group support with the aid of multidisciplinary teams. They can also initiate a special education determination at Tier 3.

Some students may actually enter school with diagnoses and special education classification based on early intervention they received before starting school through programs such as Birth to Three or Head Start or from their health care providers. Schools and families often have concerns about such children as they enter school, and those children may bypass and progress through Tier 3 into special educational programs and services without RtI interventions. Or children receiving special education Individualized Education Plan services may also receive tiered support in RtI. However, decisions about eligibility must be data- and child-driven to accurately target special services and reflect the true needs of children for such services.

RtI also seeks to reduce disciplinary incidents in school and prevent out-of-district placements through early intervention. In addition, it aims to decrease the need for costly mediated disputes about school planning by empowering families as full team participants. RtI seeks to save educational and psychological costs by encouraging schools to build collaborative, primary preventive teams that include teachers, special mental health school personnel (marriage and family therapists, school psychologists, counselors, social workers), and other special staff such as physical and occupational therapists, nurses, and parents.

As can be seen in the Figure 6.1, the RtI triangle is composed of two smaller triangles, which include an academic dimension on the left side and a behavioral dimension on the right side. These triangles both contain the three prevention tiers, but they delineate additional dimensions of instructional and behavioral supports to school achievement. The CSDE, through the Special Education Resource Center (SERC; http://ctserc.org) has adopted the term *School-Wide Positive Behavioral Interventions and Supports* (SWPBIS) to address the behavioral dimension of the RtI triangle. They note that "PBIS is not a program or a curriculum but rather a systems approach to enhance the capacity of schools and districts to adopt and sustain the use of evidence-based practices for all students" (SERC, 2009, p. 1).

Originally designed to address the needs of children with behavioral disorders within special education, PBIS has been found to have applicability for a broader range of school-based needs. The National Technical Assistance Center was established in the 1990s to build a database to support the growth of PBIS across the country. The center has completed three 5-year grant cycles to help shape the PBIS framework. It has now been incorporated into more than 18,000 schools across the United States (www.pbis.org; Sugai & Simonson, 2012).

> With PBIS, Sugai et al. (2000) note that attention is focused on creating and sustaining school environments that improve lifestyle results (personal, health, social, family, work, recreation, etc.) for all children and youth by making problem behavior less effective, efficient and relevant and making desired behavior more functional. (p. 7)

Specifically, PBIS is designed to address such outcomes as improved school climate, decreased discipline referrals and higher student achievement, all more systems-based outcomes.

As a process, PBIS addresses student outcomes, evidence- and research-based practice, a continuum of behavioral support policies and systems, and the use of data to guide decisions about school services. It fits well with the universal, group, and individual levels as well as incorporates the integration of academic and behavioral dimensions of the RtI triangle. Together RtI and PBIS constitute multitiered systems of supports (MTSS) and wraparound services to boost student achievement in positive ways (Sugai & Simonson, 2012).

Many states have made targeted efforts toward addressing school climate, proactively managing disciplinary behavioral needs, and developing evidence-based plans for integrating academic with behavioral strategies to boost student resiliency and achievement using PBIS and RtI. In the wake of the current rise in school violence, the need for collaborative work to achieve these goals has taken on a new urgency. As mentioned in Chapter 2, several school-based administrators and mental health professional developed "A Framework for Safe and Successful Schools" (Cohen, Vaillancourt, Rossen, & Pollitt, 2012). These authors called for a systems-based collaborative approach to promote school safety, integrate services to all children, and build multidisciplinary and MTSS to identify, track, and better serve children and youth in need. The Framework is discussed further in Chapter 9.

This is the domain in which the arenas of education and health care can converge in creative new ways and where multidisciplinary collaborative teams can be the most synergistic and useful. It represents a paradigm shift from merely adding on individual special education services for identified needs to incorporating a multisystemic array of elements necessary for all children to achieve in resilient ways. Schools can become a resourceful venue to remediate the duplication and fragmentation of services in health care and education through RtI-based collaborative services. The goals of ending bifurcation in domains of both general and special education and medical/behavioral health care can be efficiently addressed through multidisciplinary collaboration.

Because children spend the bulk of their time in schools, primary preventive services provided "where they live" can reach more children whose financial, cultural, or family constraints may make it difficult for them to obtain such services outside of the school day. Providing RtI collaborative behavioral health care services in schools can also help mitigate the stigmatizing labels that can accompany mental health treatment outside the "norm" of schools.

RtI shares similarities to the medical home initiative introduced in Chapter 5. As mentioned, the medical home initiative focuses on prevention and collaboration, more integrated management of chronic illnesses over time, utilization of technology to improve collaboration and communication (e-mail collaboration and e-medical records), and more comprehensive, coordinated family-centered care (American Academy of Family Physicians, American Academy of Pediatrics, American College of Physicians, & American Osteopathic Association, 2007). Both medical home and RtI initiatives emphasize time-series measurement of results to build a robust and scientific base of evidence for interventions.

Both systems incorporate components to protect the confidentiality of such collaboration. The field of education is federally mandated by the Family Education Rights and Privacy Act to allow families and eligible students to have access to their education records and to require written consent to share confidential record information (Family Policy Compliance Office, U.S. Department of Education, 2015). Likewise, hospitals and health care professionals have been similarly mandated by federal confidentiality guidelines in the American Health Insurance Portability and Accountability Act (*HIPAA 101*, 2013). This law helps ensure that all medical records, billing, and patient accounts meet certain consistent standards with regard to documentation, handling, and privacy.

In addition, each of the licensed mental health care professionals doing school-based practice is bound by the ethics codes of their respective disciplines to meet confidentiality standards on behalf of the patients they serve. This is another reason both state licensure and school certification will ensure higher quality care and collaboration among multidisciplinary team members. Several of the structural elements to ensure school-based, family-centered professional collaboration in schools are already in place or are in process of being developed. It seems an opportune time to apply the systemic logic of health care reform and RtI to the multidisciplinary collaborative systems and subsystems in schools. Many school systems across America are doing just that, and several Connecticut examples are listed in the following pages.

James H. Naylor School

The first example of building multidisciplinary RtI teams to boost student resiliency and achievement involves a K–8 urban school in downtown Hartford, Connecticut. The school has some unique characteristics in that it is a diversified urban school with a rich and varied school culture. The students speak multiple languages. The neighborhood school has had a long and close relationship with Central Connecticut State University (CCSU), with joint leadership provided by the school principal and a designated teacher from the school in partnership with professors from the university. CCSU places teachers, nurses, and special educators there each year for internship training, and many of those trainees are hired to work there after their graduation and school certification.

The leadership team from the school approached the CCSU Marriage and Family Therapy (MFT) Program director when he and other members of our Connecticut Association for Marriage and Family Therapy secured passage of school certification for MFTs in 2008. They invited CCSU to place MFT graduate students at Naylor School in their quest to build sustainable community partnerships with families of Naylor students. They were experiencing some amount of difficulty getting parents to attend school functions, and they sought the family-friendly expertise of MFTs to help them build a more active parent–school alliance. They also envisioned systemic integration of health care services into their school to complement the school nursing, psychology, and social work team established there.

Since that alliance began, CCSU has regularly placed MFTs choosing a school certification track at that school. Some of the coursework required for MFT certification is also taught there to enrich the school–university alliance and strengthen the in vivo training opportunities for MFTs. One of our first trainees placed there was a postgraduate MFT who wanted to pursue school certification. In her work with students and families, she learned that there was a sampling of students at the school who had been diagnosed with autism spectrum disorders. She initiated several child and parent group meetings that year, and she kicked off the year with a Parent–Teacher Organization–sponsored dinner that drew more than 150 children and adults from the neighborhood around the school. She celebrated the many cultures represented at the school by inviting families to bring favorite ethnic dishes to that gathering. Her work with families brought in many new parents to subsequent school events. Those parents developed closer relationships with the school staff, thereby fulfilling the community partnership quest of the school leadership team. Several of the first parent participants continue to serve leadership volunteer positions at the school.

Also that year, she and another postgraduate trainee worked with the school psychologist and social worker to begin RtI Tier 2 groups for students in the third, fifth, and sixth grades who were experiencing academic, truancy, and discipline difficulties in school. The school had coined the term *frequent flyer* to refer to the tendency of some students to remain in school bathrooms between classes and then wander around the building. It also referred to the frequency with which they had to visit the principal's office with disciplinary concerns. A few were children of gang members in Hartford, and all of the boys and girls were underachieving in school.

We developed an RtI measurement tool that year for MFTs to use in school-based practice throughout Connecticut. Our goal was to develop an evidence-based tool for RtI interventions, to be utilized by school mental health colleagues. For the school groups, we wanted to calibrate changes in behavior and achievement that the students were experiencing as a result of the group participation.

Two forms were developed to address the RtI elements of the triangle. The Referral Form included a section for reporting academic issues and another section included behavioral issues Figure 6.2). We then designed a corresponding Outcomes Form to measure changes in student behavior and achievement (Figure 6.3).

We added a section to both forms about health issues, and we developed a Likert scale to help teachers, administrators, and parents rate the severity of the referral issues. The first piloted RtI group for Naylor students was time limited to correspond to the requirements of RtI guidelines and the need for measurement at regular intervals.

School Referral Form for MFT Services

Student Name:	DOB:
Teacher:	Grade:
Parent/ Guardian:	Phone Numbers: Cell: Home:
Date:	Gender: Male Female
Name of Person Referring:	Position:

How many days has the student been absent in the last 3 months? _____

How many times has the student been suspended during the past year? _____

Please use the following scale to complete the checklist below for this student.

0 = Never; 1 = Sometimes; 2 = Often; 3 = Almost Always; or DK = Don't Know.

Academic Issues		Behavior Issues	
Attention/concentration	0 1 2 3 DK	Angry/aggressive—verbal	0 1 2 3 DK
Cheats	0 1 2 3 DK	Angry/aggressive—physical	0 1 2 3 DK
Completes class work	0 1 2 3 DK	Conflict with peers	0 1 2 3 DK
Fear of school	0 1 2 3 DK	Conflict with siblings	0 1 2 3 DK
Late to class	0 1 2 3 DK	Conflict with parents	0 1 2 3 DK
Leaves class without permission	0 1 2 3 DK	Conflict with teachers	0 1 2 3 DK
Low grades	0 1 2 3 DK	Anxious	0 1 2 3 DK
Participates in class	0 1 2 3 DK	Cultural adjustment issues	0 1 2 3 DK
Poor attendance	0 1 2 3 DK	Defiant	0 1 2 3 DK
Problems learning	0 1 2 3 DK	Depressed	0 1 2 3 DK
Refuses to attend school	0 1 2 3 DK	Grief	0 1 2 3 DK

Health Issues		Impulsive	0 1 2 3 DK
Poor hygiene	0 1 2 3 DK	Lies	0 1 2 3 DK
Medication compliance	0 1 2 3 DK	Poor decision making	0 1 2 3 DK
Substance abuse	0 1 2 3 DK	Restless, fidgety	0 1 2 3 DK
Physical complaints	0 1 2 3 DK		
Deliberately hurts self	0 1 2 3 DK		
Inappropriate sexual behavior	0 1 2 3 DK		
Issues with eating/weight	0 1 2 3 DK		
Describe the Problem (Use back if needed):			
Circle the Services Sought:			
Assessment	Family Counseling	Group	Individual Counseling
Other (please describe):			
To be completed by marriage and family therapist (MFT):			
Date received by MFT team:		MFT response:	
Name of MFT responding to referral:		Date of MFT response:	

Figure 6.2. School referral form for marriage and family therapy services. From Laundy, Ciak, & Bennett (2010). Reprinted with permission.

School Outcomes Form for MFT Services

Student Name:	DOB:
Teacher:	Grade:
Parent/ Guardian:	Phone Numbers: Cell: Home:
Date:	Gender: Male Female
Name of Person Referring:	Position:

How many days has the student been absent in the last 3 months? _____

How many times has the student been suspended during the past year? _____

Please use the following scale to complete the checklist below for this student.

0 = Never; 1 = Sometimes; 2 = Often; 3 = Almost Always; or DK = Don't Know.

Academic Issues		Behavior Issues	
Attention/concentration	0 1 2 3 DK	Angry/aggressive—verbal	0 1 2 3 DK
Cheats	0 1 2 3 DK	Angry/aggressive—physical	0 1 2 3 DK
Completes class work	0 1 2 3 DK	Conflict with peers	0 1 2 3 DK
Fear of school	0 1 2 3 DK	Conflict with siblings	0 1 2 3 DK
Late to class	0 1 2 3 DK	Conflict with parents	0 1 2 3 DK
Leaves class without permission	0 1 2 3 DK	Conflict with teachers	0 1 2 3 DK
Low grades	0 1 2 3 DK	Anxious	0 1 2 3 DK
Participates in class	0 1 2 3 DK	Cultural adjustment issues	0 1 2 3 DK
Poor attendance	0 1 2 3 DK	Defiant	0 1 2 3 DK
Problems learning	0 1 2 3 DK	Depressed	0 1 2 3 DK
Refuses to attend school	0 1 2 3 DK	Grief	0 1 2 3 DK
Health Issues		Impulsive	0 1 2 3 DK

Poor hygiene	0 1 2 3 DK	Lies		0 1 2 3 DK
Medication compliance	0 1 2 3 DK	Poor decision making		0 1 2 3 DK
Substance abuse	0 1 2 3 DK	Restless, fidgety		0 1 2 3 DK
Physical complaints	0 1 2 3 DK			
Deliberately hurts self	0 1 2 3 DK			
Inappropriate sexual behavior	0 1 2 3 DK			
Issues with eating/weight	0 1 2 3 DK			
Since the original referral, what has changed? (Use back if needed)				
Does anything still need to change? Please explain.				
Signature		Date		

Figure 6.3. School outcomes form for marriage and family therapy services. From Laundy, Ciak, & Bennett (2010). Reprinted with permission.

Results

Members from the RtI groups experienced significant academic and behavioral improvement when their progress was measured. Attendance and grades improved, "frequent flying" diminished, and the amount of disciplinary incidents decreased. Group members themselves requested to continue the group meetings, and they proceeded to meet during their school day throughout the year, with the permission of their teachers and families. The shift from documenting that such service *occurs* to recording that it *works* for students to improve educational outcomes became clear. Primary preventive services at various Tier levels of RtI made a difference in the lives of several students, teachers, and families at that school.

Two unexpected findings occurred when we analyzed the data from the forms. Teachers reported significant improvement in the climate of their classrooms as the behavior of the at-risk students improved. They reported that they were better able to teach while the at-risk students first attended the RtI groups and that those students' improved behavior over time made the classroom climate more conducive for learning. The school staff and the group agreed to resume meetings the next year with new MFT interns and postgraduates. This finding supported the PBIS notion that when school climate is addressed, positive educational outcomes can occur. Addressing this systemic layer of school health and climate is at the heart of RtI and PBIS initiatives in schools. Several LOGS model dimensions were affected positively as well, including the individual students, their families, the school, and school culture over the 2-year life cycle of that program.

The data on the Outcome Forms revealed that the changes the students had made were sustained over time. In fact, the group members and new MFT team designed a related several programs the next year. The middle and older elementary students began to mentor younger students to help them avoid some of the mistakes they had made. With the help of the MFT interns, mentoring programs for students as young as preschool and kindergarten were developed, using the theme of promoting nonviolent approaches to problem solving. All of the girls in the first young women's group for seventh and eighth graders graduated and moved on to high school the next year. These findings supported the more global systemic goal of improving school climate while improving the educational outcomes for those young women.

In addition to that group work, the next cohort of MFTs brought other new RtI programs and services to that same school. The next group saw an area of unmet need with teachers. They observed that many of the teachers were from primarily middle-class suburban backgrounds and were not adequately prepared to meet the complex social and cultural needs of some of their urban students. The challenges of managing diverse needs in an urban school setting often posed unique stress to these general education teachers, especially to those who had not had sufficient training in developing teaching skills with diverse student populations.

The MFT students obtained permission from the leadership team at the school to offer consultation sessions for elementary and middle school teachers during time set aside for weekly continuing education programs for faculty. They used techniques from Schwartz's *internal family systems model* (Breunlin, Schwartz, & Mac Kune-Karrer, 1997) to help teachers identify their areas of discomfort with academic or behavioral challenges they were experiencing with their students. When later evaluated using the Outcomes Form (Figure 6.3), these teachers reported less discomfort with behavioral challenges they faced with their students and a better fit with their teaching assignments. Fewer disciplinary referrals for RtI interventions were made that year after the RtI program the MFTs conducted with teachers. This finding provided further evidence that the shift toward demonstrating how outcomes improve with appropriate behavioral services was working.

A third example of RtI collaboration occurred during the third and fourth years of the program, when the school lost key members of its leadership team due to illness and transfer. Transitions in the healthiest of systems create stress, and institutional change takes time to settle for participants in that system. In this school, MFT interns and their supervisor noticed changes in the school climate when the principal left and key staff members were not available. More disciplinary referrals began to occur, reactive management practices started to take place, and communication among school departments became less clear and inefficient. When students at psychological risk experienced incidents of temper outbursts or other classroom disruptions, special education and RtI processes became fragmented. Referrals for special services became less coordinated among the staff members, and tension and conflict grew among various disciplines. As a result, the school climate began to suffer, and staff morale dropped.

To address this phenomenon, the new MFT training group and a former MFT graduate student, now the MFT supervisor at the school, began an RtI-based set of meetings with representative members of the teaching faculty and administration to address the broader systemic issues of keeping the school functioning through the midst of change. Over the course of school year, representative members of that group, called the Family Circle, reported that communication among departments improved. Proactive, collaborative planning replaced some of the inefficient communication that had been occurring among departmental subsystems. Although the leadership team was still in transition at the end of the school year, this group intervention helped improve the service delivery system to students and lift the morale of the teaching staff.

The three sets of interventions at the school all fall under the umbrella of RtI, and they represent three systemic layers of RtI and PBIS services that can be creatively incorporated within the RtI initiative. Such services vary from traditional special education services, which are linearly oriented toward specific students with specific diagnoses and categorized labels. Although traditional services are still needed, collaborative interventions at various systemic layers of schools can reach a wider range of students and boost student (and teacher) resiliency and achievement in significant ways. Our outcome research using the forms documented the shift in emphasis toward measuring the success of new RtI programs and services.

The next examples further demonstrate the power of shifting emphasis to measuring improved educational outcomes rather than documenting the presence of services. They add evidence to the success of boosting student achievement and enriching school climate through primary preventive programs and services across many systemic school layers.

Elementary School

A second example of multidisciplinary collaboration in schools involves the proactive integration of special with regular education services at a small suburban elementary school in Connecticut. The school principal in Westbrook was originally trained as a special education teacher. When she was hired more than two decades ago, she sought ways before the NCLB legislation to address a broader range of academic and behavioral needs of her students. She obtained training for her whole staff at the CSDE's SERC to help her teachers acquire new assessment skills to use in school. This training involved utilizing the expertise of regular *and* special education staff to identify special needs in children early in their school careers and to provide a wider variety of services to help boost student achievement.

That principal began holding biweekly meetings of elementary school teams with her school psychologist and staff, where school professionals could address concerns they had about a student. If students did not make progress with interventions they designed, the child was eventually referred for formal special education assessment. More than a decade ago, the principal began accepting MFT trainees into her school to expand her school psychology and social work staff. Their collaborative work was instrumental in creating lunch groups, parent programs, and clinical services not formerly available to students and families in her town. The success of that MFT partnership resulted in the creation of a local youth service bureau in the town that regularly places students across the school system for training, as well as provides a range of clinical services to that town's students and families. The principal served on the board of that new agency, and her leadership in supporting school and community partnerships was visionary.

That multidisciplinary partnership also resulted in decreased costs for out-of-district placements for at-risk youth, as measured by Educational Reference Group costs comparing like-sized towns. The Special Services Coordinator from that school district reported that

> the Connecticut State Department of Education Special Education Profiles for the school year 2002–2003 revealed that the total estimated costs of Westbrook's out-of-district placements by the School District of Placement by Other Agencies were $181,000 during this time. The Educational Reference Group (ERG) average for other like-sized schools was $1,000,000 during that time period. We believe that the lower costs of the Westbrook School District are attributable to the strong intervention processes we have in place for Westbrook families. (Bialicki, 2004)

His testimony to the Connecticut legislature was instrumental in helping enact the legislation that enabled MFTs to become school-certified employees in Connecticut. The principal who welcomed more collaborative mental health services for her students also helped enact that legislation. Because her elementary school was small and because that principal trained her staff to examine students' needs carefully so long ago, her school system's transition to RtI was more seamless compared with many other districts. Her work served as a visionary precursor to the RtI initiative. She incorporated collaborative RtI and PBIS principles long before they became well-known national systemic supports for students.

Since the introduction of RtI, that school system has added special service staff (psychology, counseling, social work, special education administration) to their elementary, middle, and high school, employing PBIS policies and procedures to guide their work. They hold regular RtI meetings and use evidence-based technology to track and assess student progress. Students and clinicians from the local youth service bureau under the supervision of youth service bureau clinicians currently have a robust presence throughout the school system, not solely in the elementary school where they started. Multidisciplinary mental health teams have produced myriad creative RtI and special services programs at both the school and the agency that have been effective and efficient. The success of many interventions at various subsystem levels of the school has served to build a healthy school climate and improve educational outcomes.

A final example of how the RtI initiative improves outcomes involves a model and process developed by a suburban middle school called the *consult model*. During the period when the RtI initiative was developed in Connecticut, Old Saybrook experienced several administrative changes in the middle school as well as a change of leadership in a local youth service bureau that resulted in a loss of clinical services to that school system. A colleague at the middle school partnered with her principal, her school psychologist and MFT, and several other school leaders to take advantage of special training provided by the SERC. The training was designed to prepare schools in Connecticut for adoption of RtI and PBIS.

Following that continuing education, the team developed a consult model/process that involves weekly multidisciplinary meetings with core teachers, special service teachers and staff, and administrators.

Much like medical family therapists, they collaboratively track students identified for RtI assessment and service and monitor their progress, utilizing the principles of frontloading, agency, and communion. They collaborate regularly with community clinicians on behalf of the students they serve.

Furthermore, they make extensive transition plans for their students as they enter and exit Grades 4 to 8 at the middle school. Their consultation model is amassing impressive data about the interventions they provide. Donohue (2014) examined the relationship between PBIS services and school achievement measures such as decreased disciplinary issues, improved school climate, and increased graduation rates, as viewed by school counselors across the United States. She found that there are several variables involved with institutional change and that improved outcomes with RtI and PBIS take several years to realize. However, her initial findings suggest that with sustained planning and effort, school climate can improve sufficiently to foster fewer school disciplinary referrals and other favorable educational outcomes. Because the RtI initiative is still relatively new, it will take time to realize the full potential of this systemic, institutional change.

As mentioned earlier, Connecticut is also in the process of establishing school-based health clinics in several of its urban school systems as a way of creating multidisciplinary health and education teams to comprehensively meet student needs. Some of these programs and services are developed in partnership with local social service agencies such as Child Guidance Clinics and Child and Family Agencies. Some schools are also seeking funding partnerships to provide medical and dental services in schools for children in need of such services.

All of these initiatives address RtI goals and argue for the use of licensed and certified health care teams to design and deliver collaborative services to students and families. They also incorporate broader systemic goals of incorporating emotional, social, and cultural elements to boost academic success. Much like medical family therapy that seeks to improve health by using such wider systemic variables in a primary preventive way, RtI employs similar elements.

Interest in such broader health variables has been sparked by the RtI initiative across the country, and many other groups are developing MTSS to help boost academic resiliency in schools. The former principal at Naylor School mentioned earlier left his school to join a National Center on Time and Learning (NCTL). This center is a Ford Foundation–sponsored project to support the growth of underachieving schools in the Northeast, and that former principal has become the director of school and district support in Connecticut. He consults with targeted Connecticut schools to boost student achievement on a variety of systemic levels, using multidisciplinary school teams, expanded school time, and incorporation of the arts into the educational milieu. NCTL is dedicated to building a comprehensive educational experience for a wider range of students to raise achievement standards. Having had success with systemic RtI initiatives at his urban school in Hartford, that principal requested the help of the director of the Marriage and Family Therapy Program at CCSU. He is working with school teams to develop systemic partnerships to boost student resiliency and achievement in several targeted schools across the state. He and his Boston team seek to work side by side with legislators, schools, families, and communities. Their website (www.timeandlearning.org) states that

> We build a better school day and year by expanding the school day. We support state leaders in developing policy efforts and building statewide momentum to expand learning time. We help district leaders create comprehensive planning processes that redesign the school day and year, from the ground up, to better meet the needs of the 21st century. We also assist schools that have already expanded their school day and year to help them use their learning time more effectively.

Despite these innovations, there are significant challenges to the RtI initiative in the United States. First, different school systems have unique strengths and needs, and there is enormous variability across urban, suburban, and rural school systems across the United States.

What may be relatively easy to institute in a wealthy suburban school system may seem insurmountable in a larger urban system or in a small school in a rural area with fewer financial resources, located a long distance from other districts. It is also easier to incorporate RtI tiered interventions in elementary schools, where children spend more time in one classroom than they do in middle or high school. Young children do not change classes for different subjects as frequently as they do when they progress to middle and high school classes, where instruction is departmentalized.

The shift from documenting that instruction occurs to recording that it works for students is a noble shift, but it is difficult challenge to meet for some school districts. And the shift in instruction design and emphasis from special education to general education poses dilemmas for schools trying to develop new methods of instruction with existing staff and budgets. It is difficult to measure the outcomes with new initiatives while in the midst of change from one paradigm to another. It is a bit like stepping on a moving train.

RtI is a bold initiative, however, that seeks to assess more fully and accurately the increasingly identifiable learning needs of children in schools. This goal is also of growing interest to the fields of neuroscience, psychology-related disciplines, and medicine. Technology and the evidence-based assessment tools are emerging to measure progress toward this goal. Integration of information about what contributes to student learning and resiliency will require challenging systemic effort from many disciplines across education and health care. Handled responsibly, such integration will advance the cause of comprehensive, universal education for all children as well as health care reform that enables children to learn.

Having addressed more global systemic initiatives, we now return to the microsystemic variables that profoundly affect student achievement. The next chapter addresses the convergence of mental health and education through consideration of both IDEA categories and the *Diagnostic and Statistical Manual of Mental Disorders*, Fifth Edition (*DSM–5*). Because the *DSM* is the common language of mental health and IDEA has established school categories as the common language of education, the next chapter integrates, where possible, these two major systems of evaluation of children and adolescents. The goal is to build collaborative bridges for mental health clinicians and educators between the cultures of health care and education so that children and youth may be better serviced by both systems of care.

seven

DSM-5 and Primary Disability Categories

In 2013, the Fifth Edition of the *Diagnostic and Statistical Manual of Mental Disorders* (*DSM–5*) was released. Published by the American Psychiatric Association (APA), the *DSM–5* represents its seventh attempt since 1952 to classify behaviors, thoughts, and emotions that cause significant psychological distress or dysfunction. For school-based mental health clinicians, it is important to have a working knowledge of the *DSM* because it is the standard reference that health care professionals use to guide diagnosis and treatment and communicate with each other (APA, 2013). It shares some similarities to the Individuals With Disabilities Education Improvement Act (IDEA) system of classification in education outlined in Chapter 4, but the goals, methods, and categories of each system are different.

To understand where *DSM* and IDEA converge and how they differ, it is important to become familiar with both systems of classification to understand the context within which each system was established. The reader is asked to suspend judgment about the limits of both systems until a better appreciation of the *DSM* and IDEA classification is acquired. The aim of this dense chapter is to remove collaborative constraints for professionals working with children and youth rather than to advocate for the merits of either system.

The intent of both classification systems is to form accurate assessments to provide necessary services. However, the medical *DSM–5* and the educational IDEA system of classification are organized differently, address different disorders and populations, and have different goals. Multidisciplinary collaboration to support student achievement in schools is significantly enhanced if the involved clinicians are familiar with the features of both systems. To streamline school-based collaboration, this chapter attempts to compare and contrast the two classification systems, integrating similar categories where possible. With case examples I illustrate how and why such integration can help promote collaboration between educators and health care clinicians.

The DSM lists more than 340 disorders. Although it includes child-specific diagnoses, the *DSM* addresses disorders that occur across the life span. In contrast, the IDEA classification system of U.S. public education includes only 12 categories of special needs in children and youth. Its categories address physical as well as mental disorders.

Both the *DSM* and IDEA are classification systems that seek to provide a guide to best assess, plan, and treat individuals over time. The purpose of the *DSM* is to classify mental illness and adjustment difficulties through sound *diagnosis* and *treatment*, similar to standard practice in medicine. In contrast, the purpose of IDEA is to provide *safeguards* to *all* children in schools that ensure *fair* and *equal* opportunities to benefit from public education (House, 1999). The purpose of IDEA classification is to educate all children, regardless of the constraints to learning that they may have.

In developing *DSM–5*, the APA sought in to connect its diagnoses closely with the medical classification system used internationally in the World Health Organization's (WHO's) *International Classification of Diseases (ICD)*. One goal has been to return psychiatry to its medical roots and incorporate its classification system congruently with the newest editions of the *ICD*, which is recognized worldwide. Another goal has been to improve its utility as a clinical guide for the mental health professional professions and other health care providers practicing in the United States (*DSM–5*). A third goal has been to position psychiatry to take a leadership role in diagnosis and treatment of mental disorders (Frances, 2013a).

A major focus of the *DSM–5* has been on building consensus about disorders across health care settings, so that the criteria for diagnosis and treatment can become standardized, utilized, and comprehensively researched. This focus bodes well for the future of multidisciplinary collaboration in health care and education. Unlike medical disorders, however, what is known about most mental health disorders is not firmly rooted in pathological biological processes.

Paris (2013) observes that the categories used in psychiatric diagnoses are based on signs and symptoms, and they represent syndromes rather than diseases. The *DSM–5* authors relied on agreement among the experts in their study and task groups as well as feedback from several other experts to establish the categories of the *DSM–5*. During the revision process, the *DSM–5* work groups coordinated their work with WHO Division of Mental Health, the World Psychiatric Association, and the National Institute of Mental Health to build consensus for the classification system.

Thirteen volunteer multidisciplinary working groups and six study groups were commissioned in 2006 to analyze each category of disorders and incorporate the latest information about each disorder listed in the *DSM*. Beginning in 2003, 13 invited conferences were held to refine the groups' findings and set the stage for the *DSM–5* document.

The resulting *DSM–5* has been described as "evidence-informed" rather than "evidence-based" because the etiology of many mental disorders is not known. There have thus been many criticisms about the scientific validity of the *DSM*. Neimeyer (2013) underscored the *DSM–IV* acknowledgment that "there is no assumption that each category of mental disorder is a completely discrete entity with absolute boundaries dividing it from other mental disorders or from no mental disorder" (p. 3). He added that the *DSM–5* frames the disorders as "fictive placeholders until such time as they can (selectively) be validated through largely biological markers of one sort or another" (p. 3).

Neimeyer (2013), Paris (2013), and Frances (2013a) all report that Spitzer and other early architects of the *DSM* wanted to establish an evidence base for the *DSM*. Spitzer, who is recognized as a father of *DSM* classification, established a kappa correlation coefficient of .70 as the minimum level required for reliability of the clinical use of a category. A high kappa correlation indicates agreement on diagnosis. Although a few of the categories (mental retardation and substance abuse) reached the desired kappa reliability score of .70 because they were easily observable, almost all of the other Axis I disorders fell well below that reliability standard on the *DSM–III*, however.

Allen Frances (2012), the chair of the *DSM–IV* Task Force, has criticized the reliability data collected over the past 30 years on *DSM* disorders. He noted that no improvement in reliability scores has occurred in the latest field trial results and that such low reliability undermines the credibility of *DSM–5* as a basis for diagnosis, treatment, and research. He posited that despite the low reliability and validity ratings, the decision was made to update and publish the *DSM–5* based on clinical utility, publication deadlines, and the collaborative experience and findings of the *DSM–5* work and study groups.

Clinicians are cautioned, therefore, about using the *DSM* system as an evidence-based tool with strong scientific reliability and validity. That is why multidisciplinary collaboration is so important when it comes to psychoeducational assessment of students. Several statistics quoted from the *DSM–5* manual in this chapter are based on short-term studies, and no well-designed longitudinal findings exist yet for many disorders. It is important that clinicians do not reify the categories of classification that the *DSM* posits until rigorous scientific data is generated for the support of the categories of disorders.

Nevertheless, the *DSM–5* is the most widely used classification system that currently exists about mental disorders in the United States, and its clinical utility for recognizing patterns of symptoms and behaviors is recognized across settings for the six licensed mental health professions (i.e., counseling, MFT, nursing, psychiatry, psychology, and social work). Despite controversy about the manual, the *DSM–5* is an important tool for health care clinicians to use in hospitals, outpatient clinics and treatment facilities, private practices, and schools, just as IDEA classification has been useful guide for educators. Using evaluation data collected from many sources, collaborative assessment, and diagnosis can be better appreciated and utilized across all service domains.

Several revisions and updates were made in the *DSM–5* edition, and the changes have strong implications for clinicians who do school-based collaboration. First, the *DSM–5* diagnoses were reorganized into 20 categories. The order of the categories chosen for *DSM–5* was developed on the basis of consideration of developmental and life span variables, as well as similarity of symptoms in each category to those in adjacent categories. The categories of the *DSM–5* include the following:

- Neurodevelopmental Disorders
- Schizophrenia Spectrum and Other Psychotic Disorders
- Bipolar and Related Disorders
- Depressive Disorders
- Anxiety Disorders
- Obsessive-Compulsive and Other Related Disorders
- Trauma and Stressor-Related Disorders
- Dissociative Disorders
- Somatic Symptom and Related Disorders
- Feeding and Eating Disorders
- Sleep–Wake Disorders
- Sexual Dysfunctions
- Gender Dysphoria
- Disruptive, Impulse Control, and Conduct Disorders
- Substance-Related and Addictive Disorders
- Neurocognitive Disorders
- Personality Disorders
- Paraphilic Disorders
- Other Mental Disorders (APA, 2013)

Each of these are addressed here within the context of the educational classifications described in Chapter 3.

Of importance to school-based mental health teams, a major change in this edition of the *DSM* is that the section from former editions called "Disorders First Diagnosed in Infancy or Childhood" has been eliminated. Instead, childhood disorders have been subsumed under and across the *DSM* categories to better reflect the course of each class of disorders and to better integrate each category with other disorders sharing similar symptoms. The *DSM–5* authors changed the categories to reflect a broader developmental and life span perspective for all of the disorders listed in the manual. They tried to address the temporal, severity, and spectrum dimensions of all disorders within each classification across the whole life span.

Just as some of the classification categories of IDEA in education may overlap and seem confusing at first glance, clinicians familiar with previous *DSM* editions may thus be disoriented by the changes seen in the *DSM–5* regarding childhood disorders. Many disorders share features with other disorders, such as anxiety and depression. The *DSM–5* attempted to categorize disorders on a young-to-old continuum across all of the categories, addressing developmental components of disorders within each category of classification, rather than retain a specific section devoted solely to disorders first diagnosed in children and youth. Specific cluster traits, symptoms, and/or behaviors are what characterize each major category of disorders, even though they may present differently over the course of a patient's or student's life.

For mental health clinicians working in schools, it may at first be difficult to locate data about children and adolescents in the *DSM–5*. Several of the *DSM* diagnoses have more relevance for adolescents and adults, such as the substance-related and personality disorders. Some *DSM* diagnoses are rare or nonexistent in schoolchildren, including sexual and neurocognitive disorders such as the paraphilias and dementia, and some diagnoses are more relevant for educational purposes than others. For school-based mental health clinicians and others familiar with earlier versions, it requires careful research of the *DSM–5* to use the new categories and criteria with ease and precision. That is why discussion of the *DSM* and its relevance for multidisciplinary collaboration is so important.

Because the *DSM* has dramatically changed over its various iterations, it may be tempting to reject those changes and rely on diagnoses familiar to clinicians or to use school categories alone to classify student behaviors and presenting problems. Health care clinicians practicing in schools bridge the cultures of mental health, medicine, and education, however. Well-honed "multilingual" skills are required to navigate these systems in a seamless way. Proficiency in the use of terminology from health care and education cultures is therefore necessary to train multidisciplinary teams to collaborative effectively.

Another major change in *DSM–5* is that the five diagnostic axes for diagnosis have been collapsed into one axis. In previous editions, the *DSM* axes attempted to include other systemic influences on diagnostic formulations of disorders. The axes included potential character and personality disorders, environmental stressors, related medical conditions, and levels of functioning observed in the patient or client. However, the *ICD* medical system lists only one dimension, and the *DSM–5* study and work groups attempted to collapse disorders into a single dimension to coincide better with the *ICD*. They attempted to describe features, specifiers (different presentations of a disorder), and dimensions (severity) of symptoms over time within each of the diagnostic categories to absorb this change.

Findings from neurobiological science were also updated in the *DSM–5*. Several research developments in neuroscience have occurred since the last iteration of the *DSM*. They have spawned important new information about such neurocognitive disorders as traumatic brain injury (TBI), autism, and the dementias. New findings are reflected in the *DSM–5* and have important implications for school-based mental health clinicians.

Two other major changes appear in the *DSM–5* that have significant relevance for school-based mental health clinicians. One is that under the Neurodevelopmental Disorders category, the designation of Mental Retardation has been changed to Intellectual Disability or Intellectual Developmental Disorder (APA, 2013). Spurred by Rosa's Law in the United States, which was enacted into federal law by President Barrack Obama in 2010 after a Maryland family's advocacy on behalf of their child with Down syndrome, this change mirrors the changed designation in IDEA's category to more respectfully categorize intellectual impairments. The severity levels of mild, moderate, severe, and profound still exist, and the category retains the intellectual, social, and daily living domains to capture the aspects of adaptive functioning that are necessary to assess developmental disabilities comprehensively.

Also subsumed under the Neurodevelopmental Disorders category is the changed categorization of Asperger syndrome. The disorder has been eliminated as a separate diagnosis and has been incorporated into the Autism Spectrum Disorders category to capture the dimension and severity components of the disorder on one axis. This change has sparked controversy for some who work clinically with children, youth, and adults with diagnoses of Asperger syndrome and other forms of mild autism. However, public education in the United States has categorized all levels of autism under the autism spectrum umbrella for several years, and some see this change as a clearer opportunity to form clinical partnerships across the cultures of health care and education to better diagnose and treat children with Asperger syndrome.

One of the most controversial changes in the *DSM–5* represents an example of the reification of mental disorders that was mentioned earlier in the chapter. Decades ago, there was a reluctance to diagnose children with serious mental disorders and to treat them with psychotropic medication originally designed for adults. Children grow and change rapidly, and there has been historic reticence to give serious and potentially inaccurate labels (and medications) to children that could follow them throughout their lifetimes. The rationale was that close, deliberate attention to the risks and benefits of diagnosis and treatment over time would protect the fluid nature of child development and would prevent a diagnosis of iatrogenic illness, where the treatment can be worse that the cure. The advent of managed health care in the United States and the concomitant rapid rise in psychotropic medication use with children has dramatically changed that practice.

In the last decade of the 20th century, insurance companies sought to carve out medical from mental health and substance abuse services to control the costs of such services. Insurance companies made decisions to not reimburse mental health clinicians for behavioral treatment (individual, group, family therapy) that did not meet their criteria for what they called "medical necessity." As insurance companies sought to reduce their exposure, severe restrictions were put on the frequency, reimbursement, and types of clinical mental health services that could be provided for children unless they were diagnosed with severe mental illness (such as bipolar illness and major depressive disorder). Also, some disorders such as autism were denied coverage because they were viewed as "preexisting conditions," and behaviorally based services for those children and adolescents with such chronic illnesses and disabilities were discouraged, denied, or not reimbursed.

Unfortunately, these events coincided with the effects of the community mental health movement in the United States. A large influx of untreated people with mental illness were returned from residential placement to communities without sufficient outpatient services in place to meet the needs of this population. The community mental health movement began with the leadership of President John Kennedy. It sought to close inpatient and residential treatment hospitals for the mentally ill and to develop partial, outpatient, and community-based services for those with mental illness (P. Kennedy, 2014). The goal was to develop services for these patients/clients nearer to their families and home communities. But when reimbursement for behavioral and medical services began to shrink, many of the people affected by mental illness and their families found it increasingly difficult to find the appropriate and sufficient mental health care.

Concurrently, far fewer restrictions were put on *prescribing* clinicians (MDs and advanced practice registered nurses) by insurance companies for psychotropic medicine. At the time, it seemed to be comparatively cheaper to provide than behaviorally based interventions. One result was that the diagnoses of major mental illnesses such as bipolar illness skyrocketed in the first part of the 21st century (Frances, 2012), with the full support of profit-driven policies of big pharmacology businesses. The rate of prescriptions for psychotropic medications saw a concomitant rise across all ages, despite both a dearth of outcome research to confirm their long-term effectiveness and high health risks (such as diabetes and obesity) for growing children. Frances (2012) noted that around 1997,

> drug companies brought new and expensive medicine for ADD to market and were simultaneously set free to advertise them directly to parents and teachers. Soon the selling of ADHD as a diagnosis was ubiquitous in magazines, on your TV screen, and in pediatricians' offices—an unexpected epidemic was born, and the rates of ADHD tripled. (pp. 26–27)

Another example is the antipsychotic medication aripiprazole (*Abilify*). This drug is a second-generation neuroleptic medication used for mood and neurodevelopmental disorders in children, adolescents, and adults. In an summary of an IMS Health research report on Medscape, the online psychiatry and mental health newsletter, Brooks

(2014) reported that Abilify had the highest sales of all drugs in the United States in 2013, at nearly $6.5 billion (para. 1). Psychiatric diagnoses for severe mental illness and concomitant prescription for those diagnoses grew exponentially over the past decade.

Because the *DSM–5* study and work groups were developing the fifth edition of the *DSM* at the same time, much discussion and controversy ensued about the growth of attention-deficit/hyperactivity disorder (ADHD), autism, and mood and personality disorder diagnoses and medications in youth and adolescents. Many children and adolescents acquired a diagnosis of bipolar disorder during this period of time, just as children were diagnosed with ADHD in the previous decade. The more cynical mental health clinicians tagged these phenomena as the "diagnoses du jour."

As bipolar disorder in children and youth began to be studied more carefully over the decade, there appeared to be many some diagnosed youth who did not go on to develop the more classic symptoms of bipolar I disorder as adults (Brotman et al., 2010). Such children experienced primarily irritable mood without repetitive manic cycling. In a National Institute for Mental Health (NIMH)–funded study on mania and bipolar disorder in children, Findling et al. (2011) observed: "Most young children with rapid mood swings and extremely high energy levels do not actually have bipolar disorder. However, these symptoms do cause significant problems at home, school, or with peers" (pp. 311–319).

> The *DSM–5* work and study groups (2013) decided that
> to address the potential for overdiagnosis and treatment for
> Bipolar Disorder in children, a new diagnosis, Disruptive
> Mood Dysregulation Disorder, referring to the presentation
> of children with persistent irritability and frequent episodes
> of extreme behavioral dyscontrol, is added to the Depressive
> Disorders for children up to twelve years of age. (APA, 2013,
> p. 155)

Reification and Other Controversies

Herein lies the example of reification. Were all of the children who were diagnosed during this decade truly children and adolescents with bipolar disorder? Or has the disorder become reified in children to obtain sustained medical and behavioral treatment for such children? Bipolar illness has historically not been diagnosed until late adolescence and adulthood. As many of these children (who are too often boys from minority urban backgrounds) also acquired a diagnosis of conduct disorder and/or a personality disorder such as antisocial personality disorder, are these personality disorders in children and youth real? Did medicine, pharmaceutical companies, and the *DSM* authors inadvertently collude to create a disorder or treat symptoms that belong to another disorder? Were disorder(s) created that have not been scientifically proven to exist to obtain reimbursement for psychiatric services? Did racial prejudice play a role in the escalation of such diagnoses?

Achieving consensus to establish belief in a disorder does not necessarily ensure that a diagnosis is real, and there are many health care clinicians and educators who question the proliferation of new diagnoses and lower thresholds for diagnoses in the *DSM–5*. Such diagnoses are being criticized as being scientifically unreliable and invalid, particularly when they are applied to children, who frequently experience developmental changes as they grow.

Such diagnostic labelling can be detrimental for the children. Severe mental health diagnoses tend to follow children across time, and we do not yet know the health effects of polypharmaceutical interventions on developing brains. Collaborative assessment among professionals across health care and education can help mitigate this trend. As mentioned in Chapter 5, some pediatricians, therapists, and school team members who value collaboration are beginning to experiment with such ideas as colocation, where medical and mental health clinicians practice in or near the same office. Here they can promote the notions of *frontloading, agency, and communion* with families and collaborate about cases more efficiently.

For instance, I have been a part of a pediatric consultation group for 15 years. Our Shoreline Child Study Group membership consists of health care and education clinicians from pediatrics, the six licensed mental health professions and education. We meet monthly to confer about cases with medical and mental health sequelae. Over time we have shared many cases together. Some of our private practices have begun to house both physical and mental health clinicians, and we have held joint meetings with children and families to clarify their diagnoses and support their treatment. Although we are not all in colocated offices, we sometimes hold meetings in one or another's office to confer with each other or meet with children and families. We have used a variety of collaborative levels that were described by Doherty and Baird (1987; see Chapter 5, this volume) to better serve our patients.

The following is an example of how I collaborate with our Shoreline Child Study Group. For children who eventually fulfill criteria for an autism spectrum disorder, attention problems, behavior dyscontrol, and mood dysregulation are often the first symptoms that they present as they enter preschool or kindergarten. Our collaborations have often secured an earlier diagnosis and treatment plan for some of these children. We have avoided the tendency to diagnose such children with severe mental illness and refer them for polypharmaceutical interventions.

One teen I treat, whom I will call Jeremy, was originally referred as he entered second grade. He had great difficulty sitting still in class, isolated himself from other children and had an obsession with drawing dinosaurs, marine mammals, and Pokemon figures. Jeremy had some difficulty mastering basic academic skills such as mathematics, although his drawing skills were superb. He was not overtly rejected by other students, but he preferred to work by himself and did not show interest in other children.

Jeremy's parents, having had histories of substance abuse in both of their families, were opposed to giving medication to the boy. We collaborated with his pediatrician and school team to begin a regimen of behavioral observation and intervention at school. We diagnosed him with Asperger syndrome. He was invited to join a small children's social skills group at school, and I followed him in my private practice with biweekly individual sessions. When his attention began to wander, he was given frequent study breaks to connect with his social worker at school.

With collaboration among his pediatrician, his school team, and my office, the consciousness of our whole treatment team was raised.

Jeremy's parents acknowledged that they felt strong support from our consultations, attesting to the growth of *agency* and *communion.* We were able to help Jeremy manage his symptoms without medication, and his pediatric appointments and individual therapy with me diminished as he settled into elementary school routines and began to experience academic success.

Jeremy had predictable difficulty during the transition from elementary to middle school, and then again into high school. Employing the LOGS model dimensions of individual and family life cycle, his team and family conferred, and we provided targeted individual, group, and family therapy services during these transitions. After impressive school research into educational options, Jeremy's school team referred him to a magnet school for students interested in marine biology. As a high school sophomore, he has plans for college, and I can see Jeremy as a marine illustrator in the future. He reports that he is quite happy with his school now, especially because he can focus on his love of marine creatures and be with other young scientists who share his intense passion. He recently returned for a "fifty thousand mile maintenance check" with me, requesting help to work more comfortably with fellow students on team projects.

This young man had strong family support and a collaborative school team who recognized his special needs when he was a small child. Jeremy's pediatrician was a part of our Shoreline Child Study Group, and we formed a multidisciplinary team early to support Jeremy's growth and his family's strength in advocating for him. Because his Asperger symptoms were mild, we were able to avoid medication for this boy, although this is clearly not possible for all of the children we treat and teach. However, such early intervention to support children and families may actually serve to retard or prevent the growth of diagnostic and medication inflation.

A discussion about achieving consensus in the *DSM–5* would not be complete without addressing the controversy about personality disorders. This group of disorders has historically been placed on Axis II of the *DSM* and has not been utilized for children. Childhood and youth disorders often include *features* of adult personality disorders that can become precursors to personality disorders. But the consensus of mental health clinicians (Wagner, 2014) has been that personality disorders generally do not emerge until adolescence and early adulthood, after individual's personalities become more formed and stable. Until then, behavior and growth have been historically viewed as fluid and changeable. However, Axis II disorders have been increasing applied to children and youth. Is the reification issue at play here as well? Do economic, racial, and ethnic considerations challenge and at times outweigh clinical judgment?

The controversy becomes more complex in the context of the latest *DSM–5* revision. For several years, there was a personality disorders work group established for the latest *DSM* iteration. But their results were rejected in favor of returning to a one axis framework to coincide with the *ICD*. Even though the group disbanded and their findings were dismissed from the primary section (Section II) of the *DSM–5* manual, their recommendations were included in separate category of Section III under the Emerging Measures and Models section. The findings of that *DSM–5* work group are summarized there exactly as they recommended, in a different section of the *DSM–5* verbatim.

It is curious that personality disorders were labeled as "Emerging Models" in the latest edition of the *DSM*, when they have been a major part of prior editions of the manual. Such controversy in the latest *DSM* edition speaks to the complexity of categorizing mental illness; the recent tendency to use more severe diagnoses of mental disorders in children, adolescents, and adults in recent years; as well as the tendency to reify disorders when they become more frequently diagnosed.

Allen Frances (2013b, 2013c) has written extensively about this phenomenon. Frances expresses grave concerns about the methodology of the *DSM–5* work and task groups, the transparency of the *DSM–5* work and task group findings, the short field trials, and the conflict of interest about profit-over-science issues that APA faced regarding the publication deadlines of the manual. He hypothesizes that mental health faces renewed challenges caused by diagnostic inflation and the encouragement of unnecessary treatment (Frances, 2013c).

As was addressed in the previous case example, multidisciplinary collaboration across health care and education settings can help ameliorate this challenge, as well as provide perhaps better service in the long run to the children and families. In the case of Meredith, whom we introduced in Chapter 5, her diagnosis changed many times as her symptoms worsened and she was evaluated and prescribed new medications by a variety of inpatient and outpatient providers. Her school system, psychiatrist, family, and I maintained a close collaborative relationship during that time, which helped promote the *agency* and *communion* her parents needed to endure the stress of Meredith's hospitalizations and advocate for her needs. Although Meredith's medication needs were significantly more complex than Jeremy's due to her prenatal exposure to toxic substances, we were able to track carefully which medications were prescribed through the advocacy efforts of her parents. The *agency* that her parents employed to keep track of her hospitalizations and medications probably kept Meredith's teams more accurately abreast of her medication needs than might have otherwise occurred. Rather than having their family resources depleted as so often happens in families struggling with chronic illness, Meredith's parents developed new resiliency during this time, which clearly helped Meredith, strengthened her parents' marriage, and promoted *communion* among team members.

To address psychopharmacologic concerns about the *DSM–5*, a team called the Working Group on Psychotropic Medications for Children and Adolescents was commissioned by the American Psychological Association to examine the evidence base for current mental health practices with children. In the group's book, *Childhood Mental Health Disorders: Evidence Base and Contextual Factors for Psychosocial, Psychopharmacological, and Combined Interventions*, Brown et al. (2008) traced the most frequent presenting childhood disorders, their prevalence, and the current evidence base for treatments. They defined evidence-based practice as that which includes "the integration of the best available evidence, the clinical experience and expertise of the treating clinician, and the values or preferences of the treated family" (p. viii).

In summary, they examined the risk–benefit ratio of various treatments for different childhood disorders across the *DSM* categories. They weighed the medical and psychological risks and benefits of providing behavioral *and* medication-based services to children and measured the evidence for such services. They found little scientific evidence for the efficacy (proven benefit in controlled field trials) and effectiveness (proven benefit in the community at large) of medications alone for children, some evidence for the combined use of medication and behaviorally based services for some childhood disorders, and some evidence for behavioral treatments alone. They observed a paradoxical practice that has too often occurred with children over the past decade regarding polypharmacy treatments for childhood disorders. Although they suggest that the use of multiple medications for children with childhood psychiatric disorders outstrips its efficacy, the use of combined pharmacotherapy has continued to grow. That is, although there is no ample evidence that using multiple psychotropic medications really works for children, the practice of prescribing medications concurrently has become all too frequent.

In Meredith's case, changes in medications over time have been necessary to keep her emotional and behavioral dysregulation in check. However, the close collaboration among her family and her school and clinical treatment team helped put checks and balances into the escalation of polypharmacy practices that might have damaged her health and growth.

Disorders and Categories

Having addressed some of the controversy about mental health diagnoses, I turn now to a closer examination of childhood disorders included within the *DSM–5* classification system. The syndromes in this chapter are extrapolated from the 20 categories of Section II of the *DSM–5*. I have imbedded them into the 12 educational categories of the IDEA to serve as a conceptual framework for mental health clinicians working in schools. The *DSM–5* does not base the organization of its syndromes and disorders on the frequency that the disorders appear in children and youth as IDEA does. Although I have attempted to organize the following categories under the IDEA sections of high- and low-incidence disabilities, the reader is referred to Chapter 3 for more IDEA data regarding the prevalence of the disorders according to Brown et al. (2008) and Hallahan, Kauffman, and Pullen (2009, 2012).

Descriptions of the *DSM–5* disorders and syndromes are far from exhaustive in this book, and many rare and primarily adult disorders are not included in this chapter because they may not have immediate relevance for clinicians and educators working with child and youth disorders in schools. For more specific and comprehensive information on the *DSM–5*, the reader is referred to the *DSM–5* Manual as well as Paris's (2013) book, *The Intelligent Clinician's Guide to the DSM–5–RG*. Using the same order of categories discussed in Chapter 3 on Special Education, then, the following *DSM–5* categories and diagnoses are addressed. At times the categories and diagnoses described in this chapter may read like lists. I encourage the reader to use these descriptions and my case examples as references for clinical diagnoses you may encounter in practice rather than data that needs to be memorized. They are designed to provide clinical utility for your training and practice.

High-incidence disabilities.

This section includes the disorders that have been most frequently referred for evaluations in schools. The disorders listed are intellectual and developmental disabilities/disorders, learning disabilities, and communication disorders.

Intellectual and Developmental Disabilities and Disorders

The *DSM–5* includes several categories of IDEA disorders in its first category, Neurodevelopmental Disorders. Intellectual and developmental disabilities are a set of high-incidence disorders included in this category. Similar to IDEA categorization and as was previously mentioned in this chapter, intellectual disabilities are divided into four levels of severity (mild, moderate, severe, and profound). The disorder cluster includes intellectual as well as adaptive functioning dimensions that must first be present in childhood, which also matches the IDEA criteria. The *DSM–5* adds a section on global developmental delay, referring to children under 5 years for whom the severity of the disability cannot yet be determined.

Other disabilities listed under the *DSM–5* Neurodevelopmental Disorders category include specific learning disorders, communication disorders in speech and language, autism spectrum disorders, ADHD, and motor disorders including vocal and motor tic disorders. Under the IDEA system in education, these disorders are subsumed under different categories of classification. They are therefore addressed under the appropriate IDEA categories.

Learning Disabilities. *DSM–5* establishes criteria for diagnosis of *specific learning disabilities/disorders* in similar ways as the IDEA criteria. The *DSM–5* criteria specifiers for these diagnoses include impairment in *reading* accuracy, fluency or comprehension; impairment in spelling, punctuation, or organization of *written expression*; or impairment in *mathematics* number sense, memorization, calculation, or reasoning (pp. 66–74). Each diagnosis includes severity criteria of mild, moderate, or severe.

Communication Disorders. The *DSM–5* lists an array of speech and language diagnoses in this category, including language disorders, speech sound disorders, childhood-onset fluency disorder (stuttering), social pragmatic communication disorder, and unspecified communication disorder. All refer to deficits in language, speech, and communication that can involve verbal and nonverbal behavior. Hallahan et al. (2012) note that establishing a prevalence for communication disorders is difficult because they are hard to identify, and they often appear as sequelae to other disabilities such as a brain injury or autism. Nevertheless, these authors suggest that approximately one fifth of children who are identified for special education services have a communication disorder.

The *DSM* and IDEA systems both stress the importance of context for children growing up in bilingual homes when diagnosing disorders in this category. They note that speech patterns and language nuances may be culturally different from what children experience at school and that these variables need to be incorporated when diagnosing in this category.

Since the 1960s, children with developmental delays and specific learning disabilities have received increased clinical and educational attention and support, and thus many of these students enter school with diagnoses from their pediatricians, family practice physicians, and psychologists. Over the years, school districts have employed an increasing array of skilled physical and occupational therapists, speech and language therapists, and other education specialists, and schools have developed increased sophistication about assessing learning inefficiencies early in children's lives. Frequently clinicians from private practice, agencies, and clinics are asked to attend school meetings to help school teams collaboratively design the most appropriate planning and placement services, as well as track progress for these children.

The multidisciplinary work of health and education professionals in the area of developmental and learning disabilities is an elegant example of how collaboration to boost student achievement and resiliency can function. Collaborative, family-friendly teams have successfully moved children with delays and disabilities out of institutionalized settings into mainstream education since the 1960s. Many students who once would have remained totally dependent on their families have now obtained educational, life, and work opportunities that have supported their independence and enhanced their quality of life. In my private practice, I lead a women's group for young adult women with developmental disabilities. The group is designed to be a problem-solving and social skills group. Each one of the seven group members is employed, takes public transportation, and participates in structured social activities in the community. All attended public schools in the past two decades and received mainstream education with supportive special education services. It is inspirational to witness their accomplishments.

Emotional and Behavioral Disorders.

This subsection includes childhood disorders that are listed in the *DSM–5*, including bipolar and related disorders; depression; anxiety; trauma and stressor-related disorders, disruptive, impulse control, and conduct disorders; and substance-related and addictive disorders. Many of the *DSM–5* disorders fit under this high-incidence category of IDEA classification, and their appropriate diagnosis and treatment afford rich opportunities for collaborative clinical and educational teamwork. Included here are the disorders involving thinking, feeling and behavior. They are arranged in the order of frequency for the 20 categories of Section II of the *DSM–5*.

Bipolar and Related Disorders. According to the authors of the *DSM–5*, the bipolar and related disorders are placed as a bridge between the schizophrenia spectrum disorders and the depressive disorders and include the following diagnoses: *bipolar I and II, cyclothymic, substance/ medication-induced bipolar, and related specified unspecified bipolar disorder.* These four subcategories are distinguished by the presence of manic and/or hypomanic features and contain a descending order of symptoms, which are categorized according to severity. The *DSM–5* reports a prevalence rate of the disorder in the United States to be around 0.6%.

As mentioned earlier, the *DSM–5* authors acknowledge the fluid and evolving nature of childhood and adolescence, recognizing that children and youth can experience bipolar-like symptoms that do not meet the full criteria for some of these disorders. The last categories of related specified and unspecified bipolar disorder are reserved for those symptoms. The *DSM–5* records the mean age of onset for bipolar disorder to be 18 years and indicates that there is a strong genetic link to the disorder. According Nurmburger and Foroud (2000), children with a parent or sibling who has bipolar disorder are up to six times more likely to develop the illness, although most children with a family history of bipolar disorder will not develop the illness.

DSM–5 also reports a comorbid link between the bipolar disorders and many other affective and behavioral disorders such as anxiety, ADHD, and oppositional defiant disorder. The authors acknowledge that the prevalence rate for pediatric bipolar II disorder is difficult to establish, given the lack of controlled studies and the controversy over what constitutes childhood bipolar disorder. Brown et al. (2008) add that "the expression of manic symptoms such as grandiosity, increased goal-directed activity, and excessive involvement in pleasurable activities varies on the basis of age and must be differentiated from typical childhood behaviors" (p. 88). Based on the Longitudinal Assessment of Manic Symptoms study (Findling et al., 2011), the NIMH cautions:

> Children with chronic, severe irritability and symptoms of Attention Deficit Hyperactivity Disorder (ADHD) may be misdiagnosed as having Bipolar Disorder. However, researchers

believe that it is more appropriate to label these types of symptoms as severe mood dysregulation (SMD). Evidence suggests that SMD should not be considered a form of Bipolar Disorder. Studies show that children with SMD differ from children with Bipolar Disorder in a number of ways. For example, children with SMD do not tend to develop manic episodes as they age, while children with bipolar disorder do develop mania. Rather, children with SMD are more at risk for developing anxiety disorders or depression. In addition, children with Bipolar Disorder tend to have strong family histories of bipolar disorder, but children with SMD do not. More recently, imaging studies have shown that children with SMD differ from those with Bipolar Disorder in the way their brains process facial emotions and manage attention. (p. 3)

The *DSM–5* authors therefore decided to create the disorder, which encapsulates this research as well as the consensus opinions of the task forces and study groups. As mentioned earlier in this chapter, they relabeled SMD as *disruptive mood dysregulation disorder* (DMDD) and subsumed it under the Depressive Disorders category.

Depressive Disorders. This category includes disruptive mood dysregulation disorder, major depressive disorder, dysthymia or persistent depressive disorder, premenstrual dysphoric disorder, substance/medication-induced depressive disorder, depressive disorder due to another medical condition, and other specified and unspecified depressive disorder. All are rated according to severity. What distinguishes this category of disorders is the presence of low or irritable mood that significantly interferes with a person's ability to function. The *DSM–5* reports that depressive disorders in children and youth are common and that the incidence of depression rises during early adolescence, particularly in girls. Brown et al. (2008) add that suicidal ideation happens frequently to most adolescents with depressive disorders, although suicidality is not limited to youths with depressive disorders.

Of special interest to school-based clinicians is the DMDD diagnosis introduced in the previous section. It is designed only for children up to 12 years of age, and it was moved from the Bipolar Disorders to the Depressive Disorders category because many children with a primarily irritable symptom pattern often develop anxiety and depression-based disorders rather than bipolar disorders as they enter adolescence and young adulthood. The *DSM–5* estimates that the DMDD category of disorders is more frequently diagnosed in young males than females and that the 6- to 12-month prevalence rate "probably falls in the 2%–5% range" (APA, 2013, p. 157). As with other disorders, depressive disorders all carry specifiers differentiating the intensity and the duration of the symptoms of the disorders in this category.

Anxiety Disorders. This is another group of disorders that is diagnosed frequently in children and youth. Brown et al. (2008) note that anxiety disorders are among the most frequently occurring child mental health conditions. They cite epidemiological studies suggesting at least a 10% prevalence rate. The *DSM–5* suggests that anxiety disorders occur twice as often in girls than boys.

Anxiety disorders typically start in childhood and share features of fear, anxiety, and/or anxious behavior that are excessive and/or extend beyond what is developmentally appropriate. This category includes separation anxiety, selective mutism, specific phobia, social phobia, panic disorder, agoraphobia, generalized anxiety disorder, substance/medication-induced anxiety disorder, anxiety disorder due to another medical condition, and other specified or unspecified anxiety disorder.

Obsessive-Compulsive and Related Disorders. The characteristic features of this section of anxiety disorders are *obsessions*, which are persistent or recurrent thoughts that are unwanted, and *compulsions*, which are repetitive behaviors or rituals that an individual feels driven to enact. Although the authors moved the Obsessive-Compulsive and Related Disorders from the Anxiety Disorders category to its own section, the *DSM–5* acknowledges that there is overlap in the disorders and that there are often close relationships between these categories.

The category of Obsessive-Compulsive and Related Disorders includes obsessive-compulsive disorder, body dysmorphic disorder, hoarding disorder, trichotillomania or hair-pulling disorder, excoriation or skin-picking disorder, substance/medication-induced obsessive-compulsive and related disorder, obsessive-compulsive and related disorder due to another medical condition, and other specified and unspecified obsessive-compulsive and related disorder. It is a rare category of disorders, reported with a .5% to 2% prevalence rate in children and adolescents (Rapoport et al., 2000). Brown et al. add that "it often co-occurs with disorders such as the Anxiety and Depressive Disorders, ADHD and Tic Disorders" (p. 51).

Many students with learning inefficiencies develop depressive and anxiety symptoms as they grow and as academic demands increase. Often, their symptoms are internally focused and may not be as visible in the school milieu as those in children who exhibit behavioral dysregulation, oppositionality, and other externally expressed behaviors. Because the presentation of their symptoms varies with the complexity of children and adolescents' lives, broader systemic wraparound collaborative health and educational services in schools can help normalize, identify and address those disorders during the course of students' school day.

For instance, system-wide Response to Intervention (RtI), social and emotional learning (SEL), and Positive Behavior Interventions and Supports measures that address predictable stress experiences such as exams can help keep vulnerable students from experiencing an exacerbation of anxiety and depression symptoms. In some schools where I have consulted, creative programs such as yoga and meditation have been offered to help prepare students for system-wide testing. One school mental health team trained students to give stress management tips over their public address system at the start of exams. Collaborative support services can be efficiently offered in schools, where services are colocated in an educational home.

Stigma is still too often attached to mental health services in clinics, hospitals, and agencies, and some families are reluctant to seek psychological help outside of their primary medical and educational systems of care. As my family therapy colleague Jeri Hepworth notes (personal communication, December 16, 2014), the risk of leakage grows when children and families have to seek out another physical space for care. Just as mental health and primary care doctors are now providing in colocated offices, educators can give children and families the opportunity to receive a "soft handoff" (Beck, 2015) to proper care with less stigma, if appropriate mental health services are offered within or nearby the school milieu in primary care offices.

Trauma and Stressor-Related Disorders. This category of disorders includes reactive attachment disorder, disinhibited social engagement disorder, posttraumatic stress disorder, acute stress disorder, adjustment disorders, and other specified and unspecified trauma- and stressor-related. The symptoms of this category of disorders vary significantly, but what characterizes the category itself is the exposure to a traumatic or stressful event or events. Symptoms range from internalized behaviors such as dissociation, anxiety, and depression, to externalized behaviors such as the aggressive and disruptive disorders addressed in the next section.

Because children and youth do not ordinarily initiate mental health services on their own and because many abuse and neglect circumstances are predicated on secrecy, it is difficult to speculate about the prevalence of this category of disorders in school-age populations. The *DSM–5* does not report a rate of occurrence of this general category in children, although rates of 10% to 20% of reactive attachment disorder and disinhibited social engagement disorder are reported in high risk populations of abused and neglected children. This *DSM–5* category of disorders may eventually become a more high-incidence category than we now recognize.

Many of the trauma and stress-related experiences that children experience generate symptoms which find their way into other diagnostic categories, such as anxiety and depressive disorders. Trauma-related experiences have a profound impact on children's ability to function and achieve in school. Much has been written about the impact of such tragedies as Sandy Hook on children, families, schools, and communities. Children who have endured such life experience require close team collaboration to best recognize and serve their needs over time. Years after the Sandy Hook tragedy, members of our Shoreline Child Study Group are still treating family members of survivors from that trauma. When such systems are lacking, they can actually intensify the development of the next *DSM–5* group of disorders.

Disruptive, Impulse Control, and Conduct Disorders. This category has strong implications for school-based collaborative services. *DSM–5* refers to the Disruptive, Impulse Control and Conduct Disorders as those that involve problems with emotional and behavioral control, where the rights of others are violated and the person with the disorder experiences significant conflict with social norms or authorities. It is a commonly referred category of disorders in education because children and adolescents within this group of disorders interrupt the process of education more destructively than many of the other *DSM–5*–based disorders. The category includes oppositional defiant disorder (ODD), intermittent explosive disorder, conduct disorder (CD), antisocial personality disorder, pyromania (fire starting), kleptomania (stealing), and other specified and unspecified disruptive, impulse control, and conduct disorders.

Brown et al. (2008) report that "2% to 16% of children in the US have ODD and 1% to 10% have CD, with boys at higher risk for both diagnoses" (p. 33). Frick and Loney (1999) add that children with these two disorders are at high risk for ADHD, and they often experience myriad relationship difficulties, school problems, and even incarceration as they reach adulthood. Further, Keenan, Lober, and Green (1999) suggest that girls with these disorders may be at increased risk for comorbid internalizing symptoms, which is why they may not be diagnosed as frequently with disorders in this category as boys.

This category of disorders emerges in childhood and has a chronic course. It is associated with homelessness, incarceration, many other disorders, family stressors, and environmental distress. The *DSM–5* reports a prevalence rate ranging from 1% to 11%. Because the behavioral consequences of this disorder are powerful and destructive and because systemic support for students with this set of disorders is imperative, collaborative mental health teams in schools are critically needed to address the needs of these students, boost their achievement, and help develop a positive school climate that is conducive to learning. School-based health clinics are an example of innovative contemporary multidisciplinary initiatives that involve the colocation of health and mental health services within urban schools in Connecticut.

Substance-Related and Addictive Disorders.

This *DSM–5* category of disorders includes 10 sections: substance-related disorders (including alcohol, caffeine, and cannabis-related disorders), hallucinogen-related disorders (including phencyclidine or related disorders), inhalant-related disorders, opioid-related disorders, sedative-hypnotic or anxiolytic-related disorders, stimulant-related disorders (including amphetamine, cocaine, and other stimulants), tobacco-related disorders, and non-substance-related or other [or unknown] substance disorders). It is further divided into groups of substance-use (continued use of a substance despite adverse consequences) and substance-induced (withdrawal, depression, diminished psychological functioning). It has relevance for school-based clinicians whose students become symptomatic based on substance-related problems in families, and as students themselves approach middle and high school.

Although the *DSM–5* notes that young adults aged 18 to 24 have high prevalence rates for every substance, it reports that the alcohol use disorder prevalence rate among 12- to 17-year-olds to be around 4.6%, and 8.5% among those 18 and older in the United States. Although the laws for cannabis use are changing, the *DSM–5* states that cannabinoids are currently the most widely used illicit substance in the United States, reaching prevalence rates of 3.4% among 12- to 17-year-olds and 1.5% among adults 18 years and older.

A dangerous pattern is occurring in the United States regarding the rise of opioid use disorders in teens and young adults in the last decade. Three groups of disorders are included in this category: those with addition to heroin, those adolescents and young adults who gain access to controlled opioids through prescription medications, and those health care professionals with ready access to controlled substances. Adolescents are particularly vulnerable to opioid addiction because of its highly addictive nature. The *DSM–5* reports a 12-month prevalence rate of opioid use of 1.0% among 12- to 17-year-olds in the United States, and a heroin use of less than 0.1%.

The Substance-Related and Addictive Disorders category has important implications for adolescents because substance abuse/addictions interfere significantly with the development of adaptive skills during critical periods of a teenager's life cycle. *DSM–5* describes substances' direct activation of the brain's pleasure–reward system, which inhibits the acquisition of adaptive behaviors that normally occur with cognitive and behavioral rehearsal during development. When abuse and addiction occur early in life, the opportunities to manage the challenges necessary for growth are significantly curtailed. Further, the *DSM–5* suggests that the roots of substance-abuse disorders for some persons may be seen in some behavioral disorders (ODD, DMDD, and intermittent explosive disorder) before the onset of the actual substance disorder.

Substance disorders intensify the challenges of all other disabilities and disorders listed in the *DSM–5* and IDEA categories. They are responsible for many adverse experiences for school-aged children and youth. Children who are affected by substance disorders may be underdiagnosed in schools and/or may present with other emotional or behavioral symptoms that interfere with their ability to achieve in school. Mental health teams are critical to the milieu of middle and high schools to address comprehensively the sequelae of this category of disorders.

Low-incidence disabilities.

We now turn to a brief discussion of more rare disorders that fit under the Low Incidence section of IDEA's Emotional Disturbance category. Although such disorders do not occur often in young children, their incidence becomes more complex to address in a school setting as students enter middle and high school. Schools need the support of collaborative mental health teams to support the children, their families and their teachers.

Low-incidence emotional disturbance categories.

This section includes disorders that occur less frequently in the general population as well as in schools, and includes dissociative disorders, feeding and eating disorders, and sleep-wake disorders. Although more rare, the symptoms of these disorders are important to recognize. Schools are the setting where children are often first and most available for collaborative tracking and assessment by clinical teams.

Dissociative Disorders. This category of rare disorders often occurs in the aftermath of trauma and involves an alteration of consciousness. It includes dissociative identity disorder, dissociative amnesia, depersonalization/derealization disorder, and other specified and unspecified dissociative disorder. The *DSM–5* does not cite prevalence rates for children and youth for this category of disorders but notes that it is better recognized after adolescence.

Somatic Symptom and Related Disorders. This *DSM–5* category emphasizes a diagnosis made on the basis of reported somatic symptoms that may or may not accompany a medical condition. The category includes somatic symptom disorder, illness anxiety disorder, conversion disorder (or functional neurological symptom disorder), psychological factors affecting other medical conditions, factitious disorder, and other specified and unspecified somatic symptom and related disorder. The *DSM–5* seeks to acknowledge the psychological distress and impairment that individuals experience with this set of disorders.

The prevalence of this category of disorders is not known in pediatric populations, but children, adolescents, and adults with this category of disorders are often seen in primary care settings. The *DSM–5* notes that the most common symptoms that children report are abdominal pain, headache, fatigue, and nausea, and they generally complain of one major symptom. The *DSM–5* cautions that the parents' responses to the child's symptoms are important to the child's experience of the pain. Because this category of disorders involves physiological symptoms, a collaborative relationship among a child's primary care doctor, the school system, and the family is highly recommended. Careful collaboration may help prevent the leakage that can diminish both health and education services.

Feeding and Eating Disorders. Some of the disorders of this category are quite rare. They may challenge a child or adolescent's ability to achieve academically, however, and need to be addressed by teachers and mental health staff and community health care resources when it interferes with that child's learning. The *DSM–5* lists the following disorders under the Feeding and Eating Disorders category: pica (eating nonnutritive substances), rumination disorder (regurgitation of food), avoidant/restrictive food intake disorder, anorexia nervosa, bulimia nervosa, binge-eating disorder, and other specified or unspecified feeding or eating disorder.

This category refers to disorders characterized by persistent problems with eating-related behavior that impairs ones' health or psychosocial functioning. The first two disorders appear to be more prevalent in people with intellectual disabilities than the population at large. The *DSM–5* notes that the avoidant/restrictive food intake disorder often begins in infancy and early childhood, whereas anorexia nervosa and bulimia nervosa begin to emerge in adolescence and early adulthood. These latter two disorders are more prominent among females, and the incidence rates reported by *DSM–5* are 0.4% and 1% to 1.5%, respectively.

Brown et al. (2008) cite other statistics about the emergence of anorexia and bulimia nervosa in their book on *Childhood and Mental Health Disorders.* They cite Gowers and Bryant-Waugh's findings that anorexia nervosa can appear as early as 8 years of age, whereas *Bulimia Nervosa* rarely shows up before the age of 12. Brown et al. note that depression and anxiety disorders are comorbid disorders that frequently appear with eating disorders. School-based health care teams can provide RtI groups and individual support within the course of the school day, to help students diagnosed with these disorders. Students with eating disorders are often reluctant to seek outside help for their symptoms. Collaborative support within the school day may provide a private, confidential setting to address such symptoms before they exacerbate. It can ameliorate some of the invisible suffering of affected students.

Elimination Disorders. This category of *DSM–5* disorders includes enuresis (wetting), encopresis (soiling), and other specified and unspecified elimination disorders. These disorders are usually first diagnosed in childhood or adolescence and are classified according to whether they are nocturnal (night) or diurnal (day) occurrences. They can occur voluntarily or involuntarily and are often associated with developmental delays and/or the presence of other behavioral symptoms. The *DSM–5* breaks down enuresis into primary and secondary types. Primary type refers to never reaching a stage of full bladder control. Secondary type develops after a period of urinary continence has been established. The *DSM–5* reports the prevalence of enuresis as from 5% to 10% in 5-year-olds, which falls to 1% among individuals 15 years old or older. They also note that nocturnal enuresis is more common in males, and diurnal enuresis is more common in females. Regarding encopresis, *DSM–5* reports that 1% of 5-year-olds have it and that more males have it than females. The disorder is not diagnosed in children younger than four years of age. Because these disorders can have a biological base, collaboration with the patient/client/student's primary care doctor is essential with this class of disorders.

Sleep–Wake Disorders. This is another category of *DSM–5* disorders that calls for multidisciplinary collaboration to diagnose, treat, and track symptoms. Some occur rarely in children and adolescents, and some are more common. *DSM–5* includes 10 disorders in this category: insomnia disorder; hypersomnolence disorder (excessive sleepiness); narcolepsy; breathing-related sleep disorders (obstructive sleep apnea, central sleep apnea, sleep-related hypoventilation); circadian rhythm sleep–wake disorders; and the parasomnias of non–rapid eye movement sleep arousal disorders, nightmare disorder, rapid eye movement sleep behavior disorder, restless legs syndrome, and substance/medication-induced sleep disorder. Because sleep deprivation can trigger many other psychological stressors, these disorders often co-occur along with other *DSM–5* disorders. They have psychological as well as physical components, and thus collaboration with primary care physicians and sleep specialists is imperative.

Although the *DSM–5* does not report the prevalence of sleep disorders in children and adolescents with much specificity, insomnia, circadian rhythm sleep–wake disorders, and several of the parasomnias such as nightmares are known to occur children with anxiety disorders and adolescents with an array of challenges to their sleep as they experience puberty. Substance-related sleep–wake disorders in adolescence can affect concentration in school and therefore significantly interfere with academic achievement.

Evolving categories.

This section includes two categories of disorder that have seen an explosion of diagnosis in the past few decades. Originally categorized as low-incidence disorders, the two evolving categories of the ADHDs and autism spectrum disorders (ASD) have received increasing attention and service in schools and in health care settings.

ADHD. The *DSM–5* retains the general criteria for diagnosis for ADHD that were in previous editions of the manual, but they include the ADHDs in the Neurodevelopmental Disorders section of the manual. IDEA subsumes this category of disorders under its Other Health Impaired (OHI) category. The symptoms of this disorder can present in three ways: with a predominantly inattentive presentation, a predominantly hyperactive/impulsive presentation, or a combined presentation. Severity criteria include mild, moderate, or severe, and specifiers may also include whether the symptoms are in partial remission. The *DSM–5* also includes two other subsections of the disorder (Other Specified and Unspecified) that may not meet the full criteria for inclusion into one of the subtypes of ADHD. IDEA makes less distinction among types of ADHD.

Both classification systems recognize that the diagnosis of ADHD has increased significantly in the past two decades and that it has moved from a low-incidence disability to a more frequently diagnosed disorder. Every experienced school nurse, teacher, and school team will attest to this trend. Reporting on a randomized study of children with ADHD, Biederman, Lopez, Boellner, and Chandler (2002) suggested that approximately 5% of school-age children in the United States can be diagnosed with ADHD, with boys outnumbering girls in ratios from 2:1 to 6:1. As mentioned previously, ADHD was originally classified under the OHI category of disability in school systems. Many school districts and clinicians are reconsidering how to best currently classify and treat the increasing diagnostic incidence of this disorder. Given the diagnostic and pharmacological inflation issues mentioned previously, multidisciplinary collaboration among medical providers, mental health clinicians, and educators is essential.

ASDs. As discussed earlier in this chapter, the *DSM–5* now subsumes Asperger syndrome into the ASD category of disorders to address a fuller range of symptoms in a comprehensive way. Severity of the ASDs is rated along three specifiers which include social communication and interaction (lack of social reciprocity), restricted or repetitive/

stereotyped patterns of behavior, and known genetic or environmental etiology. The diagnosis further clarifies whether the presence of intellectual and/or language impairments are present and how much support a person needs in order to function.

Some high-functioning children on the ASD spectrum (with Asperger syndrome or a pervasive developmental disorder) are not fully diagnosed until middle school, when higher order mental and social skills become more necessary for academic and social success. In my experience, many bright children who later receive an ASD diagnosis are first diagnosed with ADHD. Byron Rourke (1989), a Canadian neuropsychologist who helped develop the category of nonverbal disability, evaluated children who could often process information in sequential fashion quite well. In fact, he noted that such children learned to read well, and they enjoyed the structure of early elementary school where children learn in step-by-step fashion. It was when they were confronted with unstructured information where they had to process simultaneously (such as learning to navigate a playground at recess or entering a school lunchroom) that such children tended to emotionally regress and decompensate, and at that point, inattention and hyperactive behavior were observed.

What Rourke found was that such children had difficulty processing information that is presented all at once. When children were psychologically evaluated, testing showed significant discrepancies between their right and their hemisphere scores. Rourke posited that the corpus callosum section of the brain in such children was compromised. This is the area of the brain where associations among concepts are made, information is simultaneously processed, and complex information is integrated. Although many of the children he tested scored well above the average range on verbal comprehension subtests, their ability to process information simultaneously was significantly compromised. Rourke called this disorder a nonverbal learning disability.

Research has targeted other areas of the brain, such as the amygdala and mirror neurons (Baron-Cohen et al., 2000; Ramachandran & Oberman, 2006), for diagnostic clues about children with ASDs. It is this area of the ASDs that has seen a significant jump in diagnosis and educational classification in the past decade. With early diagnosis and comprehensive support, these children are able to meet with success in school and many are able to achieve college degrees.

I lead an adult ASD group with five members. Four hold college degrees, yet all are struggling to activate their plans for their adult lives, which include independent living, supportive work and satisfying social lives. Much of the clinical work with this group involves helping them understand aspects of their diagnosis, such as why it took longer for them to complete their education; develop social skills; and address why they was not diagnosed when they were young children. As I collaborate with their physicians and families, some group members and their families report that their sense of *agency* and *communion* has improved and that their hopes have risen regarding what they can accomplish in their lives.

Low-incidence disabilities.

Many of the disabilities listed in the remaining IDEA and *DSM–5* categories involve disorders that include combined medical, neuro-psychological, and other physiological components. I have included the following *DSM–5* categories and disorders under IDEA's low-incidence disabilities. They include Schizophrenia Spectrum and Other Psychotic Disorders and Gender Dysphoria.

Schizophrenia Spectrum and Other Psychotic Disorders. The key diagnostic features that define the psychotic disorders are delusions, which involve rigid and fixed beliefs and hallucinations, which are perceptual experiences that occur without an external stimulus. The *DSM–5* adds that speech and motor movements may be disorganized, and negative symptoms also characterize this category of disorders. Negative symptoms refer to diminished emotional expression; a decrease in purposeful, self-initiated activities; and diminished ability to experience pleasure. The Schizophrenia Spectrum Disorders include the following diagnoses: schizotypal, delusional, brief psychotic, schizophreniform, schizophrenia, substance/medication-induced psychotic disorder, and catatonia. Specifiers involving duration and severity are also listed in this section.

Brown et al. (2008) suggest that Schizophrenia Spectrum Disorders are relatively rare in children and youth, although such symptoms as social withdrawal, isolation, and some disruptive behavioral disorders often appear before diagnosis. As with many disorders, the earlier symptoms begin to appear, the higher the risk becomes for a more pernicious and chronic course for the disorder. Paris (2013) explains that this is due more to temperamental rather than environmental factors that are predominant in children with early-onset disorders. The treatment for this class of disorders typically involves a combination of behavioral and psychopharmacological interventions, although Brown et al. caution about the risks and benefits of using neuroleptic medications that can cause weight gain and metabolic problems in children. Although they express optimism about the promise of newer medications, these authors offer due warning about the risks of serious health side effects in children with antipsychotic medications.

Gender Dysphoria. The *DSM–5* defines the term *gender* as the lived role that an individual plays in society and/or the identification one assumes as a male or a female. It recognizes that some males and females develop an identity that is different from their anatomic biological indicators.

In the *DSM–5*, Gender Dysphoria refers to the significant discontent and distress or impairment that an individual may experience regarding the incongruence between one's experienced and one's assigned gender and/or the medical processes to reconcile these differences (p. 451). This category includes the diagnoses of gender dysphoria and other specified and unspecified gender dysphoria and requires duration of 6 months of distress before diagnosis. It is organized along developmental lines. The section on children requires six symptoms for diagnosis and well as a specifier about the presence of a disorder of sexual development such as the *ICD* classifications of congenital adrenal hyperplasia or androgen insensitivity. For adolescents and adults, the diagnosis requires the presence of two symptoms as well as a specifier about whether an individual has made the medical and legal transition to the desired gender.

The *DSM–5* reports prevalence rates of from 0.005% to 0.014% for males and from 0.0002% to 0.0003% in females. The *DSM–5* also notes the persistence of gender dysphoria symptoms once they appear. They report a range from 2.2% to 3.0% in males and 1.2% to 5.0%

in females as children mature into adolescence and adulthood. The *DSM–5* does not list specific prevalence rates for children. It does suggest that gender dysphoria symptoms are first seen in clinics between the ages of 2 and 4 and that there appear to be two trajectories to the disorder: includes early and late onset.

One of the most painful issues children face in schools is bullying, especially as children move into middle and high school and experience puberty. Adolescence is a time when identity becomes a major developmental task, and the cognitive rehearsal for this period in students' lives takes place within the academic and social life of schools and other youth-based organizations. Although there is growing acceptance of sexual identity variability, school system professionals are well served to be alert to the presence of bullying and gender dysphoria, particularly as children approach adolescence.

Deaf and Hard of Hearing, Blindness and Low Vision, and Low-Incidence, Multiple and Severe disabilities. The *DSM–5* does not include these categories directly in its classification system. It does, however, include Neurocognitive Disorders, which are addressed subsequently. Children with multiple disabilities require significant support to achieve academically. School-based support is critical to the success of students with these categories of disability. In addition, because these disorders are complex and chronic, the potential for anxiety, depression, and behavioral and other *DSM–5* disorders is high in families of children who fall into these IDEA categories. It is because of the advocacy efforts of families and educators over the years that children with multiple disabilities are being educated in public schools today. The emotional toll on families whose resources are challenged at every turn with chronically disabled and ill children is enormous. Collaborative mental health teams in schools and collaborative consultation with health professionals in the community can play a critical role in supporting families through their children's school careers and across affected families' life cycle.

Neurocognitive Disorders. The *DSM–5* lists the following disorders in the Neurocognitive Disorders category: delirium and major and mild neurocognitive disorders (major or mild Alzheimer disease, fronto-temporal disorder, Lewy bodies disorder, vascular, TBI, HIV infection, prion, Parkinson disease, Huntington disease, and disorders due to another medical condition or to multiple etiologies). The biological causes and courses of these disorders are increasingly being identified and treated in modern medicine. Most of these disorders affect individuals in later life who are well past childhood and adolescence. Delirium typically happens in hospitals and is associated with high fever and disorientation. It can occur in ill children with elevated fevers.

This category of disorders is not often seen in children and adolescents and is associated more with aging populations. TBIs, however, can happen to people of all ages, and a percentage of young adults with Down syndrome are now being diagnosed with forms of fronto-temporal and Alzheimer type dementia (Stanton & Coetzee, 2004). The *DSM–5* notes that NCDs with childhood and adolescent onset have broad repercussions for social and intellectual development. These are the children and youth who get classified within the IDEA category as having multiple disabilities.

OHIs. As mentioned earlier, the ADHDs are often included in this OHI category of disability, along with such physical disorders as allergies, asthma, and orthopedic impairments. The ADHDs have been addressed previously. Other physical disabilities that IDEA includes are not addressed in the *DSM–5* unless psychiatric symptoms accompany a medical disorder or disability.

Motor Disorders. The *DSM–5* lists several disorders under this category, which fits within IDEA's OHI category of disabilities. They list a developmental coordination disorder, which involves significant delayed motor skills that interferes with a child's ability to perform and execute motor tasks. The *DSM–5* notes that this disorder has an early developmental onset but is one that is not better explained by another developmental disability or neurological condition such as cerebral palsy. The *DSM* reports the prevalence of this disorder in children aged 5 to 11 years as 5%.

A related disorder is stereotypic movement disorder, which co-occurs with many severe and complex disabilities. This disorder involves repetitive, driven, and purposeless motor behavior such as head-banging, hand shaking, or waving. The specifiers in this disorder include whether a movement is self-injurious or not, and the disorder can be mild, moderate, or severe in presentation. The *DSM–5* notes that stereotypic movements start early and are common in infancy and early childhood but that complex stereotypic movement disorders are much less common in children, occurring in 3% to 4% of children, primarily in children with developmental disabilities.

Tic Disorders. This final category of *DSM* disorders that fits within the OHI category of IDEA includes Tourette syndrome, chronic motor or vocal tic disorder, provisional tic disorder (less than 1 year in duration), and other specified and unspecified tic disorders. Onset of these disorders occurs before age 18 years, and the course may wax and wane in frequency. In Tourette syndrome, both motor and vocal tics are present, although not always at the same time. The disorders involving either or both forms of tics develop usually before school age, and often the symptoms begin to decline in adolescence. *DSM–5* states that the prevalence of tics is estimated to be rare, ranging from 3 to 8 per 1000 in school-age children.

Conclusions

It is my contention that collaborative multidisciplinary teams in and near schools can diminish the ranks of untreated mental illness in childhood, adolescence, and adulthood. Such teams can provide early detection, intervention, and support to children and families in ways that prevent students' needs from becoming invisible. Such multitiered systems of support in education have the potential to prevent school tragedies and untold mental distress.

The tragic life of Adam Lanza might have been altered if he had not fallen through the systemic cracks of contemporary U.S. education and mental health. In the report by the Office of the Child Advocate in Connecticut, authors identified several missed chances during his life to collaboratively address his symptoms and support effective home, school, and clinical teamwork on his behalf (to view the full text of the report, see courant.com/lanzareport; see also Griffin, Kovner, & Altimari, 2014). As it happened, his extreme isolation from his family, school, and society over time became an iatrogenic trigger that fueled Adam's murderous rampage.

Adam's untreated mental symptoms represent an unintended consequence of the community mental health laws of the 1960s that were not accompanied by the development of collaborative outpatient support systems of care. Rachel Pruchno, a professor of medicine at Rowan University in New Jersey who has written a memoir of mental illness and family secrets, noted in the *Hartford Courant* that as inpatient programs for children and adolescents with disruptive disorders have dwindled,

> the lack of progress made toward improving life for people with mental illness is shameful. Today, too many people with mental illness are imprisoned or roaming the streets homeless. Caring families must watch helplessly as their loved ones spiral out of control. We owe those who suffer severe mental illness, and their families, more. (Pruchno, 2014, p. C2)

It is far easier to evaluate specific omissions and mistakes retrospectively than to plan ahead collaboratively to prevent tragedies from happening. As stated throughout this book, early diagnosis of disorders is made more comprehensive by assessment teams. Most health professionals generally have a working understanding of mental health disorders and categories, often based on the *DSM*. They need to understand how educators assess student functioning and how the IDEA categories apply to their patients. Bridging diagnostic cultures across health care and education can help foster better collaborative assessment and treatment. We as health care providers and educators owe our children more. To provide that "more" to children and to help clinicians appreciate the context of school-based evaluation of children who experience constraints to academic achievement, we turn in the next chapter to school-based assessment.

eight

Assessment: Where We Start

As was addressed in earlier chapters, children's school progress has historically been measured by individual achievement scores. This chapter tracks the evolution of assessment from its individualized roots in special education to the systemic measures currently utilized to evaluate student resiliency and achievement in all children. Collaborative, multidisciplinary school assessment increasingly fulfills the "frontloading" criteria that teams use to formulate collaborative plans for the health care and educational needs of all students. This chapter is about the use and value of multidisciplinary assessment in schools, whether for individualized or wider systemic purposes.

All students are evaluated regularly though assignments, quizzes, and tests. Customarily, the results are shared with families during parent–teacher conferences and at other times throughout the year. School children also take group mastery tests during specific years of their school career to further evaluate their performance. However, such group mastery tests still focus on whether individual achievement scores measure up to local, state, and national norms for student progress.

Individual psychoeducational assessment is typically administered to students who are eligible for and/or receiving special education services. Such testing is conducted to assess and track the progress of individual students with special needs' abilities, needs, and achievement across their school careers. That process was first addressed in Chapter 3. Since the P.L. 94-142 law was enacted in the United States, the special education assessment process has become more sophisticated, more multidisciplinary, and more integrated across elementary, middle, and high school grade levels.

Psychoeducational testing refers to the process of administering and summarizing a series of measures to determine a student's aptitude and achievement levels. Along with special educators and school counselors, school psychologists and neuropsychologists have led the psychoeducational testing process in the United States for more than half a century. Professionals in health care and education recognize the importance of psychometric assessment in diagnosing such disorders as developmental and learning disabilities, cognitive disorders, and autism. A strong cadre of educational and psychological assessment measures has been developed to meet the complex ways that disabilities present themselves. Schools have developed a growing ability to identify and service children with an array of special needs because of these well-researched and well-normed measures.

Multidisciplinary Assessment

In his text for mental health clinicians in schools, House (1999) makes a careful distinction between *testing* and *assessment*. Whereas testing involves the mechanical process of tabulating a series of test scores, assessment involves a *higher* level of systemic integration of data about a student. House notes that for assessment to be comprehensive, an awareness of contextual issues (cultural, developmental, family, medical, psychiatric, school, psychoeducational, etc.) must be integrated with an understanding of each individual case over time.

As he applies *DSM* diagnoses to children in school settings, House notes that psychiatric classification "interacts with many other systems of behavior, codes of ethics and values, and people" (p. 178). All licensed mental health professionals have graduate training with the *DSM* system, and each can link student behavior with mental health diagnosis and categorization when necessary. Those clinicians with additional systems training use broader longitudinal overview of growth in systems (LOGS) model elements to assess a wider range of needs and design interventions.

In the years since P.L. 94-142 was enacted, the medical, mental health, speech and language, and physical and occupational therapy professionals have joined psychologists and special educators in the assessment process. School collaborative teams use a combination of *direct observation, self-report measures,* and *testing* to assess student biopsychosocial functioning. Collaborative assessment of a child's abilities, strengths, and needs represents a more systemic evaluation of a student's functioning than traditional academic scores alone.

Gregory Bateson (1972), a father of family therapy and an anthropologist who studied cybernetics, the interwoven nature of all phenomena, would say that this process reveals the "patterns that connect." The patterns that emerge during a comprehensive assessment reveal a fuller profile of the whole child than simply one or a few measures. IDEA endorses such collaborative "frontloading" to address and track the progress of students in need of special services over time.

Carefully assessing these patterns to establish a child's learning profile is clearly labor-intensive, but comprehensive assessment represents a valuable investment in children that can prove to be of great preventive benefit to students. Multidisciplinary assessment can help clarify what a student specifically needs to achieve to the best of his or her ability and can help prevent a cycle of failure that begets dysfunction for that child and possibly the school system to which that child belongs.

In the current health care environment in the United States, far too many children and youth do not have ready access to psychological assessment and support through private insurance, clinics, or community agencies. Because schools have witnessed the exponential growth of special education knowledge and expertise since 1975, schools have become a logical and appropriate setting for high-quality assessment where licensed and school-certified multidisciplinary teams can offer a continuum of services to students over time. Assessment can thus be offered to students "where they live," providing primary preventive support within a child's natural environment. Frontloading services early in a child's school career can help avoid inappropriate labeling, costly and difficult-to-access services in the community, out-of-district placements, and potentially serious health problems later in a student's life.

As with the last chapter, a caveat regarding the lists of assessment measurements described in this chapter needs to be made here. Some mental health clinicians may receive training in these instruments in their graduate coursework. Indeed, such training forms the bulk of school psychologists' graduate education. However, for other mental health and medical disciplines, such individualized assessment measures may not be familiar. Because psychological assessment measures are used frequently in schools and form the context for the newer, more systemic initiatives such as Response to Intervention (RtI) and Positive Behavior Interventions and Supports, it is important for readers to receive an introduction to the tools used for school-based assessment.

Individualized Psychoeducational Assessment Measures

This section highlights some assessment tools that are currently used to measure and address student needs. It includes how traditional special education assessment procedures have evolved with RtI into system-wide measures that are being introduced to schools. The goal of this section is to encourage a model of best practice for multidisciplinary assessment in schools to promote student achievement and resiliency.

The assessment measures introduced in this section are by no means exhaustive, and examples are intended to be illustrative of the domains being evaluated. School systems vary according to student populations, available staff, and preferred measurements. Assessment procedures should be used based on each school district's needs, requirements, clinician preferences, and affordability of the assessment tools. The traditional psychological assessment instruments listed in this chapter are well tested and have appropriate validity and reliability. Many of the newer measures afford creative ways to capture needed additional information while providing clinical and educational utility. As with the *Diagnostic and Statistical Manual of Mental Disorders (DSM)*, newer measures should help to develop a foundation for better evidence-based services in schools. A detailed resource list of measures is located in "Appendix A: Index of Resources." Interested readers can investigate which measures are appropriate for multidisciplinary school teams in their districts to use for school-based assessment. A list of companies that publish these assessment measures is also included in Appendix A.

School individual assessment typically involves a prereferral process in which several self-report checklists are collected from teachers, allied health care clinicians, parents, and students to establish a basis for a psychoeducational evaluation. Examples of these measures are the Conner's' Rating Forms and the Behavior Assessment Scales for Children (BASC). They include versions for parents, teachers, and students to complete. Data from these measures are integrated with group aptitude and achievement records during the prereferral process.

Formal testing typically includes an evaluation of a student's aptitude and achievement using the Wechsler Intelligence Scale for Children, Fifth Edition (WISC–V), the Wechsler Abbreviated Scale of Intelligence (WASI), and the Kaufman Assessment Battery for Children (KABC) or the Kaufman Brief Intelligence Test (K–BIT). These tests measure a child's abilities in cognitive domains such as verbal comprehension, working memory, nonverbal aptitude, visual/motor abilities, and processing speed. Aptitude testing is accompanied by achievement testing with measures such as the Kaufman Test of Educational Achievement—3 (K-TEA–3) or the Wechsler Individual Achievement Test, Third Edition (WIAT–III). Achievement measures are increasingly being administered by special education professionals on the assessment team.

Many school psychologists also incorporate personality assessment into evaluations. These are less structured projective measures that collect data about a student's emotional state and coping skills. Measures often included in projective assessment are the Rorschach Inkblot Test, the House-Tree-Person, the Thematic Apperception Test, and the Sentence Completion Test. Projective assessments also include self-report measures such as the Beck Inventories and the Reynolds Scales. The Reynolds Scales include an assessment of bully victimization as well. These measures include self-report inventories of mood and behavior for children and youth. The Millon Clinical Inventories and the Minnesota Multiphasic Personality Inventory (MMPI) are also useful self-report measures for students of preadolescence age through adulthood.

Mental health clinicians practicing in schools who work with families incorporate relationship-based self-report measures into their assessments. Examples of these include the Parenting Stress Index, Fourth Edition (PSI–4), The Parent Report Card for children and adolescents, and the Parent–Child Relationship Inventory (PCRI). Data from such measures can be particularly useful for school teams partnering with parents of children with chronic disabilities to measure the success of collaborative planning and service over time.

Neuropsychological screening measures (examples include the NEPSY [which stands for A Developmental NEuroPSYchological Assessment], the Beery Buktenica Test of Visual-Motor Integration [VMI], the Bender-Gestalt, the Benton Visual Retention Test, Fifth Edition, and the California Verbal Learning Test) are used to identify specific perceptual strengths and needs such as executive functioning, visual and auditory processing, left and right hemisphere functioning, sensory-motor processing, and memory.

Other specific measures and rating scales are used by school psychologists and other team members to investigate specific areas of concern about the student. For instance, to assess the presence of autism symptoms, several measures including the Autism Diagnostic Observation Schedule and the Pervasive Developmental Disability Behavior Inventory are useful. For concerns about the presence of attention-deficit/hyperactivity disorder, school professionals often use the Brown ADD Scales and Conner's Comprehensive Behavior Rating Scales. Specialized speech and language and physical and occupational therapy measures are administered as necessary to measure other targeted areas of disability. These include measures such as the Arizona Articulation Proficiency Scale, Test of Auditory Processing Skills, Beery VMI, Bender-Gestalt, Otis-Lennon, and Test of Written Language, for example.

For students with neurodevelopmental disabilities, measures of adaptive functioning such as the Adaptive Behavior Assessment System and the Vineland Adaptive Behavior Scales, Second Edition, are used to evaluate domains of communication, daily living skills, socialization, and motor functioning. Testing companies rank the qualifications that allied health care clinicians need to administer specific assessment instruments. Master's level teachers and allied mental health clinicians currently receive training to administer certain instruments from the testing companies and/or through online and professional seminars.

Schools use health and mental health clinicians in their districts to conduct assessments, and they can also contract with health care clinicians in the community to provide these services. Federal law mandates that schools must fund one outside assessment from a psychologist or neuropsychologist if such an evaluation is requested.

Mental Health Assessment: New Tools

With the advent of the *DSM–5*, new measures have been developed for mental health assessment that can be incorporated into school-based clinical work. They are called cross-cutting measures, and they are designed to cut across and be used for the range of disorders listed in the manual. The Level 1 Cross-Cutting Symptoms Measure (American Psychiatric Association [APA], 2013) is a 25-question survey of 12 domains for children, adolescents, and adults. Symptoms are rated and scored according to severity on a Likert scale. Some of the questions involve questions about suicidal ideation/suicide and substance abuse items. They are rated on a "Yes/No/I Don't Know" scale. The measure is administered directly or through an informant such as a parent or guardian and can be accessed at www.psychiatry.org.dsm5.

Much like other measures used in triennial reviews, cross-cutting measures were developed to be administered at the beginning and across the treatment process to track progress over time. The *DSM–5* reports that these measures have clinical utility and were found to have promising reliability in pediatric populations across the United States and Canada during the short time they were field tested (APA, 2013). Although the validity of these results has been questioned (Frances, 2013a, 2013b) because of their short history of use, clinical utility should grow as multidisciplinary mental health professions use these instruments across settings and over time. Usage should boost reliability estimates and help build a scientific base of evidence for collaborative assessment of child and youth disorders.

Mental health licenses all require training in assessment, which incorporates elements of health histories and mental status examinations to address the quality of one's thinking, emotions, and behavior. The depth, breadth, and focus of assessment training varies across disciplines, but all mental health professionals are trained to conduct assessments. In schools, this has historically involved addressing aspects of a student's functioning to help determine the appropriate disability category for a student's Individual Education Plan.

RtI and Newer Assessments

As No Child Left Behind legislation was passed in 2001 and RtI began to roll out across the country in 2004, school professionals started to consider other variables besides cognitive aptitude and disability that can interfere with student learning and achievement. The IDEA reauthorization and the Safe Schools Acts that were passed in the wake of the Columbine, Sandy Hook, and other shootings have mandated higher expectations for schools to provide safer, healthier environments for students and teachers. School bullying, family stressors, dual languages spoken in the home, preschool readiness preparation, immigrant and/or minority culture differences, poverty, and exposure to violence are all recognized as constraints to learning and achievement. Individualized psychoeducational assessment is labor intensive, and that individualized process is not always necessary or sufficient to evaluate all constraints to student achievement accurately. Many students without innate disabilities experience *relational* barriers to achievement, and the RtI initiative sought to address broader constraints to learning.

As described in Chapter 6 on RtI, schools are including several new levels of school system culture to assess needs and provide targeted support and promote a nurturing milieu for all students who experience constraints to learning. School-Wide Positive Behavioral Intervention and Supports (SWPBIS or PBIS) is an intervention system for reinforcing desired behavior that grew out of the reauthorization of IDEA in 1997 and has developed within the RtI initiative. Based on principles of applied behavioral analysis that was originally designed for students with severe learning problems in special education, PBIS is designed to enhance the capacity of schools to support achievement more comprehensively for all children. PBIS is a broad initiative that uses evidence-based practices to address relational and environmental systemic layers of the school milieu that serve as constraints to school achievement. Horner, Sugai, and Anderson (2010) report that PBIS/SWPBIS

> is not a formal curriculum but a 2–3 year process of leadership team training intended to establish local or school capacity for adoption of effective and preventive behavioral interventions, high implementation integrity, continuous use of data for decision making, embedded professional development and coaching to establish predictable, consistent, positive and safe social contingencies at the whole school level. (p. 4)

The RtI initiative and PBIS integrate well with each other, and together they afford many opportunities for collaborative mental health teams to assess student needs and design services at several systemic levels. As described in Chapter 6, RtI assesses both behavioral and academic dimensions of student functioning and incorporates three tiers of intervention in the classroom (whole class, small group, and individual interventions for students) to support students who need such service. PBIS is designed to assess and address even broader systemic layers of school culture and is based on *prevention*. Horner et al. (2010) address three levels of prevention as they describes PBIS. They include *primary prevention* as occurring at the school-wide level, *secondary prevention* as occurring in the classroom, and *tertiary prevention* as occurring at the individual level. All are designed to improve lifestyle results (personal, health, social, family, work, recreation) for all children and youth by making problem behavior less effective, efficient, and relevant and desired behavior more functional

PBIS emphasizes four elements of supports that school personnel need to create a positive and safe school climate:
1. Team-based leadership
2. Data-based decision making
3. Continuous monitoring of student behavior

4. Effective ongoing professional development (www.pbis.org, 2014)

The PBIS website suggests that school districts and states incorporate these elements by establishing training teams to learn how to integrate PBIS into their RtI programs with fidelity. To do this, they suggest that these teams engage in a process of preparation for PBIS by taking the following steps: (a) examine their school data to define and specify the need for services and (b) secure buy-in from their systems' staff and leadership to move forward with PBIS. They then recommend that a facilitator from the teams be identified who can move the implementation process forward (www.pbis.org). The website lists many ways to obtain the training to create PBIS within RtI. An extensive PBIS network for training exists, and information can be obtained from the home page of the PBIS.org website, under "Important Links."

In collaboration with national colleagues and aided by funding from the National Technical Assistance Center on Positive Behavioral Interventions and Supports through the Office of Special Education Programs (OSEP), the Sugai team from the University of Connecticut has partnered with the Special Education Resource Center of Connecticut (SERC) through the Connecticut State Department of Education. Together they have developed a model and a continuum of PBIS training and assistance for more than 65 school districts in Connecticut since 2000 (SERC, 2009).

Chapter 6 described some examples of how Connecticut schools are implementing PBIS within RtI. Districts such as Westbrook have sought and obtained SERC training for key staff from their schools, creating teams of regular and special educators, mental health staff, and administrators who meet regularly to track students, provide needed services, and address broader systemic needs to promote achievement. School counselor Margaret Donohue joined the PBIS initiative with her Old Saybrook Middle School 5 years ago to prepare her staff for broader systemic PBIS/RtI interventions to promote school achievement. Donohue (2014) reported that the consultation process they developed resulted in better identification of student needs, evolved teacher attitudes, and more collaborative school practices. Their consultation model has now been incorporated into weekly meetings within the school day and includes a multidisciplinary team of regular and special educators, mental health staff, and administrators as well. Both school systems report better coordinated special and regular education services, improved school climate, and decreased disciplinary referrals.

In Sugai and Simonson's (2012) report on national PBIS history and outcomes, they note that more than 18,000 school teams have been trained in PBIS as of 2012 in the United States, and the National Center has enjoyed three successful 5-year grant cycles to conduct research and hold leadership and dissemination conferences. Regarding PBIS impact, schools are reporting improved teacher expectations, decreased school discipline referrals, lowered incidence of bullying, and better school climate and organizational health.

To assess the need for and the effectiveness of these newer levels of intervention, grades and school individual and group achievement scores will continue to be the standard for achievement progress in education. The assessment measures described earlier in this chapter are also useful to gauge student progress. PBIS also recommends that curriculum-based measures be used. Several of these can be downloaded from www.aimsweb.com, a division of Pearson Education, Inc. These measures are primarily for school teams to collaboratively assess and track the educational progress of students within the three intervention tiers of RtI.

Schools can develop their own baseline and outcome assessment measures as well. For our MFTs who train and practice in Connecticut schools, we developed the *Referral* and *Outcomes* forms for teachers that were illustrated in Chapter 6 on RtI (see Figures 6.2 and 6.3). We designed the forms to develop Tier 2 individual and group interventions for students, teachers, and families. We then measured individual student and wider system progress over the course of the school year. Supportive Tier 2 programs for parents, teachers, and students have been offered in different school systems where needed to build positive school relationships and build capacity for student achievement. Our preliminary research affirms other findings that schools experience fewer disciplinary referrals and less absenteeism after these PBIS interventions, and school climate improves.

Together PBIS and RtI represent the *multitiered systems of support* (MTSS) that operate in conjunction with special education processes. Multidisciplinary teams of teachers, administrators, and specialists form PBIS teams in schools. They develop collaborative plans and work with school personnel and families to provide support to all levels of the school community. In addition to providing comprehensive assessment of different dimensions of school culture, mental health teams offer additional value-added component to education. They help diminish the bifurcation of special and regular education that has challenged many school systems and budgets. With PBIS training, multidisciplinary school teams have been assembled to assess need within the three tiers of RtI as well as traditional special education services in schools that were described at the beginning of the chapter. Mental health teams are beginning to serve leadership roles with educators in managing such assessment and service.

In the wake of increasing school violence nationally, the "Framework for Safe and Successful Schools" was developed and endorsed by a national educational/mental health mental health collaborative that was established to address school safety. In their executive summary, Cowen, Vaillancourt, Rossen, and Politt (2013) report that this group issued a joint policy statement endorsing the value of MTSS. They offered six recommendations for supporting effective school safety. First introduced in Chapter 3 for this text, these recommendations include the following:

1. Allow for blended, flexible use of revenue streams in educational and mental health services
2. Improve staffing ratios to allow for the delivery of a full range of services and effective school–community partnerships
3. Develop evidence-based standards for district-level policies to promote effective school discipline and positive behavior
4. Fund continuous and sustainable crisis and emergency preparedness, response, and recovery planning and training that uses evidence-based models
5. Provide incentives for intra-and interagency collaboration
6. Support multitiered systems of support (p. 1)

What is also noteworthy about the work of this collaborative is its membership. It includes an impressive multidisciplinary array of educators and mental health leaders and their national organizations, including the American School Counselor Association, the National Association of School Psychologists, the National Association of Elementary School Principals, the National Association of Secondary School Principals, the National Association of School Resource Officers, and the School Social Work Association of America. Their policy statement integrates current literature about best practices in schools, helps delineate some of the roles played by different mental health professionals on school teams, and advocates for collaboration across school systems to promote school safety and create fertile learning environments in schools for children.

Horner et al. (2010) describe several systems of early evaluation and intervention for the various tiers of the RtI triangle. These are all designed to provide positive and preventive implementation alternatives for SWPBIS. They cite *Check and Connect* from the University of Minnesota, which links students with select adults to provide targeted support that students might need. They also list a daily report card that improves access to academic and social support called *Check-in/Check Out*, or *CICO*. Another individualized program to train children to reduce problem behavior is called *First Step to Success (FSS) Think Time*, developed by Nelson and Carr (2000), is another program developed for teachers and students to stop negative interaction and help students plan. Horner et al. (2010) describe research indicating a decline in disciplinary referrals and other problem behaviors.

These assessment and intervention programs all contain behavioral elements that have relevance for school-based mental health practice. They are thriving relatives of the applied behavioral analysis programs that were developed for students who are intellectually disabled or behaviorally challenged and are now being incorporated into general education. Mental health clinicians can provide strong support to teachers and provide leadership as these initiatives unfold across schools. The relative contributions from the allied professions of counseling, marriage and family therapy, nursing, psychiatry, psychology, social work, and other health care professionals are strong, and the RtI initiative affords creative opportunities to fully integrate mental health service with school-based student educational evaluation and planning.

Early, comprehensive assessment of children is complex and labor intensive, however. Schools are increasingly challenged by learning and safety concerns, behavioral issues that present themselves, the logistics of leading the assessment process, and financial and other challenges that tax the resources of school systems. Some would argue that mental health teams add too much complexity to schools and that education of children should be the sole responsibility of school systems. The next chapter addresses these challenges and concerns.

nine

Challenges and Constraints

Developing multidisciplinary professional support in education to boost student achievement has many challenges. This chapter addresses a sampling of the constraints and dilemmas that schools face as they seek to build multidisciplinary teams and adopt best practices to support student resiliency and performance. Armed with information about the challenges, the goals of this chapter are to (a) demonstrate the value of using a systems approach to dilemmas that constrain student achievement, (b) promote multidisciplinary team assessments and service to children in need across their school careers, and (c) urge that family members be respectfully included as team members. I recommend that an *educational home* be established in schools, which is the setting where children spend the bulk of their childhood outside of time with their families. With support from teachers, families, and community, an educational home can foster collaborative planning and nurture student achievement while systemically addressing constraints to learning. The educational home concept is much like promoting the medical home in medicine, where better health outcomes are sought through collaboration.

Four main constraints challenge the ability to build collaborative multidisciplinary teams in schools: (a) guild issues and silos, (b) language boundaries and barriers, (c) the need to shift from linear to systemic thinking, and (d) financial and administrative logistics. Each constraint is addressed in the following pages, and solutions to address and mitigate them are offered. The first constraint refers to the complexity of six licensed mental health professions that exist in the United

States (see Chapter 2). The section about this constraint consumes the bulk of this chapter. It is one of the more challenging constraints to mitigate, but the fruits of effective multidisciplinary collaboration can be powerful for students and school teams. The remaining constraints are related to the first, and discussion about them follows.

Guild Issues and Silos

An interesting paradox occurs for human service professionals who obtain graduate educational degrees. Specialized graduate education in human services often forces students to forego other avenues of study in the pursuit of that specialized training. The more education and licensure/certification that is required for a specialization, the more distanced students can become from other bodies of knowledge and expertise. As this phenomenon occurs, silos of knowledge can be created, where specialized knowledge is developed yet the boundaries among various bodies of knowledge deepen.

It is tempting to claim exclusive ownership of models and key concepts when they are studied and learned in silos. If deliberate attempts are not made to bridge those silos with open minds, perceptions can become reified. From Galileo to Einstein, science has struggled with changing epistemologies in the context of established "truths," which are later discredited with broader research and new knowledge.

This paradox is played out within and among the six licensed professions that practice in mental health, and guild issues that emerge from siloes of training can easily thwart the integrity of collaborative school assessment and service. For instance, a curious artifact of history currently challenges the young profession of marriage and family therapy. Despite its multidisciplinary history, marriage and family therapists (MFTs) across the United States (with the help of the American Association of Marriage and Family Therapy) have recently completed the linear task of obtaining licensure in all states. Concurrently, many of the psychiatrists, psychologists, and social workers who started the field of relationship-based systemic therapy with dual licenses have begun to retire from practice, tempting newly licensed MFTs to claim systemic orientation as being their exclusive domain.

The dangers of reification can serve as a constraint for MFTs, because systems theory as applied to human relationships has been adopted by interested clinicians from all six of the licensed mental health groups. MFTs' history of multidisciplinary training and membership has helped them to bridge guild issues among health care and education settings where overlapping skill sets converge. But that history may not continue to serve MFTs for current and future school-based collaboration if guild issues prevail, now that MFTs are licensed in every state. Older mental health disciplines have similar issues as they have created special interest groups and divisions for their members. The American Psychological Association, for example, has more than 50 divisions with interests that frequently overlap but at times function as silos of special interest.

Each of the six licensed mental health disciplines brings unique clinical skills to school-based practice, based on the length (from 2 to 8 years) and content of the specialized graduate training. In general, school counselors are the professionals who have the most familiarity with school curriculum, and they are trained to link the psychosocial elements of student functioning to school curricular achievement for all students. School counselors have historically also helped to guide students into secondary and postsecondary education and training that matches their talents and interests. They have had a long history of service in the field of education. At Central Connecticut State University (CCSU) where I teach, the graduate school of professional studies houses the Counselor Education, and it offers specialized training in school counseling, rehabilitation counseling, and mental health counseling. It is a combined department with our MFT Program, and it is called the Counselor Education and Family Therapy Department.

School-based MFTs incorporate generations of family psychological, cultural, and other layers of systemic influence that have relevance for student achievement. Their special expertise lies in helping to cultivate relationships between families and schools. MFTs are often referred to as the "WD-40" of school teams, greasing the wheels of communication across the systemic levels of student, school, and family. Systems training is the clinical cornerstone of all MFT graduate education.

School nurses and physicians/psychiatrists link the medical influences on child behavior with school behavior and help educational colleagues to appreciate how medical issues can affect children's health and learning. School psychologists, neuropsychologists, and clinical psychologists are experts at psychosocial testing and assessment, and they are the mental health professionals who clarify the nature of students' cognitive, neuropsychological, and psychosocial constraints to learning. They are often leaders in researching and reporting the effectiveness of clinical practice in schools, and they have been valued school employees in American schools since the end of the Second World War.

School social workers are experts at linking resources with student needs, both within the school system and with community agencies outside of the school. Having started as a helping profession with disenfranchised immigrant populations in the United States, social workers are well equipped to address cultural diversity needs and issues in schools. They have had historic expertise in addressing the financial, social, and emotional needs of individuals and families.

Four of the six groups (counseling, MFT, nursing, and social work) require a master's degree for state licensure and school certification. Psychiatry and psychology require a doctoral degree for state licensure, although typically states allow school psychologists with masters' degrees to become certified for school-based practice.

Although each of the mental health professions offers unique services, there is also significant overlap in the skill base of the six licensed mental health groups. For instance, MFTs have been a distinct profession since the 1970s, but as mentioned earlier, the field was originally developed in the 1950s by psychiatrists, psychologists, and social workers who sought more comprehensive, systems-based ways of addressing mental health than individual diagnosis and treatment alone. Some school counselors, psychologists, psychiatrists, nurses, and social workers have added systems-based training to their skill base (Cowan et al., 2013; Gerrard & Soriano, 2013).

Above and beyond individual licensure and certification, clinicians from each of the mental health disciplines often develop overlapping interests and areas of expertise (such as treating trauma-related disorders, applied behavioral analysis, or medical family therapy). These "necessary redundancies" are what equip mental health professionals to offer collaborative assessment and treatment services across the continuum of school system layers. Mental health clinicians can offer traditional individualized services as well as address broader systemic issues such as school climate and school violence. Mental health teams can work directly with students, teachers, and administrators to address broader environmental variables through group and whole system interventions. Each licensed mental health professional can assess and treat within the scope of their license, and members from each group can develop specialty skills in certain areas across individual, group, and whole system layers of service within school communities.

There are varied pools of mental health professionals available to schools across urban, suburban, and rural settings and elementary, middle, and high school age levels. Schools should have the authority and freedom to hire available licensed and certified multidisciplinary teams that best support their unique needs. For instance, the shoreline Connecticut town where I held my first school-based position faced two challenges in the early 1970s. The town housed a residential facility for developmentally disabled children and was seeking ways to provide community-based education for its residents as the facility was closing. It was also the era of civil rights legislation when laws were being passed that prohibited schools from denying educational opportunities for children from minority backgrounds or with special needs. At the end of the Vietnam War, the town was also facing new challenges regarding the influx of psychedelic drugs into the shoreline communities. I was hired because my special education, substance abuse, and social work training met the needs of that community at the time.

Each school system and district has specific needs for multitiered systems of support (MTSS) that address that system's unique needs. Current national initiatives such as Common Core, Response to Intervention (RtI), and Positive Behavior Interventions and Supports (PBIS) require a broader and deeper analysis and planning process for the initiatives to achieve the goals of improving student achievement. Mental health professionals are in a key position to raise the consciousness of school colleagues about the roles and value of social and emotional competence and learning. Standards for mental health professionals need to be raised to best meet these needs and challenges.

Raising licensure and school certification standards for mental health professionals is not without controversy and complexity. Because of the nature of silo training and tendency towards linear thinking that prevails in education, hiring sufficient and appropriate multidisciplinary mental health staffs contains both internal and external challenges. Allied mental health professionals often experience the guild dilemma of seeing other mental health colleagues as competitors for rare job positions in schools rather than as collaborators. Because schools do not typically require state licensure for masters' level mental health professionals to become school certified, many of those nonlicensed mental health professionals can practice only in school settings currently. Competition for school-based mental health positions is therefore high.

Despite the initial investment of time and money, however, raising the standards of school mental health services by hiring sufficient *licensed* and *school-certified* mental health teams has significant value. The cost of obtaining licensure and certification lies with the professionals seeking those qualifications, not the school systems that hire those clinicians. Although the salaries for some licensed and certified staff may be initially larger for the school system (such as doctoral-level psychologists who specialize in school psychology rather than masters level clinicians trained in school psychology), the preventive value of using higher standards should result in better outcomes. Comprehensive early identification and collaborative tracking of children at risk and/or with special needs by more highly credentialed professionals can help prevent costly out-of-district placements that occur when untreated problems escalate.

Careful systemic intervention can prevent children with unmet needs from becoming "invisible" students who later generate violent and other emergent situations for schools. As has been addressed in this book, where inpatient and other psychiatric services have diminished and become fragmented, far too many children have not had access to needed psychiatric residential and community services. Because schools have become the de facto setting for the mental health services that children receive, it seems wise to provide sufficient, well-qualified, and appropriate services in the setting where children spend the majority of their lives outside of the home. Licensed multidisciplinary mental health teams have functioned effectively in hospital and outpatient community settings for many decades. As community residential and inpatient mental health programs and services have become fragmented and less easily available to families with psychiatric needs, it makes sense to strengthen those services for children at risk closer to their educational home.

The multidisciplinary initiative mentioned in Chapter 8, "A Framework for Safe and Successful Schools," recommends eight "best practices" to create safe and successful schools. The practices operationalize the six policy recommendations and incorporate many systemic elements to comprehensively address school structure, climate, and culture. Their recommended best practices include the following elements:

1. Integrate all initiatives and services through collaboration among school staff and with community providers. This model seeks to reduce redundant services, frame behavioral services within the context of school culture and learning, and support strong leadership and whole-staff commitment.

2. Implement MTSS, which include universal screening, prevention and wellness promotion, implementing gradually more intense evidence-based interventions as needed, and monitoring student progress. PBIS and RtI are the primary methods of MTSS, but the goal is to also incorporate both school-employed and community-based services that are holistically integrated.

3. Improve access to school-based mental health supports, which includes addressing shortages.

4. Integrate school safety and crisis prevention, preparedness, response and recovery.

5. Balance physical and psychological safety.

6. Employ effective, positive school discipline.

7. Allow for consideration of context to design interventions that fit the school system's needs.

8. Acknowledge that sustainable and effective improvement takes time. (pp. 4–8)

It is significant that many national mental health and educational organizations as well as many state associations of school-based mental health professions have signed on as supporters of this multidisciplinary initiative. Clearly, a growing number of school-based professionals are calling for an effective, systemic, and multidisciplinary response to the rising rate of school violence, as well as for recognition of the importance of carefully identifying and servicing all children with mental health needs in schools.

Kazdin and Blase (2011) caution that exclusive focus on traditional face-to-face mental health treatment delivery is insufficient to address the unmet psychological needs of individuals across all settings. School leaders are increasingly recognizing the need to address social and emotional learning issues on several tiers of school structure beyond traditional individual and group counseling alone. Schools provide a rich milieu for designing collaborative mental health team support for behavior and academics as well as school climate. It is encouraging that the mental health disciplines are moving beyond guild concerns to address school safety and achievement in comprehensive ways through policy initiatives such as the *Framework*.

New initiatives recognize the need for teachers to understand and utilize social and emotional learning constructs in their classrooms that call for the collaborative expertise of mental health teams to help teachers implement these constructs. Yoder (2014) summarizes social and emotional learning (SEL) as "the educational process that focuses on the development of social-emotional competencies (which are) the skills, behavior and attitudes students and adults need to effectively manage their affective, cognitive and social behavior" (p. 2). SEL promotes five competencies that include self-awareness, self-management, social awareness, relationship management, and responsible decision making (Yoder, 2014).

Following the Sandy Hook tragedy, Connecticut adopted legislation in 2013 mandating that these constructs be incorporated into general teacher training in Connecticut state schools. A multidisciplinary team from CCSU was appointed to design teacher training modules for SEL to be incorporated into general education training. The next chapter addresses that initiative in more depth, but the role of multidisciplinary mental health teams is growing, and the need for collaboration is also increasing. It is a window of opportunity for mental health teams in schools to promote academic readiness and achievement.

Each profession in health care and education has developed its own vocabulary for communication that can be difficult to decipher outside of the unique setting where such services are delivered, however. This is why specific vocabulary from education, psychology, and health has been detailed in this book. Language differences can pose additional challenges for collaborative planning and service, which is the topic of the next section.

Language Boundaries and Barriers

In my classes at CCSU, I give a midterm exam that is composed of vocabulary terms used by clinicians and other professionals in medicine, mental health, and education. I ask my students to define several terms and to use those that vocabulary in a short response that demonstrates their understanding of it. I tell graduate students that it can be a disadvantage to participate in clinical or educational staff meetings with a "deer in the headlights" expression caused by unfamiliarity with language used at such meetings. Part of the preparation for that midterm exam is to become familiar with vocabulary from all three fields so that meaningful and productive collaboration can occur. All health care professions have jargon that is well understood within each field but less comprehensible outside of that professional circle. Several of these terms are listed and defined in Appendix B.

If approached respectfully, professional jargon can be learned, used, and appreciated. If not approached thoughtfully, language barriers among the professional groups can become constraints to collaborative assessment, planning, and service. Those constraints extend to students and families as well. Many families are intimidated by the language of assessment and planning procedures in schools. Family members can experience discomfort that challenges their confidence to participate in school meetings in informed ways.

This can also happen in medicine when families are dealing with acute and chronic health care conditions such as asthma, allergies, and obesity. Families interact with health care professionals who are trained to relay medical results and dictate prescriptive medications or procedures to address the illness without ensuring that those results and recommendations are understood or accepted. Medical appointments leave little time to ensure that patients and their families are willing and able to follow a treatment plan. Like education, the language of medicine is complex and has its jargon that is well understood by trained health care professionals, but it is not easily understood by all patients and families, and the hierarchical nature of medicine can be intimidating.

To address this constraint, medical family therapists have borrowed a practice called *motivational interviewing* (MI) from Miller and Rollnick (2013), who developed it as an early step to help people engage in treatment for alcoholism. McDaniel, Doherty, and Hepworth (2014) describe motivational interviewing as a form of structured counseling, where the interviewer works to draw out the side of the patient that wants to change, rather than using the prescriptive methods typically practiced in health care and education. The authors recommend MI as a communication technique that clinicians can use to engage patients more effectively. The goal is to clarify communication between medical providers and patients and families by minimizing jargon, listening for understanding about what treatment is offered, and offering support about the patient's readiness to obtain treatment. The strategy of MI is to "join with" rather than "prescribe to."

McDaniels et al. (2014) describe four principles in MI: (a) expressing empathy, (b) developing a discrepancy between an unhealthy behavior and one's broader values and goals, (c) using empathy with whatever resistance is shown to help the patient work through his or her ambivalence, and (c) supporting the patient's decision to make or not make change at that moment in time. The authors suggest that MI gives health care teams a common language to address challenges that patients and their families bring to health care settings.

The principles of MI can be adapted for schools, with mental health clinicians helping to teach those communication skills to school teams. Herman, Reinke, Frey, and Shepard (2013) published a valuable text for such adaptation. These authors describe how to apply MI across the K–12 spectrum, offering valuable suggestions about how to engage students, parents, and teachers in talking about the language of change. They address barriers to motivation and outline the four-stage process of engaging, focusing, evoking, and planning that is central to motivational interviewing. Their text outlines how to integrate principles of MI with various school programs that schools offer, to help increase the effectiveness of those programs. MI can be a powerful communication tool to bridge language constraints with families and among collaborative school teams. It can help mitigate communication challenges and can contribute to developing the PBIS elements that characterize a positive school climate. Just as immigrant populations develop impressive skills in new cultures by being willing and motivated to become bilingual, bridging cultural professional language barriers through effective communication techniques such as motivational interviewing can make collaborative team planning in schools positive and productive.

From Individual to Systems

Significant advances have occurred in education and in medicine as learning, resilience, illness, and wellness have been examined over the years. Medical progress has been made with such conditions as low birth weight, asthma, neurodevelopmental disorders, and many other conditions. Such advances have extended the life spans and quality of life of children with special needs in immeasurable ways.

The progress that has been made in special education regarding children's health, diagnoses and psychosocial functioning has also been exponential. For instance, a diagnosis of dyslexia no longer prohibits a child from academic achievement if that child receives early evaluation and support in school. Children with Down syndrome, who until 1975 could be prohibited from attending public schools, are now graduating from high school and training programs and moving into gainful employment. We have more tools to evaluate and support the growth of children than we have ever had in the United States. Analytical research of the individual variables necessary for children to grow and learn has helped to make that happen. Such linear attention to individual constraints to learning has clearly spurred the growth and success of education for students with special needs in the United States over the past half century.

The establishment of individual and specific special education services for each of the categories of disability has helped many children with those specific handicaps, but because the growth of special education services and budgets developed separately from general education, that separation has also contributed to the bifurcation of special education from mainstream education. This has inadvertently resulted in increased yet at times disparate, costly, ineffective, and inaccurate program planning and services for students, as well as painful labeling for students with special needs. As discussed in Chapter 6 on RtI, individualized special education evaluations are labor-intensive and are not necessarily appropriate for all students.

Broader assessment and systemic support for all students are what emerged from the No Child Left Behind Act of 2001 and the resulting RtI initiative in 2004. Educators have begun in the past decade to make the shift from simply adding individualized special services in linear fashion to integrating school-based academic and behavioral services efficiently for all students.

As was addressed in the last chapter, many variables contribute to achievement, and it is often the relative contribution of these variables that accounts for achievement variance among children. There is room for both linear and systemic thinking in diagnosis, treatment, and education of children. A child newly arrived from another country may, for instance, be dyslexic, undernourished, and bullied by other children. All of these variables affect that child's readiness and ability to achieve at school. It is the relative and the "both–and" components of assessment, treatment, and education that form the focus of this chapter. That is why the longitudinal overview of growth in systems (LOGS) model, discussed in Chapter 4, was developed—to help conceptualize and prioritize those components for students in education. The prioritization of those components may change over time as children grow, and outcome measures such as the one for RtI services illustrated in Chapter 6 can be used to measure program and service effectiveness.

School system resources and the ability and willingness to address those variables judiciously are also important variables to consider. Part of the challenge for health and education professionals is how to become "multilingual" in different ways of thinking. For health care professionals working in educational settings, learning to address health care needs in a setting where education is the major goal requires learning about school language and culture. For teachers, it means developing sophistication about how social and emotional regulation and learning are precursors for academic achievement.

It also means raising consciousness about the importance of teacher impact on positive school environment. Such a systemic para-digm shift broadens the scope to offers a wider pool of "best practice" and evidence-based opportunities in schools to meet student needs. It means that individualized programs and services need to be integrated with systemic thinking and planning for all students where appropri-ate so that school systems can work "smarter rather than harder" to promote student achievement.

Learning *when* to use different lenses to address those compo-nents as appropriate is another important variable to consider. For instance, using testing instruments to assess specific students' learning inefficiencies provides important linear ways to design individualized support for those students. Attending to broader variables such as bul-lying, teacher morale, and parental support to that assessment may expand the validity of that individual assessment. Employing broader systemic lenses where needed may potentially increase the success of the MTSS that those students receive.

Financial and Administrative Logistics: Money, Organization, and Capacity

A key consideration for school systems to foster student achieve-ment and resiliency is to create the multidisciplinary teams that work collaboratively to meet the needs of all students and families in afford-able ways. Schools vary across many dimensions. Educational needs in children also vary across dimensions such as ages of children served;

the particular needs that occur in towns or districts; types of rural, suburban, or urban communities served; cultures served; and available community resources and support. Initiatives evolve, schools run out of money, and key personnel often change during crucial times.

Research suggests that it is also more difficult to institute systemic initiatives such as PBIS in middle and high schools, where classes and courses are more specialized, than in elementary school, where education occurs more holistically (Horner et al., 2010; Sugai & Simonson, 2012). In school systems with scarce or dwindling financial resources, guild and language issues are further reinforced by real financial constraints. Furthermore, school administrators whose orientation has not been grounded in health influences on student achievement may also question the need for and costs involved in hiring licensed, certified mental health teams in schools. All of these administrative logistics must be addressed to build sustainability in collaborative team building.

Power, Blum, Guevara, Jones, and Leslie (2013) articulate some of the further barriers to collaboration between school systems and community-based primary care clinicians and health/mental health providers. They cite such administrative constraints for clinicians in private practice as the lack of reimbursement by insurance companies for collaboration. These codes are what are used to define specific services, and insurance companies use them to determine reimbursement. The passage of the No Child Left Behind Act in 2001 raised expectations for accountability in schools for both student and teacher performance. Meeting those expectations such as the Common Core Standards for students has challenged teachers' time and energy. For many, it has constrained their potential willingness to invest in collaboration.

Power et al. (2013) also cite the lack of current mechanisms to coordinate services among providers and educators. They view the laws governing the confidentiality of communication, a lack of continuity of care in both education and health care, as well as underresourced families and schools struggling with poverty as additional administrative and fiscal barriers to collaboration across systems.

Comer and Barlow (2014) cite additional constraints to broad implementation of evidence-based mental health treatment across community settings including schools. In their article on the role of specialty care in the delivery of psychological treatments, they address the crisis of availability, accessibility, and sustainability of psychological services across treatment milieus. They point out that overworked and underfunded community agencies are often challenged by high staff turnover and that the sustainability of individually administered evidence-based treatments is hard to organizationally maintain across settings. They also highlight the shortage of available mental health professionals, particularly in remote regions, and how that affects care for those with rare disorders such as Tourette disorder. Comer and Barlow (2014) call for better utilization of telehealth and other technology-based specialty care services to reach a broader range of individuals with mental health needs.

Solutions

Peek and Heinrich (1995) offer a way to view health care systems that fosters appreciation for the complexity of educational needs yet is adaptable for clinical service in schools. They describe "three world-views" of health care systems, which include the clinical enterprise, the operational management of the enterprise, and the financial components of the system. They argue that all three dimensions operate simultaneously and are necessary for success and sustainability of collaborative health care systems. If any dimension is not well managed, the health care system suffers. The clinical enterprise refers to the quality of the health care provided and the achievement of health goals. The operational dimension addresses the structures and procedures designed to help the system function on a day-to-day basis. The financial dimension addresses the value, costs, and accounting of the health care system.

Applying these dimensions to school systems, educating children, and promoting achievement are akin to improving health care quality and goals as the clinical dimension, and the operational dimension involves the policy and program structure that school administrators develop to best achieve education and achievement goals. The financial dimension is similar to health care, where staff salaries, budgets, and the costs of running the school system are developed and executed.

All stakeholders in education need to have an appreciation of these three worldviews and the time and energy required to integrate these three dimensions with fidelity and obtain "buy-in" from all stakeholders (school staff, families, and community). Innovative educational initiatives and frameworks such as SWPBS/PBIS and MTSS need careful clinical, administrative, and financial consideration as well as coordinated planning to be successful.

It takes time, data-driven collaboration, and effort to be successful. In her exploration of PBIS outcomes with school counselors across the United States, Donohue (2014) found that favorable results did not become apparent for the counselors in her research sample for 3 or more years after PBIS was initiated. That is, school climate and relationship and behavior variables among students, faculty, and administration are difficult to measure as well as slow to change. Results do not always emerge clearly until PBIS procedures and services are initiated and followed with fidelity for some time. Horner et al. (2010) echo this finding, calling PBIS

> a 2–3 year process of leadership team training intended to establish school capacity for adoption of effective and preventive behavioral interventions, high implementation integrity, continuous use of data for decision making, embedded professional development and coaching to establish predictable, consistent, positive and safe social contingencies at the whole school level. (p. 4)

These authors report that the features of PBIS draw from integrated research in the fields of education, mental health, and behavior analysis and that the real contributions of initiatives such as SWPBS and MTSS are their systemic focus on the whole school as the dimension of analysis and intervention, rather than solely traditional individualized work with students identified with special needs. Results of use of that systemic framework are complex to evaluate, but they are beginning to emerge.

Horner et al. (2010) report a growing body of evidence suggesting that implementation of PBIS is associated with reductions in problem behavior in students and the lowering of office discipline referrals and school suspensions. Although they caution that causal relationships are not yet to be inferred, the expectation is that improving social behaviors and school climate contributes to readiness and availability to instruction. That is, making school milieu more positive helps engage students more productively so that they can learn and improved academic outcomes can become more likely. These authors are beginning to affirm the positive effects of social and emotional learning in education.

Power et al. (2013) offer additional creative suggestions to bridge collaboration between schools and community health and mental health care practices. They call for the development of mechanisms to better coordinate care over time, including such innovations as colocation of primary and mental health care and health/mental health and education into the same setting. I referred to the problem of "leakage" in earlier chapters, where referred students and their families are not seen outside of schools due to financial, insurance, cultural, or other constraints. Connecticut and other states are currently experimenting with school-based health clinics, where health care professionals are placed and services are offered in schools within the school day. Connecticut also places many agency mental health clinicians from youth service bureaus and child guidance clinics in schools for ongoing mental health programs.

Another innovative Power et al. (2013) suggest is training specialists to link systems of care though case managers, with mental health and health care professionals from many disciplines trained to collaborate across systems to address complex needs. Such professionals could be colocated in schools or in easily accessible community practices and agencies, where school-based teams of mental health employees are not affordable.

These authors also view primary care practices and schools as major milieus for the delivery of mental health services, but they concur that the schools and community health care practices need systemic mechanisms to better coordinate the necessary care for families struggling with chronic health and mental health needs. They agree that the roles the two systems play can be complementary. Many schools are already equipped with technological tools for such collaboration, and many are adopting systems of providing and tracking behavioral health services through RtI, PBIS, and special education services.

It takes leadership, patience, and systemic commitment to develop and sustain collaborative school-based teams to create such system-wide services. It also takes an appreciation of the complexity involved in evolving health care to become more effective for children and families. However, the cost savings of such preventive "frontloading" as suggested in medical family therapy can be significant. Collaborative, preventive planning, and coordinated services can help mitigate the need for disciplinary measures and costly out-of-district placements for children at risk for behavioral and mental health disorders. The value-added quality of promoting positive school climate where students, teachers, and families are nurtured is immeasurable for all stakeholders and can prevent costly due process hearings, out-of-district placements, and other expensive litigation. Building collaborative health care teams in schools can build organizational capacity for both systems of care.

A key value of systemic collaboration is prevention. The RtI initiative identifies the three levels of primary, secondary, and tertiary prevention within three tiers of whole classroom, group, and individualized support services. Here is where academic and behavioral assistance is more comprehensively integrated into the education milieu through MTSS. I often tell my students, "We know we are successful by the statistics that do not happen." Prevention is difficult to measure, but it is critically important for successful student and teacher outcomes.

There are many complex logistic issues to manage, but the value of many professional eyes on children and the collective team support that it provides to families cannot be underestimated. Failure to plan can create an unbearable drain on the energy, hope, and creativity of the families and professionals working with these students. Conversely, proactive collaborative planning early in a child's life can prevent physical and mental health issues from developing or intensifying and can help avoid untold complications later. Conflict cannot always be avoided, but a collaborative "ounce of prevention" by a multidisciplinary school-based team can provide "a pound of proactive cure" for children with complex health and educational needs.

It is challenging in social science research to determine precisely what the relative contributions of each mental health discipline are to favorable educational outcomes. As has been described throughout this book, all mental health clinicians provide some degree of psychological support services to students, their families, and in schools. Their collective skills need to be fully utilized to help education move to the next level of promoting student achievement and resiliency.

The development of collaborative mental health teams in schools does not happen without careful planning. It takes good leadership within school systems, as well as careful and knowledgeable supervision to mentor new clinicians-in-training for school-based practice. The closing chapter is devoted to supervision.

ten

Supervision of School-Based
Mental Health Clinicians

Beyond traditional diagnostic, counseling, and psychotherapy skills that all mental health professionals are trained to provide, school-based mental health practice requires some unique skills. It is important for those who supervise mental health clinicians in schools to understand the components of those skills to provide appropriate supervision to mental health clinicians-in-training. American Psychological Association President Nadine Kaslow (2014) observed that many psychologists learn to supervise by emulating the lead of favored supervisors, by avoiding the negative behaviors of supervisors that were not helpful, or a combination of these. She advocates for the development of supervision as a distinct professional competency, organized on several domains that are addressed later in this chapter. Lee and Everett (2004) echo the need for integrated skill sets in supervision.

Some of the mental health professions have formal training tracks to prepare clinicians to become supervisors. Marriage and family therapists (MFTs), for instance, must obtain specific postgraduate training to become an American Association of Marriage and Family Therapy (AAMFT) approved supervisor, which is typically a 2-year process. To become AAMFT approved supervisors, licensed MFTs must undergo didactic and experiential training to achieve nine competency objectives, similar to the domains introduced by Kaslow. Supervisory training includes a review of the literature on supervision and submission of a "philosophy of supervision" paper. Approved supervisory update training is required every 5 years; it involves conducting updated current literature reviews and receiving training in supervisory mentorship and instruction in the development of supervisory contracts.

The profession of social work has traditionally included supervision in all of its clinical settings, and the discipline has a rich supervision history in adoptions, corrections, schools, social agencies, and other milieus where social workers practice. These examples of specific training in supervision illustrate supervisory initiatives and practices in mental health. They are meant to be illustrative rather than exhaustive summaries of how supervision is offered in the six mental health professions.

Each mental health organization has special interest groups within their professional organizations, and school-based practice is one of them. Supervisors become better able to mentor supervisees in knowledgeable ways when they are well oriented in specific practice milieus. Supervisors interested in school-based clinical work and supervision should contact their professional organization for more information and direction regarding school-based supervision. Contact information regarding the six mental health professions is included in Appendix A. State Department of Education websites are also included in Appendix A.

Although not all mental health disciplines require formal supervisory training, supervisory training is recognized as important to obtain where it is offered. The American Psychological Association recently created a Task Force to create guidelines for clinical supervision in psychology (DeAngelis, 2014). The goal is to make supervision a more evidence-based part of psychology training. Kaslow (2014) summarized seven domains of supervisory skill that the Task Force recommended as necessary for practice, particularly in new and unique settings such as school systems. The domains include supervisor competence; diversity competence; supervisory relationship competence; professionalism, and assessment/evaluation feedback competence regarding clinical growth and effectiveness in supervisees; addressing professional competence issues; and consideration of ethics, legal, and regulatory matters.

This chapter addresses both the skills that are needed for mental health school-based practice as well as the competencies that are important for supervisors of school-based mental health practitioners. The skill set mental health clinicians need includes the following components: obtaining the necessary coursework and training required for school certification by state departments of education across the United States, being well versed in systems theory as it applies to education, recognizing the *initial* role of mental health clinicians as "guests" in the milieu of education as they join school teams, and embracing collaborative multidisciplinary teams as a preferred mode of service to children and families.

Supervisors need to know the regulations about school-based certification in the state where their supervisees practice. Familiarity with systems-based school theory, developmental and learning theory, and regular as well as special education history is necessary for supervisors to support student learning in supervisees. It is important that supervisors recognize that mental health professionals are often initially viewed as "guests" in schools but that a major goal of supervision is to help steward the notion that good mental health is an essential prerequisite for learning. Supervisors need to help supervisees learn to participate in collaborative school teams to foster supervisees' growth as well as appreciate the value of multidisciplinary collaboration. Each of these components is addressed in the following sections.

Certification Laws and Regulations Regarding Coursework

Following passage of the first MFT school certification law in the United States in 2007, the Connecticut State Board of Education developed training and experience regulations required for school-based MFT certification that can serve as a reasonable model for all mental health practitioners in schools. MFT applicants for school certification must be licensed by the Department of Public Health in their specialty field, pass a Praxis Exam (required of all educators), fulfill a minimum of 300 of hours of supervised experience in public schools, and complete graduate coursework in special education, developmental, learning, and school-based systems theory. This coursework and experience is required in addition to the MFT graduate education required for state licensure with the Department of Public Health.

With the exception of the licensure and school-based systems theory requirements, these regulations are somewhat similar to those that other mental health clinicians (counselors, school psychologists and social workers) must meet to become school certified. Licensure by the state Public Health Department is not yet required for the other mental health groups who become certified by the state departments of education to practice in schools. However, the Connecticut State Department of Education expressed its intent to upgrade future standards for all mental health professionals who practice in schools when the certification law for MFTs was enacted in 2008. State licensure and certification are both important to raise the standards of mental health practice in schools to comprehensively address contemporary educational needs. Clinicians' supervisors need to be familiar with their particular state's requirements for certification for mental health professionals employed in schools.

Systems Orientation

School-based counselors, MFTs, psychologists, and social workers all need to be trained in systems theory to incorporate mental health practice successfully into contemporary U.S. schools. As has been discussed throughout this book, several new systemic support systems and initiatives have been developed in the past decade to efficiently track and provide needed attention to all children.

Multitiered systems of support (MTSS) initiatives are emerging to better serve students with special needs in education as well as create seamless layers of support for children in general education who are not formally identified with an Individualized Educational Plan/ Program (IEP). New behavioral and academic opportunities for children are becoming available to cultivate academic and behavioral resiliency through MTSS. These include both traditional individualized, group and family services, Response to Intervention (RtI)-based tiered layers of support for students in and out of in the classroom, as well as continuing education/professional development for teachers in social and emotional readiness for learning. System-wide team building and service opportunities are being initiated through PBIS across the country to ensure that safe, positive, and effective educational climates can position children better for academic learning and success.

These initiatives all require the systematic application of psychoeducational knowledge and skills to various subsystems of school culture. They represent a way to end the historic bifurcation of specialized services for children in need from children in general education, and they offer strong opportunities for mental health clinicians to play a recognized leadership role in schools. The goal is to address children's needs and readiness for academic and emotional/social growth by offering seamless and comprehensive systems of support "where children live" during the school day, in their educational home.

The goal of education is to teach children in the least restrictive environment (LRE), and the role of the mental health professional in schools is to apply psychological principles and practices to equip children to learn. At one point, a clinician's service may entail boosting parental support of a child's IEP with a first-generation immigrant family. At another time, the clinician may design a group for several students to encourage the development of social skills. The longitudinal overview of growth in systems or LOGS model, described in Chapter 4, offers a systemic framework to address the wide range of determinants of a child's functioning across time, and it illustrates versatile opportunities for mental health professionals to support a child's education across his or her school career. Supervisors need to comprehend the similarities and differences between targeted schoolbased practice and practice in other clinical settings to provide the support and direction that school-based mental health clinicians need to practice effectively in schools.

Mental Health Clinicians as "Guests" in Education

Unlike mental health agencies and clinics where assessment and individual, group, and family counseling/therapy are the primary service offered, the primary focus in education is educational achievement. The goals of mental health clinical services are to seek improvements in psychological, social, and emotional functioning, whereas the goals of education are promote achievement and academic resiliency. In many school systems where collaborative mental health teams have functioned successfully, mental health services are valued, and clinicians are perceived to be integral members of the school community. However many school systems have minimal or no mental health staff or have not yet incorporated mental health teams into the mainstream of their school culture.

A first step is to recognize that mental health professionals might be initially viewed as "guests" in the educational milieu, where their skill set and expertise might not be understood by other staff members. Traditional counseling/therapy services are often difficult to observe and appreciate because they are predicated on confidentiality. Often, wider, systemic interventions are required over time to introduce and market how mental health services can be effectively integrated into education, based on unique school needs and the particular talents of the mental health staff. To "graduate" from guest status to full participation in school culture and become fully assimilated into the educational community, mental health clinicians need to penetrate many layers of school subsystems. That takes time, creativity, and solid systemic supervision.

It has long been known that relationships cultivated over time promote collaboration. We find it useful for supervision to be provided at the school districts where students train and clinicians practice. For instance, in our school-based systems theory and practicum courses, my colleague Barbara Bennett and I travel to our students' school placements to observe meetings and provide supervision. Students report that the supervision has been useful for them and collaborative for their school colleagues. We have developed a strong appreciation for the educators we have met, the services they provide, and the difficult work they do. The number of districts where our students are placed has grown significantly since we began this practice. But there are many more who are still unfamiliar with MFT school-based practice and the value of multidisciplinary collaboration.

For instance, when we surveyed 154 teachers, special educators, allied mental health colleagues, support staff, and administrators in five urban and suburban schools shortly after MFT school certification in Connecticut (Laundy, Nelson, & Abucewicz, 2011), we learned that allied mental health clinicians and special educators were the specialists who reported the most familiarity with services that MFTs offer. The vast majority of respondents (72%) were aware of MFT services and 74% responded that MFTs help support teachers to improve student outcomes and are valued school employees.

In contrast, although *general* educators welcomed MFTs into their schools, they had the *least* familiarity (66%–69% agreement) with the roles that MFTs play with students who have identified special education needs as well as students within general education. Perhaps due to the bifurcation of special education from general education that continued to permeate many school systems across the country until RtI and PBIS began to be introduced, these findings may not be surprising. Because Connecticut was the first state to certify MFTs for school-based practice, we viewed this finding as reflecting the newness of MFT school certification in the United States as well.

In our study, we also addressed the temporal dimension of how opinions of MFT roles evolve over time. As MFT school certification was new at the end of the past decade, we compared opinions about MFT clinical services between schools where such services were new with schools where services had been operating for some time. Survey participants from one elementary school where MFTs have practiced for a decade "provided compelling evidence for the relationship between active multidisciplinary school collaboration over time and appreciation for clinical services and support for the roles MFTs play in education" (Laundy et al., 2011, pp. 9–10).

These findings may be replicated for mental health clinicians practicing in schools where RtI, PBIS, and MTSS are not yet fully incorporated into the culture of schools or where mental health services are new. As mentioned in previous chapters, it often takes a number of years of school commitment to RtI and PBIS initiatives with fidelity before results are known and appreciated.

Particularly for mental health clinicians-in-training, learning to integrate the clinical theory necessary for licensure with clinical practice in schools may be challenging where mental health service is not the major service provided in the educational milieu. Supervision entails both supporting new clinicians to integrate mental health theory and practice within the context of education and mentoring them into their respective mental health professions.

In our survey, we found that collaborative experience breeds better understanding about the various roles MFTs can play in schools, similar to Donohue's (2014) findings in her research with PBIS services and counselors. As collaborative support teams work with school systems to develop and execute PBIS, RtI, and MTSS services over time, the more teachers and administrators learn to value, understand, and utilize mental health services.

In schools where there are not yet enough school-based mental health employees, practicum, and internship positions can also be created in social agency settings to operate collaboratively with mental health school staff. As is a common practice in Connecticut, schools often use contracted support from youth service bureaus and child guidance clinics to create collaborative mental health services for students during the school day. In some instances, such collaboration has resulted in funding new mental health positions in schools and fostered the colocation of agency staff within local school buildings. Supervision of students and clinicians serving schools in this way entails focused attention to agency and school-based clinical practice.

Adapting mental health services to school milieus is a critical skill for mental health professionals to have, and supervisory support to develop this skill is necessary. Recognizing our beginning roles as "guests" in schools helps mental health professionals better join with school teams to start "where they are" to support student achievement and functioning. It helps pave the way for development of more traditional counseling and therapy as the time becomes ripe and opportunities are created to establish mainstream mental health programs and services in schools. Receiving direction and support from supervisors helps mental health clinicians-in-training achieve that goal more effectively with confidence.

Commitment to Multidisciplinary Exposure and Collaboration

A historic event occurred in Connecticut after the school violence tragedy in Newtown. As mentioned previously, Connecticut legislators in 2012 amended teacher preparation coursework to mandate the inclusion of training in evidence-based classroom and behavior management and assessment and social and emotional development and learning of children (House Bill No. 6292, Public Act No. 13-333, An Act Concerning Teacher Education Programs). The bifurcation of special education from general education will be further alleviated by this law. It will equip teachers in general education to collaborate with mental health teams in schools to better meet the needs of at-risk students.

A major feature of the CCSU faculty task force is the recognition of the importance of multidisciplinary input to student learning and achievement. The task force demonstrates the collective value and role that all academic and behavioral professions have in promoting student and teacher academic success. The multidisciplinary authors of "A Framework for Safe and Successful Schools" (Cohen, Vaillancourt, Rossen, & Pollitt, 2012) and many other partners in mental health and education also agree that collaborative multidisciplinary collaboration can offer powerful support to children in schools. Collaborative support is becoming better recognized as a potent resource to help children succeed, as well as a force over time to prevent "invisible" constraints to learning from festering into volatile and violent outcomes.

Borrowing from medical family therapy that was addressed in Chapter 5, such collaboration can foster effective "communion" with families and prevent burnout among students, families, and teachers when chronic needs present themselves. Supervisors need to have an appreciation of the potency of collaboration to provide the necessary support that mental health clinicians-in-training and those who are certified need to thrive in schools.

As another part of their school-based training, our CCSU MFT Program requires that our graduate students have school-based supervision by a mental health school employee belonging to another allied mental health profession. Our goal is to instill the value of multidisciplinary collaboration and teamwork from the time our students enter their school-based practicum experience. The combined supervision they receive from the MFT faculty helps reinforce both the socialization into the MFT profession and an appreciation of the value of multidisciplinary team building in education. It is designed to better prepare students for clinical school interventions across many systemic layers and with several allied school partners.

Supervisors can play a vital role to help supervisees learn how to function collaboratively in school settings. They can help clinical trainees learn the value, boundaries, and opportunities of multidisciplinary team collaboration, while helping shape the specific skills they need to practice in their mental health specialty field. Supervisors can help trainees to appreciate the "necessary redundancy" skills that all mental health clinicians possess while helping trainees cultivate the unique clinical skills that each has to offer within the educational milieu.

Summary of Training and Supervision Content

Mental health professionals make unique and timely contributions to school systems. Training in the multiple dimensions of individual, family, group, community, and cultural systems makes mental health professionals valuable assets to educators. It enables them to join educators as colleagues at many levels. Systems-based training equips mental health clinicians to normalize the need for mental health support in schools and collaborate with multidisciplinary teams, initiatives, and processes in education.

Counselors, MFTs, school psychologists, and school social workers address many varied clinical needs in schools. As has been mentioned several times in this text, each mental health profession has areas of overlapping clinical training as well as unique skills and areas of interest. It is important that supervisors model and show support for both our "necessary redundancies" as well as the unique skill base of each of our professions. Refer back to the mental health matrix in Chapter 2 (Figure 2.1) as an example of the shared and unique competencies of master's level school counselors, MFTs, school psychologists. and social workers. All mental health professions are also bound by their codes of ethics, which set the boundaries for scope of practice within each profession's range of competency.

Effective School Supervision

Finally, accessing supervisees' strengths to support growth at varied stages of training and development is a goal of all supervision. To support supervisees with varied backgrounds, we find it useful to supervise in groups, where diversity of experience is apparent and appreciated. Group members can model varied ways mental health clinicians can join children, families, and school colleagues to provide services.

For instance, one of our graduate MFT students is young and bilingual. She has endeared herself to students and young families in her urban school because of her enthusiasm and her command of languages. Another student is a postgraduate licensed MFT with teenagers of her own. She has designed a support group for grandparents raising grandchildren. She also has a background in art and has made invaluable contributions to "marketing" clinical services with flyers and a newsletter announcing those services. Another student has extensive background in education as a former school psychologist. She has contributed to the development of MFT collaborative practice with other school professionals, helping ease some of the cultural anxiety new teachers experience as they encounter students from other cultures. A fourth graduate MFT is a licensed and seasoned practitioner who has served as a mentor for newer clinicians. Their varied skills have worked synergistically over time, and in a few short years, MFT services grew into a recognized department in that urban school system.

Connecticut now ensures that schools have access to a full range of behavioral health services by certifying four of the allied mental health clinical groups including MFTs, school counselors, school psychologists, and social workers. Licensed psychiatrists and advanced practice nurses provide the other two mental health professional services by contract. Many more states are initiating similar legislation. It is timely and necessary to provide mental health clinicians with training and supervision opportunities in schools so that they can function effectively in education as certified practitioners. It is important to train supervisors in school-based work as well to competently and ethically mentor mental health clinicians into a choice of school-based clinical practice. Raising the standards of collaborative mental health practice in schools through licensure, certification, and building an evidence base for best practices may not only more effectively address the apparent as well as invisible needs of vulnerable students in education. It may prevent untold tragedy.

In the later decades of the 20th century, exponential progress has been made in health care and education, which more clearly reveals the variables that help children grow and thrive. We have learned a great deal about the physical, neuropsychological, and psychosocial constraints that challenge that growth. Multidisciplinary school-based teams who integrate those elements with learning to collaboratively support children's ability to grow and achieve are a generative and potent resource for education. This book was written to help mental health clinicians operationalize their collective strengths to help teachers foster more comprehensive and effective education. The time is ripe for the development of the educational home in school systems across the United States.

Appendix A

Commonly Used Assessments and
Assessment Company Index

This appendix includes a sampling of several psychological assessment companies in the United States. It also includes the websites of organizations that can provide helpful assessment and other data collection information. The list is meant to be illustrative rather than exhaustive, and the reader is encouraged to research other avenues for data collection instruments.

Assessment Instruments

Behavioral screening measures.

Behavioral Assessment Scale for Children (BASC)

Conners Comprehensive Behavior Rating Scales (CBRS)

Developmental Profile, Third Edition (DP–3)

Miller Assessment for Preschoolers (MAP)

Parent-Child Relationship Inventory (PCRI)

Pervasive Developmental Disability Behavioral Inventory (PDDBI)

Intelligence/aptitude.

Kaufman Assessment Battery for Children, Second Edition (KABC–II)

Kaufman Brief Intelligence Test (K–BIT)

Wechsler Abbreviated Scale of Intelligence (WASI)

Wechsler Intelligence Scale for Children—V (WISC–V)

Woodcock–Johnson Tests of Cognitive Abilities (WJ–IV)

Achievement.

Kaufman Test of Educational Achievement (K–TEA)

Wechsler Individual Achievement Test, Third Edition (WIAT–III)

Woodcock–Johnson IV (WJ–IV) Tests of Achievement

Adaptive Behavior.

Adaptive Behavior Assessment System, Second Edition (ABAS–II)

Vineland Adaptive Behavior Scales

Personality (Projective) Assessment.

House-Tree-Person

Rorschach

Sentence Completion Test

Thematic Apperception Test (TAT)

Specialized Assessments.

Adaptive Behavior Interview (ADI)

Autism Diagnostic Observation Schedule, Second Edition (ADOS–2)

Beery–Buktenica Developmental Test of Visual-Motor Integration, Sixth Edition (VMI)

Bender Visual-Motor Gestalt Test, Second Edition (Bender–Gestalt II)

Parent–Child Relationship Inventory (PCRI)

Parent Report Card for children and adolescents

Parenting Stress Index, Fourth Edition (PSI–4)

There are many more specialized assessments that target specific areas of learning and aptitude. The school team can access these instruments as they are relevant for their particular school system's needs. Instruments can be accessed from the following assessment companies.

Assessment Companies

American Guidance Service (AGS)

AGS provides assessment and educational tools designed for mental health professionals, paraprofessionals, teachers and parents to effectively address psychological and behavioral issues affecting children and adolescents.

Contact

4201 Woodland Road, P.O. Box 99, Circle Pines, MN 55014-1796

Tel: (800) 328-2560

Website: http://www.agsnet.com

Cross-Cutting Diagnostic Measures (from the *DSM–5*; American Psychiatric Association, 2013)

Contact

American Psychiatric Association, 1000 Wilson Blvd., Ste. 1825; Arlington, VA. 22209-3901

Tel: (703) 907-7300

Website: www.psychiatry.org/dsm5

PAR, Inc.

PAR publishes psychological materials for intelligence, achievement, adaptive behavior, career, and personality assessment and includes assessment materials for behavioral and health care disorders such as autism, depression, trauma, eating disorders, and chronic pain.

Contact

16204 North Florida Avenue, Lutz, FL 33549.

Tel: 800-331-8378

Website: *www.parinc.com*

Pearson Assessments

Pearson publishes psychological assessment materials for intelligence, achievement, adaptive behavior, vocational, early childhood functioning. It also administers AIMSweb, an RtI assessment system to track student progress.

Contact

19500 Bulverde Road, San Antonio, Texas 78259

Tel: (800) 627-7271

Website: *www.pearsonassessments.com*/PearsonClinical.com/Psychecatalog

PRO-ED, Inc.

PRO-ED is a publisher of
- standardized tests (assessments)
- books (resource and reference texts)
- curricular and therapy materials
- professional journals

In the following areas:
- Speech-language pathology
- Special education and rehabilitation

- Psychology and counseling
- Occupational and physical therapy
- Early childhood

Contact

8700 Shoal Creek Boulevard, Austin, TX 78757-6897

Tel: 800-897-3202

Website: http://www.proedinc.com

Riverside Publishing, a Division of Houghton Mifflin Harcourt

Riverside Publishing provides educational and clinical and special needs assessment tools for mental health professionals and educators.

Contact

3800 Golf Road, Suite 200, Rolling Meadows, Illinois 60008

Web site: www.riversidepublishing.com

WPS, formerly Western Psychological Services

WPS provides resources for mental health professionals (particularly psychologists), as well as occupational therapists, speech-language pathologists, and special educators.

Contact

625 Alaska Avenue, Torrance, CA 90503

Tel: (800) 648-8857

Website: www.wpspublish.com

Appendix B

Resources for Special Education, RtI, and

PBIS/SWPBIS Programs and Services

U.S. Department of Education: To access your state's department of education, visit www.ed.gov for a listing of each state's contact information.

Connecticut State Department of Education

The Connecticut State Department of Education can be accessed for valuable information about certification regulations and useful special and general education links.

The contact information is: Connecticut Department of Education, State Office Building: 165 Capitol Avenue, Hartford, CT 06106.

Tel: 860-713-6543; Toll-Free: (800) 465-4014; Fax: (860) 713-7001

Website: http://www.sde.ct.gov

Framework for Safe and Successful Schools

This multidisciplinary initiative can be accessed at www.nasponline.org/schoolsafetyframework. The contact information is: National Association of School Psychologists, 4340 West Highway, Ste. 402l, Bethesda, MD. 20814. Tel: (866) 331-NASP

National Center on Time and Learning

This is an innovative initiative in New England designed to improve outcomes of underachieving schools by extending the school day and enriching the school curriculum. It can be accessed at the National Center on Time & Learning 24 School Street, 3rd Floor, Boston, MA

02108. Tel: (617) 378-3900. Their web address is: www.timeandlearning.org

Positive Behavior Interventions and Supports (PBIS)

Housed in Oregon, the PBIS implementation team has developed surveys, evaluations, and other research instruments to develop, track, and evaluate PBIS programs in schools across the United States. The center and can be accessed at www. pbis.org.

Social and Emotional Learning

This initiative promotes social and emotional learning to enhance academic achievement in school. The contact information is: Collaborative for Academic, Social, and Emotional Learning (CASEL), 815 W. Van Buren St. Ste. 210, Chicago, IL 60607-3567. Tel: 312-226-3770

National Organizations for the Mental Health Professions

American Association for Marriage and Family Therapy: www.AAMFT.org

112 South Alfred Street; Alfred, VA 22314-3061. Tel: (703) 838-9808
American Psychiatric Association: www.psych.org

1000 Wilson Blvd., Ste. 1825; Arlington, VA. 22209-3901. Tel: (703) 907-7300
American Psychological Association: www.apa.org

750 First St. NE; Washington, D.C. 20002-4242. Tel: (800) 374-2721
American School Counselor Association: ASCA: www.NSCA.org

1101 King St., Ste. 625; Alexandria, VA 22314. Tel: (703) 683-ASCA
National Association of School Nurses: www.nasn@nasn.org

1100 Wayne Ave., #925; Silver Spring, MD 20910 Tel: (240) 821-1130
National Association of School Psychology: www. nasponline.org

4340 East West Hwy., Ste. 402; Bethesda, MD 20814. Tel: (301) 657-0270
National Association of Social Workers: www.naswdc.org

750 First Street, NE, Ste. 700; Washington, DC 20002. Tel: (202) 408-8600

Appendix C

Glossary of Terms

The following are some of the more frequent terms used by health care providers and educators. The list is not intended to be exhaustive but rather a representative sampling of the language that educators and health care providers use. Educators and clinicians-in-training may find it useful to help bridge some of the language barriers in both fields and promote the integration of health care within educational settings. Sources used for this glossary are included at the end of the glossary as well as in the reference list.

Accommodation

Without changing the content standards or expectations for the general education curriculum, this concept creates an *equal opportunity* for children to "show what they know" by changing instruction, materials or tasks to better support what a child is learning.

Adequate Yearly Progress (AYP)

This term refers to the determination of whether a student is progressing through his or her education curriculum sufficiently.

Baseline

In education, this refers to the level of student performance before interventions. In health care, it refers to an initial measurement of one's functioning as a comparison point over time.

Behavioral Intervention Plan (BIP)

Similar to an Individual Education Plan in special education, this refers to a plan developed under Response to Intervention in which children's targeted behaviors that interfere with learning and achievement are identified.

Benchmarks

These are the expected outcomes and goals for students within a specific domain (reading, math, etc.) or grade within the course of the school year. These benchmarks set the norm for designing Response to Intervention and other services.

BID. *See* Quaque Die

Consult Model/Process

This is the process created by the No Child Left Behind Act through the Response to Intervention initiative. It is designed to provide early, preventive, and positive interventions to students who are struggling in specific areas, based on data collected about student functioning and achievement. The consult process identifies the specific area of concern and develops and tracks interventions, assessments, and strategies to promote student growth. Only when and if interventions do not meet with success are students then referred for more formal special education assessment.

Current Procedural Terminology (CPT)

This health care term refers to codes used for the specific service a health care clinician is providing to a patient/client. In mental health, the codes include individualized, group, and family therapy; diagnosis; and collaboration services. There are additional CPT codes for psychologists, psychological, and neuropsychological testing codes.

Curriculum-Based Measures (CBMs)

These are the monitoring measures to gauge student progress. These measures can be locally developed, but generic CBMs are also available for free download or purchase from such sources as DIBELS or AIMSweb.

Data or Consult Teams

These are the multidisciplinary teams of school professionals who collect and analyze data and make decisions about student progress under Response to Intervention. Teams operate across district, school, and grade levels as well as curriculum content areas.

Diagnosis (Dx)

This health care term refers to the condition that providers confer on a patient/client based on signs and symptoms. The *Diagnostic and Statistical Manual of Mental Disorders* (*DSM–5*), an American Psychiatric Association (2013) publication, is in process of aligning itself more with the World Health Organization's *International Classification of Diseases*, which includes both medical and psychiatric diagnoses. Whereas former editions of the *DSM* used six axes to address the variables that determine a diagnosis, the *DSM-5* bases diagnosis on only one axis, which is designed to align with the *ICD* use of a single axis. Psychiatric diagnosis in *DSM-5* is now organized in spectrum fashion into categories of mild, moderate, and severe.

Differentiated Instruction

This refers to a Response to Intervention approach within general education that includes using various ways to meet the differing needs of students (visual, auditory, hands-on, small group, etc.). It is used as an important part of Tier I and II instruction and involves using varied teaching materials and differing ways of presenting teaching elements to maximize teaching opportunities for children with varied learning needs.

Due Process

This is the process mandated by the Individuals With Disabilities Education Act (IDEA) that requires schools and families to work together to determine the most appropriate educational plan and program for children with special needs.

Emotionally Disturbed (ED)

A broad educational category of disability that includes the majority of emotionally handicapping conditions which interfere with learning and achievement in public education.

English as a Second Language (ESL)

This is a category of need and special services that are provided to students who are learning English after learning a mother language in another country.

Evidence Based

To provide the best treatment and practice base for disorders, building a research-based rationale for that practice is critical. Evidence-based practice represents a shift in both education and health care from documenting that services are being provided to ensuring that those services actually work.

Family Education Rights and Privacy Act (FERPA)

This is a 1974 federal act that establishes the standards that schools must follow to manage student records. Parents have the right to inspect student records for accuracy, and schools must have written parent permission to release school records to outside agencies.

504 Plan

This plan is a result of Part H, an amendment to Public Law 94-142, the special education law. Part H guarantees access to school-based support for all children with physical and other health-related handicaps. It requires less formal assessment and tracking than Individualized Education Plans.

Flexible Grouping

Adapting grouping of students flexibly to the changes in instructional needs of individual students over time.

Free and Appropriate Public Education (FAPE)

This term refers to what is guaranteed by Public Law 94-142. It is the language of the special education law that mandates free and specific appropriate educational services for children who need special education services.

Functional Behavioral Assessment (FBA)

This refers to an assessment made by a special education professional, a behavioral consultant or mental health professional. It targets specific behaviors that interfere with learning and achievement. These behaviors are then incorporated into a Behavior Intervention Plan in Response to Intervention or special education to track the progress of interventions and behaviors over time.

Health Insurance Portability and Accountability Act (HIPAA)

This 1996 federal act set national standards to protect the confidentiality of health records. The law addresses how and when confidential patient information can be disclosed. It is designed to protect privacy rights while insuring high-quality health care and protecting public health and well-being.

Homogeneous Grouping

Grouping students with like instructional needs together (such as spelling, reading, and math groups).

Hora Somni (HS)

This is a Latin term meaning "at bedtime," referring to the time when a prescribed medication should be ingested.

Individual Education Plan/Program (IEP)

This IDEA term refers to services offered to children aged 3 to 21 years. It is a specific special education plan devised for each student determined to need special education services and is a legal document.

Individualized Family Service Plans (IFSP)

This IDEA term refers to the service plan offered to children from birth to 3 years of age with special needs. It refers to the special education plan designed for families with small children who have been identified with special needs early in their lives. It includes children with developmental disabilities and handicaps who have received early diagnoses.

Individualized Transition Plan (ITP)

This IDEA term refers to the transitional education plan created for students with aged 16 to 21 who need extended services following their high school graduation. It follows the legal guidelines of an IEP.

Individuals With Disabilities Education Act (IDEA)

This 1975 federal law is another term for Public Law 94-142, which provided national support for the development of special education services in the United States. It has been reauthorized several times with amendments to ensure that children with special learning needs are allowed access to public education.

Intellectual Disability (ID)

This term replaces the antiquated term *mental retardation.* It refers to children, adolescents, and adults with developmental disabilities.

International Classification of Diseases, Ninth and Tenth Revisions (ICD)

This is the World Health Organization's classification of diseases that includes medical as well as psychiatric diagnoses (by contrast, the *Diagnostic and Statistical Manual of Mental Disorders* [*DSM*] includes only psychiatric diagnoses). The latest version of the DSM, *DSM–5*, is designed to coincide better with *ICD* terminology to promote more universal understanding of diseases and disorders.

Learning Disability (LD)

A learning disability can occur in any one or a combination of the five senses: sight, hearing, taste, smell, and touch. LDs can be manifested as a receptive (blindness) or an expressive (cerebral palsy) learning disability or a combination of these.

Least Restrictive Environment (LRE)

This is a special education requirement that children must be provided education in the environment that provides the most conducive milieu for learning based on their special education needs. The goal is to provide the best education possible for student with special needs without unduly restricting the milieu where they learn.

Modification

An actual change in the curriculum content standards or expectations that affects what a student learns and the degree to which the student is expected to demonstrate mastery. Those changes can involve either the amount of concepts or performance expectations within a given grade level standard, or a change in the level of performance standard.

Multitiered Systems of Support (MTSS)

This term refers to the growing need for support for school safety and achievement at many levels of school system operations. MTSS is a term utilized by a multidisciplinary group of education/administration and school mental health professionals to promote school safety and success.

No Child Left Behind (NCLB)

This legislation, enacted in 2001, shifted emphasis from mandating that specific curricular requirements occur to documenting that student learning is occurring, based on evidence-based learning and practice.

Nonverbal Learning Disability (NLVD)

This is a pervasive developmental disability that affects many areas of the brain, primarily the right hemisphere. Many students with high functioning autism and Asperger syndrome exhibit symptoms of an NLVD. NLVD is neuropsychological in origin and means that skills relating to sequential processing skills (such as reading) are better developed than those skills needed for processing and integrate stimuli that are perceived simultaneously.

Not Otherwise Specified (NOS)

This is a psychiatric term that is used as a modifier for diagnoses when not all criteria for a full diagnosis are fulfilled. This term has been replaced in the *DSM–5* with the term "Conditions Not Elsewhere

Classified" (CNEC). It means that a client or patient may exhibit *features* or *symptoms* of a disorder but not sufficiently to make a full diagnosis of that disorder.

Occupational Therapist (OT)

Health care professionals who are often part of multidisciplinary teams in public schools. They provide specialized therapeutic services to help students learn, improve, or master activities of daily living to students who need them.

Other Health Impaired (OHI)

This education classification category includes several chronic health conditions such as obesity, cancer, and asthma. It also includes attention-deficit/hyperactivity disorders (ADHDs).

Pervasive Developmental Disability (PDD)

A pervasive developmental disability is one that challenges a person over many domains in his or her life and lasts as a chronic disorder over the course of one's life.

Physical Therapist (PT)

Health care professionals who are often members of multidisciplinary teams in public schools. PTs provide specialized therapeutic services to remediate physical impairments, disabilities, or limitations to students who need them.

Planning and Placement Team (PPT)

The primary assessment and program vehicle for special education. This school team meets to assess student needs, determine and categorize eligibility for special education, and track student progress over time.

Positive Behavioral Support (PBS) or Positive Behavioral Interventions and Supports (PBIS)

This represents an approach to changing behaviors that emphasizes students' capabilities and strengths. The initiative puts a positive focus on what students can do, as well as creates opportunities for improving the quality of school climate.

Positive School Discipline

Establishing a school climate that is clear, consistent, nonpunitive (as in zero tolerance), and reinforces positive behaviors. The goals are to promote optimal learning environments in schools and promote school safety and achievement.

Progress Monitoring

This refers to using data teams and data to track student progress.

Pro Re Nata (PRN)

This is a Latin term meaning "as circumstances require," or "as needed." It refers to the frequency with which medication can or should be taken.

Public Law 94-142 (P.L.94-142)

Established in 1975, P.L. 94-142 established the federal right of all children to a public education in the least restrictive environment possible. It the major special education law that mandated schools to provide academic services and accommodations to all children, regardless of their cultural, health, or cognitive needs.

QID. *See* Quaque Die

Quaque Die (QD), Bis in Die (BID), Ter in Die (TID), and Quarter in Die (QID)

These are Latin terms that refer to the frequency by which medication should be ingested. The terms include every day, twice daily, thrice daily, and four times daily.

Rule Out (R/O)

This is a term derived from medicine that refers to eliminating all competing hypotheses about a disorder before a diagnosis is reached. Ideally, the rule-out process continues until clarity is reached, so that appropriate and sufficient treatment can occur.

Response to Intervention (RtI)

This is a national initiative that developed from the No Child Left Behind Act of 2001 in which more accountability for student achievement and more support within general education were established. It is designed to establish a system of tiered services and tracking within general education to help all students succeed in school, not solely those children who had formal special education support. The RtI initiative includes three increasing levels of intervention that include both academic and behavioral dimensions. Close monitoring of interventions across these levels is designed to better document and streamline the provision of services for children in need of services to boost their achievement. *See also* Tier I, Tier II, and Tier III.

School Resource Officer (SRO)

This is a school security professional who optimally can support positive school discipline in the way a crossing guard does. An SRO works with students and school professionals to ensure school safety.

Scientific Research-Based Interventions (SRBI)

Connecticut's term for implementing the No Child Left Behind Act. It refers to using instructional practices and interventions for students that have been researched and determined to improve student learning outcomes.

School Wide Positive Behavioral Interventions and Supports (SWPBIS). See Positive Behavioral Interventions and Supports

Severely Emotionally Disturbed (SED)

This educational classification category is reserved for a small number of children with psychological/behavioral disorders with severe symptoms.

Social-Emotional Learning

This term refers to learning that promotes self-awareness, the ability to regulate emotions and behavior, as well as social awareness and competency regarding responsible decision making and relationship management.

Speech and Language Pathologist (SLP)

Health care professionals who are part of multidisciplinary teams that in public schools and provide specialized speech and language services to students who need them.

TID. *See* Quaque Die

Tier I

The first level of RtI support, using the core general education curriculum with differentiated instruction (academic and behavioral supports as needed) for all students.

Tier II

The second level of RtI support for students not achieving expected educational benchmarks. This level provides short-term individual and small group interventions within the general education system.

Tier III

The third, most intensive and individualized short-term intervention system of support for students not achieving benchmarks after receiving Tier I and II support. Tier III interventions fall within the last tier of general education before a referral for special education assessment and intervention is made.

Universal Common Assessments

Those assessments given routinely to all students in their grades to assess progress towards educational benchmarks. These include such assessments as mastery tests and common core testing that are similar across grades, districts, and states.

Sources for Appendix B

Alexander, K., & Alexander, M. D. (2012). *American public school law* (8th ed.). Belmont, CA: Wadsworth CENGAGE Learning: www.centgage.com

American Association for Marriage and Family Therapy: www.aamft.org

American Psychiatric Association: www.psychiatry.org

American Psychological Association: www.apa.org

American School Counselor Association: www.schoolcounselor.org

American Speech and Language Hearing Association: www.asha.org

Connecticut Parent Advocacy Center, Inc: www.cpacinc.org

Connecticut State Department of Education, Bureau of Special Education materials (2014): www.ct.gov/sde; www.sde.ct.gov/sde/cwp/view.asp?a=2626&q=320730

Cowan, K. C., Vaillancourt, K. I., Rossen, E., & Pollitt, K. (2013). Executive summary. In *A framework for safe and successful schools* [Brief]. Bethesda, MD: National Association of School Psychologists. Retrieved from http://www.nasponline.org/resources/handouts/Framework_for_Safe_and_Successful_School_Environments.pdf

Merriam-Webster's Collegiate Dictionary. (2002). Springfield, MA: Merriam-Webster.

National Association of School Nurses: https://www.nasn.org

National Association for School Psychologists: www.nasponline.org

National Association of Social Workers: www.naswdc.org

Special Education Resource Center (SERC): www.ctserc.org

Taber's Cyclopedic Medical Dictionary. (1997). Philadelphia: F.A. Davis Company.

Yoder, N. (2014, January). *Teaching the whole child: Instructional practices that support social and emotional learning in three teacher evaluation frameworks* (rev. ed.; Research to Practice Brief). Washington, DC: Center on Great Teachers & Leaders at American Institutes for Research. Retrieved from http://www.gtlcenter.org/sites/default/files/TeachingtheWholeChild.pdf

References

American Academy of Family Physicians, American Academy of Pediatrics, American College of Physicians, & American Osteopathic Association. (2007, March). *Joint principles of the patient-centered medical home.* Retrieved from www.medicalhomeinfo.org/Joint20%statement.pdf

American Association of Marriage and Family Therapy. (2000). *Readings in family therapy supervision.* Alexandria, VA.

American Psychiatric Association. (2000). *Diagnostic and statistical manual of mental disorders, Fourth Edition, Text Revision (DSM–IV–TR).* Washington, DC: Author.

American Psychiatric Association. (2013). *Diagnostic and statistical manual of mental disorders, Fifth Edition (DSM–5).* Washington, DC: Author. Retrieved from http://dx.doi.org/10.1176/appi.books.9780890425596.dsm14

Anderson, W., Chitwood, S., & Hayden, D. (1997). *Negotiating the special education maze: A guide for parents and teachers.* Bethesda, MD: Woodbine House.

Austin, A. E., & Herrick, W. W. B. (2014, May). *The effect of adverse childhood experiences on adult health: 2012 North Carolina Behavioral Risk Factor Surveillance System Survey* (SCHS Studies: A Publication of the State Center for Health Statistics; No. 167). Retrieved from http://www.schs.state.nc.us/schs/pdf/SCHS_Study_167_FIN_20140505.pdf

Baio, J. (2014, March). *Prevalence of autism spectrum disorder among children aged years- autism and developmental disabilities monitoring network, 11 sites, United States, 2010. 63* (SS02), 1–21. Retrieved from http://www.cdc.gov/ncbdd/autism/data.html

Baron-Cohen, S., Ring, H. A., Bullmore, E. T., Wheelwright, S., Ashwin, C. Y., & Williams, S. C. R. (2000). The amygdala theory of autism. *Neuroscience & Biobehavioral Reviews, 24,* 355–364.

Barron, J. (2013, October 25). Almost a year after massacre Newtown begins razing Sandy Hook School. *The New York Times.* Retrieved from http://www.nytimes.com/2013/10/26/nyregion/almost-a-year-after-massacre-newtown-begins-razing-sandy-hook.html?_r=0

Bateson, G. (1972). *Steps to an ecology of mind: Collected essays in anthropology, psychiatry, Evolution and epistemology.* Northvale, NJ: Jason Aaronson.

Beck, M. (2015, January 12). Tot therapy: Psychiatrists join up with pediatricians: Families are more receptive to treatment in a pediatrician's office than in a mental-health clinic. *The Wall Street Journal.* Retrieved from http://www.wsj.com/articles/tot-therapy-psychiatrists-join-up-with-pediatricians-1421105535)

Becvar, D. S., & Becvar, R. J. (2008). *Family therapy: A systemic integration* (7th ed.). New York, NY: Allyn & Bacon.

Bialicki, C. (2004, October). Correspondence sent to State of Connecticut House of Representatives, Honorable Brian O'Connor, from Ralph Cohen and Kathleen Laundy. Copy in possession of Kathleen C. Laundy.

Biederman, J., Lopez, F. A., Boellner, S. W., & Chandler, M. C. (2002). A randomized, double-blind, placebo-controlled, parallel-group study of SL1381 (AdderallXR) in children with attention-deficit/hyperactivity disorder. *Pediatrics, 110,* 258–266.

Boyd-Franklin, N., & Hafer Bry, B. (2000). *Reaching out in family therapy: Home-based, school, and community interventions.* New York, NY: Guilford Press.

Boyle, C. A., Boulet, S., Schieve, L. A., Cohen, R. A., Blumberg, S. J., Yeargin-Allsopp, M., . . . Kigan, M.D. (2011). Trends in the prevalence of developmental disabilities in US children, 1997–2008. *Pediatrics, 127,* 1034–1042. doi: 10.1542/peds.2010-2989

Bradley, R., Danielson, L. C., & Hallahan, D. P. (2002). Identification of learning disabilities:

Research to practice. Washington, DC: Lawrence Erlbaum. Retrieved from www.apbs.org/new_apbs/interventionreferences.aspx

Breunlin, D. D., Schwartz, R. C., & Mac Kune-Karrer, B. (1997). *Metaframeworks: Transcending the models of family therapy.* San Francisco, CA: Jossey-Bass.

Brooks, M. (2014, January 30). Top 100 selling drugs of 2013. *Medscape Medical News.* Retrieved from http://www.medscape.com/viewarticle/820011

Brotman, M. A., Rich, B. A., Guyer, A. E., Lunsford, J. R., Horsey, S. E., Reising, M. M., . . . Leibenluft, E. (2010). Amygdala activation during emotion processing of neutral faces in children with severe mood dysregulation versus ADHD or bipolar disorder. *American Journal of Psychiatry, 167,* 61–69.

Brown v. Board of Education of Topeka, 347 U.S. 483 (1954).

Brown, R. T., Antonuccio, D. O., Dupaul, G. J., Fristad, M. A., King, C.A., Leslie, L. K., . . . Vitiello, B. (2008). *Childhood mental health disorders: Evidence base and contextual factors for psychosocial, psychopharmacological, and combined interventions.* Washington, DC: American Psychological Association.

Campbell, T., & McDaniel, S. (1987). Applying a systems approach to common medical problems. In M. Croach & L. Roberts (Eds.), *The family in medical practice: A family system primer* (pp. 112–139) Berlin and Heidelberg, Germany: Springer-Verlag.

Carr, A. (2000). Evidence-based practice in family therapy and systemic consultation: I. Child-focused problems. *Journal of Family Therapy, 22,* 29–60.

Centers for Disease Control and Prevention. (2014). CDC estimates 1 in 68 children has been identified with autism spectrum disorder. Retrieved from http://www.cdc.gov/media/releases/2014/p0327-autism-spectrum-disorder.html

Comer, J. S., & Barlow, D. S. (2014). The occasional case against broad dissemination and implementation: Retaining a role for specialty care in the delivery of psychological treatments. *American Psychologist, 69*, 1–18. doi: 10.1037/a0033582.

Connecticut State Department of Education, Bureau of School and District Improvement. (2008, February). *Using scientific research–based interventions: Improving education for all students.* Retrieved from http://www.sde.ct.gov/sde/lib/sde/pdf/pressroom/SRBI

Cowan, K. C., Vaillancourt, K. I., Rossen, E., & Pollitt, K. (2013). Executive summary. In *A framework for safe and successful schools* [Brief]. Bethesda, MD: National Association of School Psychologists. Retrieved from http://www.nasponline.org/resources/handouts/Framework_for_Safe_and_Successful_School_Environments.pdf

DeAngelis, T. (2014). Help, support, advice & guidance. *Monitor on Psychology, 45*, 43–45.

Doherty, W. J., & Baird, M. A. (1987). *Family-centered medical care: A clinical casebook.* New York, NY: Guilford Press.

Donohue, M. D. (2014). *Implementing School Wide Positive Behavioral Interventions and Supports (SWPBIS): School counselors' perceptions of student outcomes, school climate and professional effectiveness.* Unpublished doctoral dissertation, University of Connecticut, Storrs.

Donovan, M. S., & Cross, C.T. (Eds.). (2002). Minority students in gifted and special education. *The National Research Council Panel on Minority Overrepresentation in special Education.* Washington, DC: National Academy Press.

Education for All Handicapped Children Act of 1975. Pub. L. 94-142. (1975).

Family Policy Compliance Office, U.S. Department of Education (2015). Retrieved from www2.ed.gov/policy/gen/guid/fpco/index.html

Feinstein, S. (Ed.). (2014). *From the brain to the classroom: The encyclopedia of learning.* Santa Barbara, CA: ABC-CLIO.

Feldman, A. M. (2011). *Understanding health care reform: Bridging the gap between myth and reality.* Boca Raton, FL: CRC Press.

Findling, R. L., Youngstrom, E. A., Fristad, M. A., Birmaher, B., Kowatch, R. A., Arnold E, . . . Horwitz, S. M. (2011). Characteristics of children with elevated symptoms of mania: The Longitudinal Assessment of Manic Symptoms (LAMS) Study. *Journal of Clinical Psychiatry, 21,* 311–319.

Fletcher-Janzen, E., & Reynolds, C. R. (Eds.). (2008). *Neuropsychological perspectives on learning disabilities in the era of RTI.* Hoboken, NJ: Wiley.

Frances, A. (2012). How many billions a year will the *DSM–5* cost? *Bloomberg.* Retrieved from http://mobile.bloomberg.com/news/2012-12-20/how-many-billions-a-year-will-the-dsm-5-cost-.html

Frances, A. (2013a). *Saving normal: An insider's revolt against out-of-control psychiatric diagnosis, DSM–5, big pharma, and the medicalization of ordinary life.* New York, NY: HarperCollins.

Frances, A. (2013b). *Essentials of psychiatric diagnosis, revised edition: Responding to the challenge of DSM.* New York, NY: Guilford Press.

Frances, A. (2013c). The new crisis in confidence in psychiatric diagnosis. *Annals of Internal Medicine, 159,* 221–222. Retrieved from http://annals.org/article.aspx?articleid=1722526

Frick, P. J., & Loney, B. R. (1999). Outcomes of children and adolescents with oppositional defiant disorder and conduct disorder. In H. C. Quay & A. E. Hogan (Eds.) *Handbook of disruptive behavior disorders* (pp. 507–524). New York, NY: Kluwer Academic.

Genel, M., McCaffree, M. A., Hendricks, K., Dennery, P. A., Hay, W. W., Jr., Stanton, B., . . . Jenkins, R. R. (2008, May 3). A national agenda for America's children and adolescents in 2008: Recommendations from the 15th annual public policy plenary symposium, Annual Meeting of the Pediatric Academic Societies. *Pediatrics, 122,* 843–849.

Gerrard, B., & Soriano, M. (Eds.). (2013). *School-based family counseling: Transforming family–school relationships.* San Francisco, CA: Institute for School-Based Family Counseling.

Grey, G. (2014, January 30). Letter from the Connecticut Board of Regents for Higher Education to Miller, J., President, Central Connecticut State University, New Britain, Connecticut.

Gowers, S., & Bryant-Waugh, R. (2004). Management of child and adolescent eating disorders: The current evidence base and future directions. *Journal of Child Psychology and Psychiatry, 45,* 63–83.

Gould, E. (February 23, 2012). *A decade of declines in employer-sponsored health insurance coverage* (EPI Briefing Paper No. 337). Washington, DC: Economic Policy Institute. Retrieved from www.epi.org/publication/bp337-employer-sponsored-health-insurance

Griffin, A., Kovner, J., & Altimari, D. (2014, November 22). Sandy Hook massacre: So many warnings. *The Hartford Courant,* pp. 1, 6–7. Retrieved from http://www.courant.com/news/connecticut/hc-newtown-adam-lanza-child-advocate-report-20141121-story.html#page=1

Hallahan, D. P., Kauffman, J. M., & Pullen, P. C. (2009). *Exceptional learners: An introduction to special education* (11th ed.). Boston, MA: Pearson.

Hallahan, D. P., Kauffman, J. M., & Pullen, P. C. (2012). *Exceptional learners: An introduction to special education* (12th ed.). Boston, MA: Pearson.

Hardman, M. J., Drew, C. J., & Egan, M. W. (2008). *Human exceptionality: School, community and family* (9th ed.). Boston, MA: Houghton Mifflin.

Health Insurance Portability and Accountability Act of 1996. P.L. 104-191. (1996).

Herman, K. C., Reinke, W. M., Frey, A. J., & Shepard, S. A. (2013). *Motivational interviewing in schools: Strategies for engaging parents, teachers and students.* New York, NY: Springer Publishing Company.

HIPAA 101: Guide to Compliance Rules and Laws. (2013). Retrieved from http://www.hipaa-101.com

Hoffman, L. (2002). *Family therapy: An intimate history.* New York, NY: Norton.

Homer, C. J., Klatka, K., Romm, D., Kuhlthau, K., Bloom, S., Newacheck, P. . . . Perrin, J. M. (October, 2008). A review of the evidence for the medical home for children with special health care needs. *Pediatrics, 122,* 3922–3937.

Horner, R. H., Sugai, G., & Anderson, C. M. (2010). Examining the evidence base for School-Wide Positive Behavior Support. *Focus on exceptional children, 42*(8), 1–14House, A. E. (1999). *DSM–IV diagnosis in the schools.* New York, NY: Guilford Press.

Individuals With Disabilities Education Act of 1997 (IDEA). 20 USC §1400 et seq. (1997). Available at http://thomas.loc.gov/home/thomas.php

Karaca-Mandic, P., Choi Yoo, S. J., & Sommers, B. D. (2013). Recession led to a decline in out-of-pocket spending for children with special health care needs. *Health Affairs, 32,* 1143–1152.

Kaslow, N. J. (2014). Becoming a better supervisor. *Monitor on Psychology, 45,* 5.

Kazdin, A. E., & Blase, S. L. (2011). Rebooting psychotherapy research and practice to reduce the burden of mental illness. *Perspectives on Psychological Science, 6,* 21 – 37. doi: 10.1177/17456916 10393527

Keckley, P. D. (2010). Deloitte Center for Health Solutions. (2010). *The medical home: Disruptive innovation for a new primary care model.* Retrieved from http://www.deloitte.com.assets. Dcom-UnitedStates/LocalAssets/Document/us_chs_MedicalHome_w.pdf

Keenan, K., Loeber, R., & Green, S. (1999, March). Conduct disorder in girls: A review of the literature. *Clinical Child and Family Psychology Review, 2*(1), 3–19.

Kelson, S. (2007). *An introduction to the health care crisis in America. How did we get here?* Center for Full Employment and Price Stability (CFEPS). Retrieved from http://www.cfeps.org/health/chapters/html/ch1.htm

Kennedy, P. (2014, November/December). There is no health without mental health. Symposium conducted at the 2014 American Association for Marriage and Family Therapy Conference, Milwaukee, Wisconsin. *Family Therapy Magazine, 13,* 21–22.

Kirk, S., Gallagher, J. J., Coleman, M. R., & Anastasiow, N. (2009). *Educating exceptional children* (12th ed.). Boston, MA: Houghton Mifflin.

Knudsen, E. I., Heckman, J. J., Cameron, J. L., & Schonkoff, J. P. (2006). Economic, neurobiological, and behavioral perspectives on building America's future workforce. *Proceedings of the National Academy of Science USA*. 103(27), 10155-10162.

Laundy, K. C. (1990). *The relationship between family psychosocial functioning and compliance with treatment for familial hyperlipidemia* [Doctoral dissertation]. *Dissertation Abstracts International*, 50–10B, 4774. University Microfilms No. 8923642.

Laundy, K. C. (2009). Supervisory bulletin: Family therapy in schools. *Family Therapy magazine, 8*, 41–43.

Laundy, K. (2013). Connecticut MFT models for school-based family counseling: Medical family therapy and the Longitudinal Overview of Growth in Systems (LOGS). In B. Gerrard & M. Soriano (Eds.), *School-based family counseling: Transforming family–school-relationships* (pp. 741–752). San Francisco, CA: Institute for School-Based Family Counseling.

Laundy, K. C., Nelson, W., & Abucewicz, D. (2011). Building collaborative mental health teams in schools through MFT school certification: Initial findings. *Contemporary Family Therapy, 33*, 384–399. doi: 10:1007/s10591-011-9158-2.

Laundy, K. C., Ciak, M., & Bennett, B., Rivard-Lentz, C., Tomala, G., & Rosa, S. (2010). School referral forms for MFT services. Unpublished manuscript, Department of Counseling and Family Therapy, Central Connecticut State University, New Britain, Connecticut.

Laundy, K. C., Ciak, M., & Bennett, B., Rivard-Lentz, C., Tomala, G., & Rosa, S. (2010). School outcome forms for MFT services. Unpublished manuscript, Department of Counseling and Family Therapy, Central Connecticut State University, New Britain, Connecticut.

Lee, R. E., & Everett, C. A. (2004). *The integrative family therapy supervisor.* New York, NY: Brunner-Routledge.

Lerner, J., & Johns, B. (2009). *Learning disabilities and related mild disabilities: Characteristics, teaching strategies and new directions.* New York, NY: Houghton Mifflin/Harcourt.

McAllister, J., Sherrieb, K., & Cooley, C. (2009). Improvement in the family-centered medical home enhances outcomes for children and youth with special healthcare needs. *Journal of Ambulatory Care Management, 32,* 188–196.

McCarthy, D., Mueller, K. & Tillman, I. (July, 2009). Group health cooperative: Reinventing primary care by connecting patients with a medical home. *The Commonwealth Fund.* Retrieved from http://long-termscorecard.org/~/media/files/publications/case-study/2009/jul/1283_mccarthy_group-health_case_study_72_rev.pdf

McDaniel, S., Doherty, W., & Hepworth, J. (2014) *Medical family therapy and integrated care,* (2nd ed.). Washington, DC: American Psychological Association.

McDaniel, S. H., Hepworth, J., & Doherty, W. J. (1992). *Medical family therapy: A biopsychosocial approach to families with health problems.* New York, NY: Basic Books.

Miller, W. R., & Rollnick, S. (2013). *Motivational interviewing: Helping people change* (3rd ed.). New York, NY: Guilford Press. (See also www.motivationalinterview.org)

National Association of State Directors of Special Education, Inc. (2014, April 3). *Multi-tier system of support (MTSS).* Retrieved from http://www.nasdse.org/Projects/MultiTierSystemofSupportsMTSS/tabid/411/Default.aspx

National Association of State Directors of Special Education, Inc. (2008). *Intervention: Blueprints for implementation.* Retrieved from http://www.nasdse.org/portals/0/district.pdf

National Reading Panel. (2000, April). *Teaching children to read: An evidence-based assessment of the scientific research literature on reading and its implications for reading instruction.* U.S. Department of Health and Human Services Public Health Service, National Institutes of Health, National Institute of Child Health and Human Development. NIH Pub. No. 00-4769. Retrieved from http://www.nichd.nih.gov/publications/pubs/nrp/pages/smallbook.aspx

Neimeyer, G. (2013, September). *DSM–5* Workshop. Connecticut Psychological Association Workshop. Gaylord Hospital, Wallingford, Connecticut.

Nelson, J. R., & Carr, B. A. (2000). *The Think Time strategy for schools.* Longmont, CO: Sopris West.

Nichols, M. P., & Schwartz, R.C. (2001). *Family therapy concepts and methods* (5th ed.). Boston, MA: Allyn and Bacon.

Novotney, A. (November, 2014). Psychology's roles in patient-centered medical homes. *Monitor on Psychology, 45,* 38–40.

Nurnberger, J. I., Jr., & Foroud, T. (2000). Genetics of bipolar affective disorder. *Current Psychiatry Reports, 2,* 147–157.

Olszewski-Kubilius, P., Limburg-Weber, L., & Pfeiffer, S. (2003). *Early gifts: Recognizing and nurturing children's talents.* Waco, TX: Prufrock Press.

Paris, J. (2013). *The intelligent clinician's guide to the DSM–5–RG.* Montreal, Canada: Oxford University Press.

Peek, C. J., & Heinrich, R.L. (1995). Building a collaborative healthcare organization: From idea to invention and innovation. *Family Systems Medicine, 13,* 327–342.

Power, T. J, Blum, N. H., Guevara, J. P., Jones, H. A, & Leslie, L. K. (2013). Coordinating mental health care across primary care and schools: ADHD as a case example. *Advances in School Mental Health Promotion, 6,* 68–80.

Pruchno, R. (2014, December 21). Op-Ed: Mental health laws at fault in Newtown. *The Hartford Courant,* p. C2. Retrieved from http://www.courant.com/opinion/op-ed/hc-op-pruchno-mental-health-issue-newton-1221-20141219-story.html

Ramachandran, V. S., & Oberman, L. M. (2006). Broken mirrors: A theory of autism. *Scientific American: Special Section: Neuroscience.* Center for Brain and Cognition: University of San Diego. Retrieved from http://cbc.ucsd.edu/pdf/brokenmirrors_asd.pdf

Rapoport, J. L., Inoff-Germain, G., Weissman, M. M., Greenwald, S., Narrow, W. E., Jenson, P. S. . . . Canino, G. (2000). Childhood obsessive-compulsive behavior in the NIMH MECA study: Parent versus child identification of cases. *Journal of Anxiety Disorders, 14,* 535–548.

Rapoport, J. L. & Ismond, D. R. (1996). *DSM –IV training guide for diagnosis of childhood disorders.* New York: Brunner-Routledge.

Raymond, E. B. (2008). *Learners with mild disabilities: A characteristics approach* (3rd ed.). Boston, MA: Pearson.

Rolland, J. S. (1984). Toward a psychosocial typology of chronic and life-threatening illness. *Family Systems Medicine, 2,* 245–262.

Rolland, J. S. (1994). *Families, illness, and disability: An integrative treatment model.* New York: Basic Books.

Rones, M., & Hoagwood, K. (2000). School-based mental health services: A research review. *Clinical Child & Family Psychology Review, 34,* 223–241.

Rothstein, R., & Johnson, S. F. (2010). *Special education law* (4th ed.). Thousand Oaks, CA: Sage.

Rourke, B. P. (1989). *Nonverbal learning disabilities: The syndrome and the model.* New York, NY: Guilford Press.

Rourke, B. P., & Tsatsanis, K. D. (2000). Nonverbal learning disabilities and Asperger syndrome. In A. Klin, F. R. Volkmar, & S. S. Sparrow (Eds.), *Asperger syndrome* (pp. 231–254). New York, NY: Guilford Press.

Sams, C. (2012). A spring in Singapore: The importance of maintaining balance in the lives of gifted children. *The Torch,* 18–19.

Seaburn, D. G., Lorenz, A. Gunn, W., Gawinski, B., & Mauksch, L. B. (1996). *Models of collaboration: A guide for mental health professionals working with health care practitioners.* New York, NY: Basic Books.

Seligman, M., & Darling, R. B. (2007). *Ordinary families, special children: A systems approach to childhood disability* (3rd ed.). New York, NY: Guilford Press.

Shaywitz, S. (2004). *Overcoming dyslexia: A new and complete science-based program for reading problems at any level.* New York, NY: Vintage Books.

Shaywitz, S. E., & Shaywitz, B. A. (2008). Paying attention to reading: The neurobiology of reading and dyslexia. *Developmental Psychopathology, 20,* 1329–1349. Retrieved from http://dyslexia.yale.edu/Research.html

Sparrow, S. S., Cicchetti, D. V., & Balla, D. A. (2005). *Vineland—II Adaptive Behavior Scales: Survey forms manual* (2nd ed.). Circle Pines: AGS Publishing.

Sprenkle, D. H., & Piercy, F. P. (2005). Pluralism, diversity and sophistication in family therapy research. In D. H. Sprenkle & F. P. Piercy (Eds.). *Research methods in family therapy* (pp. 3–18). New York, NY: Guilford Press.

Stanton, L. R., & Coetzee, R. H. (2004). Down's syndrome and dementia. *Advances in Psychiatric Treatment, 10, 50–58* doi: 10.1192/apt.10.1.50

State Education Resource Center. (2009, March). *Positive Behavioral Support data report and summary: A look at Connecticut.* Middletown, CT: Author. Retrieved from http://www.pbis.org/common/cms/files/pbisresources/0309pbsdatact.pdf

Stichter, J. P., Conroy, M. A., & Kauffman, J. M. (2008). *An introduction to students with high-incidence disabilities.* Retrieved from http://www.coursesmart.com/an-introduction-to-students-with-high-incidence/janine-p-stichter-maureen-a-conroy-james/dp/9780135011904

Storm, C. L., & Todd, T. (2003). *The reasonably complete systemic supervisor resource guide.* Lincoln, NE: iUniverse.

Sugai, G., & Horner, R. R. (2006). A promising approach for expanding and sustaining school-wide positive behavior support. *School Psychology Review,* 35(2), 245. doi:10.1111/j.1746-1561.1999.tb06354.x

Sugai, G., & Horner, R. H. (2010). School-wide positive behavior support: Establishing a continuum of evidence based practices. *Journal of Evidence-based Practices for Schools. 11*(1), 62–83.

Sugai, G., Horner, R. H., Dunlap, G., Hieneman, M., Lewis, T.J., Nelson, C.M., … Ruef, M. (2000). *Applying positive behavior support and functional behavioral assessments in schools.* Retrieved from http://digitalcommons.calpoly.edu/cgi/viewcontent.cgi?article=1031&context=gse_fac

Sugai, G., & Simonson, B. (2012). *Positive Behavioral Interventions and Supports: History, defining features, and misconceptions.* Storrs, CT: Center for Positive Behavioral Interventions and Supports, University of Connecticut. Retrieved from http://www.pbis.org/common/pbisresources/publications/PBIS_revisited_June19r_2012.pdf

Tsatsanis, K. D., & Rourke, B. P. (1995). Conclusions and future directions. In B. P. Rourke (Ed.), *Syndrome of nonverbal disabilities: Neurodevelopmental manifestations* (pp. 476–496). New York, NY: Guilford Press.

Turnbull, R. H. (1993). *Free and appropriate public education: The law and children with disabilities* (4th ed.). Denver, CO: Love Publishing.

U.S. Department of Education (2001). *NCLB/Overview Executive Summary.* Retrieved From www2.ed.gov/nclb/overview/intro/execsumm.html

U.S. Department of Health and Human Services, National Institute of Mental Health (2012). NIH Publication No.12-6380.

Wagner, K. D. (2014). Age in school cohort, borderline personality disorder, and neurofeedback. *Journal of Clinical Psychiatry, 75,* 528–529.

Watzlawick, P., Weakland, J., & Fisch, R. (1974). *Change: Principles of problem formation and problem resolution.* New York, NY: Norton.

Wright, P. W. D., & Wright, P. D. (2007a). *Wrightslaw: Special education law* (2nd ed.). Hartfield, VA: Harbor House Law Press.

Wright, P. W. D., & Wright, P. D. (2010). *Wrightslaw: From emotions to advocacy: The special education survival guide* (2nd ed.). Hartfield, VA: Harbor House Law Press.

Yapko, D. (2003). *Understanding autism spectrum disorders.* London, England: Jessica Kingsley.

Yell, M. L. (2012). *The law and special education* (3rd ed.). Upper Saddle River, NJ: Pearson Education.

Yoder, N. (2014, January). *Teaching the whole child: Instructional practices that support social and emotional learning in three teacher evaluation frameworks* (rev. ed.; Research to Practice Brief). Washington, DC: Center on Great Teachers & Leaders at American Institutes for Research. Retrieved from http://www.gtlcenter.org/sites/default/files/TeachingtheWholeChild.pdf

Ysseldyke, J. E., & Algozzine, B. A. (1995). *Special education: A practical approach for teachers* (3rd ed.). Boston, MA: Houghton Mifflin.

Index

assessment
    developed for *DSM–5*, 161–62
    individual psychoeducational assessment, 155–56, 158–61
    measures, 158–61
    multidisciplinary, 156–58
    and Positive Behavior Interventions and Supports, 165
    and Response to Intervention, 162–68
asthma, 43, 49, 65, 76, 80–81, 82–83, 152
attention-deficit/hyperactivity disorder (ADHD), 49, 147
    assessment of, 160
    care utilization and, 80–81
    comorbidity, 139, 141
    increased incidence of, 43, 49, 126
    misdiagnosis, 136
    prevalence, 49, 147
Autism and Developmental Disabilities Monitoring Network (ADDM), 47
autism spectrum disorders (ASDs), 37, 38, 42, 43, 66, 102, 123–24, 128,
    134, 147–49
    categorization of, 47, 123–24
    definitions of, 47
    and denial of insurance coverage, 124
    diagnosis and assessment of, 48, 160
    evolution of, 46, 123, 146–49
    high-functioning, 148
    and IDEA, 47–49
    incidence of, 47–48, 49, 126
    and IQ, 48
    and pragmatics of speech, 44
    and psychoeducational testing, 156
    research on, 47–49, 148–49
    symptoms of, 47

baseline (education), 207
Behavioral Intervention Plan (BIP), 207
benchmarks, 97, 208

violence in schools, xi, 11–12, 15, 17, 152–153
 and collaborative/multidisciplinary care, 26, 45–46, 100, 153, 166, 173, 176, 199
 and students with disabilities, 56–57
Virginia Tech, 11
visual impairment, 50

World Health Organization (WHO), 118–19, 209

Youth Service Bureaus, 21

CPSIA information can be obtained
at www.ICGtesting.com
Printed in the USA
LVOW11s1543140717

541341LV00001B/13/P

9 780990 3445